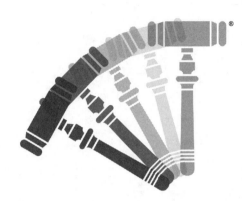

Casenote® Legal Briefs

EVIDENCE

Keyed to Courses Using

Fisher's
Evidence
Third Edition

Wolters Kluwer
Law & Business

This publication is designed to provide accurate and authoritative information in regard to the subject matter covered. It is sold with the understanding that the publisher is not engaged in rendering legal, accounting, or other professional services. If legal advice or other expert assistance is required, the services of a competent professional person should be sought.

> — From a Declaration of Principles adopted jointly by a Committee of the American Bar Association and a Committee of Publishers and Associates

SFI Certified Chain of Custody
Product Line Contains At Least
20% Certified Forest Content
www.sfiprogram.org
SFI-00756

About Wolters Kluwer Law & Business

Wolters Kluwer Law & Business is a leading global provider of intelligent information and digital solutions for legal and business professionals in key specialty areas, and respected educational resources for professors and law students. Wolters Kluwer Law & Business connects legal and business professionals as well as those in the education market with timely, specialized authoritative content and information-enabled solutions to support success through productivity, accuracy and mobility.

Serving customers worldwide, Wolters Kluwer Law & Business products include those under the Aspen Publishers, CCH, Kluwer Law International, Loislaw, Best Case, ftwilliam.com and MediRegs family of products.

CCH products have been a trusted resource since 1913, and are highly regarded resources for legal, securities, antitrust and trade regulation, government contracting, banking, pension, payroll, employment and labor, and healthcare reimbursement and compliance professionals.

Aspen Publishers products provide essential information to attorneys, business professionals and law students. Written by preeminent authorities, the product line offers analytical and practical information in a range of specialty practice areas from securities law and intellectual property to mergers and acquisitions and pension/benefits. Aspen's trusted legal education resources provide professors and students with high-quality, up-to-date and effective resources for successful instruction and study in all areas of the law.

Kluwer Law International products provide the global business community with reliable international legal information in English. Legal practitioners, corporate counsel and business executives around the world rely on Kluwer Law journals, looseleafs, books, and electronic products for comprehensive information in many areas of international legal practice.

Loislaw is a comprehensive online legal research product providing legal content to law firm practitioners of various specializations. Loislaw provides attorneys with the ability to quickly and efficiently find the necessary legal information they need, when and where they need it, by facilitating access to primary law as well as state-specific law, records, forms and treatises.

Best Case Solutions is the leading bankruptcy software product to the bankruptcy industry. It provides software and workflow tools to flawlessly streamline petition preparation and the electronic filing process, while timely incorporating ever-changing court requirements.

ftwilliam.com offers employee benefits professionals the highest quality plan documents (retirement, welfare and non-qualified) and government forms (5500/PBGC, 1099 and IRS) software at highly competitive prices.

MediRegs products provide integrated health care compliance content and software solutions for professionals in healthcare, higher education and life sciences, including professionals in accounting, law and consulting.

Wolters Kluwer Law & Business, a division of Wolters Kluwer, is head-quartered in New York. Wolters Kluwer is a market-leading global information services company focused on professionals.

Format for the Casenote® Legal Brief

Nature of Case: This section identifies the form of action (e.g., breach of contract, negligence, battery), the type of proceeding (e.g., demurrer, appeal from trial court's jury instructions),or the relief sought (e.g., damages, injunction, criminal sanctions).

Fact Summary: This is included to refresh your memory and can be used as a quick reminder of the facts.

Rule of Law: Summarizes the general principle of law that the case illustrates. It may be used for instant recall of the court's holding and for classroom discussion or home review.

Facts: This section contains all relevant facts of the case, including the contentions of the parties and the lower court holdings. It is written in a logical order to give the student a clear understanding of the case. The plaintiff and defendant are identified by their proper names throughout and are always labeled with a (P) or (D).

Palsgraf v. Long Island R.R. Co.

Injured bystander (P) v. Railroad company (D)

N.Y. Ct. App., 248 N.Y. 339, 162 N.E. 99 (1928).

NATURE OF CASE: Appeal from judgment affirming verdict for plaintiff seeking damages for personal injury.

FACT SUMMARY: Helen Palsgraf (P) was injured on R.R.'s (D) train platform when R.R.'s (D) guard helped a passenger aboard a moving train, causing his package to fall on the tracks. The package contained fireworks which exploded, creating a shock that tipped a scale onto Palsgraf (P).

🏛 RULE OF LAW
The risk reasonably to be perceived defines the duty to be obeyed.

FACTS: Helen Palsgraf (P) purchased a ticket to Rockaway Beach from R.R. (D) and was waiting on the train platform. As she waited, two men ran to catch a train that was pulling out from the platform. The first man jumped aboard, but the second man, who appeared as if he might fall, was helped aboard by the guard on the train who had kept the door open so they could jump aboard. A guard on the platform also helped by pushing him onto the train. The man was carrying a package wrapped in newspaper. In the process, the man dropped his package, which fell on the tracks. The package contained fireworks and exploded. The shock of the explosion was apparently of great enough strength to tip over some scales at the other end of the platform, which fell on Palsgraf (P) and injured her. A jury awarded her damages, and R.R. (D) appealed.

ISSUE: Does the risk reasonably to be perceived define the duty to be obeyed?

HOLDING AND DECISION: (Cardozo, C.J.) Yes. The risk reasonably to be perceived defines the duty to be obeyed. If there is no foreseeable hazard to the injured party as the result of a seemingly innocent act, the act does not become a tort because it happened to be a wrong as to another. If the wrong was not willful, the plaintiff must show that the act as to her had such great and apparent possibilities of danger as to entitle her to protection. Negligence in the abstract is not enough upon which to base liability. Negligence is a relative concept, evolving out of the common law doctrine of trespass on the case. To establish liability, the defendant must owe a legal duty of reasonable care to the injured party. A cause of action in tort will lie where harm,

though unintended, could have been averted or avoided by observance of such a duty. The scope of the duty is limited by the range of danger that a reasonable person could foresee. In this case, there was nothing to suggest from the appearance of the parcel or otherwise that the parcel contained fireworks. The guard could not reasonably have had any warning of a threat to Palsgraf (P), and R.R. (D) therefore cannot be held liable. Judgment is reversed in favor of R.R. (D).

DISSENT: (Andrews, J.) The concept that there is no negligence unless R.R. (D) owes a legal duty to take care as to Palsgraf (P) herself is too narrow. Everyone owes to the world at large the duty of refraining from those acts that may unreasonably threaten the safety of others. If the guard's action was negligent as to those nearby, it was also negligent as to those outside what might be termed the "danger zone." For Palsgraf (P) to recover, R.R.'s (D) negligence must have been the proximate cause of her injury, a question of fact for the jury.

▶ ANALYSIS
The majority defined the limit of the defendant's liability in terms of the danger that a reasonable person in defendant's situation would have perceived. The dissent argued that the limitation should not be placed on liability, but rather on damages. Judge Andrews suggested that only injuries that would not have happened but for R.R.'s (D) negligence should be compensable. Both the majority and dissent recognized the policy-driven need to limit liability for negligent acts, seeking, in the words of Judge Andrews, to define a framework "that will be practical and in keeping with the general understanding of mankind." The Restatement (Second) of Torts has accepted Judge Cardozo's view.

———

Quicknotes

FORESEEABILITY A reasonable expectation that change is the probable result of certain acts or omissions.

NEGLIGENCE Conduct falling below the standard of care that a reasonable person would demonstrate under similar conditions.

PROXIMATE CAUSE The natural sequence of events without which an injury would not have been sustained.

———

Party ID: Quick identification of the relationship between the parties.

Concurrence/Dissent: All concurrences and dissents are briefed whenever they are included by the casebook editor.

Analysis: This last paragraph gives you a broad understanding of where the case "fits in" with other cases in the section of the book and with the entire course. It is a hornbook-style discussion indicating whether the case is a majority or minority opinion and comparing the principal case with other cases in the casebook. It may also provide analysis from restatements, uniform codes, and law review articles. The analysis will prove to be invaluable to classroom discussion.

Issue: The issue is a concise question that brings out the essence of the opinion as it relates to the section of the casebook in which the case appears. Both substantive and procedural issues are included if relevant to the decision.

Holding and Decision: This section offers a clear and in-depth discussion of the rule of the case and the court's rationale. It is written in easy-to-understand language and answers the issue presented by applying the law to the facts of the case. When relevant, it includes a thorough discussion of the exceptions to the case as listed by the court, any major cites to the other cases on point, and the names of the judges who wrote the decisions.

Quicknotes: Conveniently defines legal terms found in the case and summarizes the nature of any statutes, codes, or rules referred to in the text.

Wolters Kluwer Law & Business is proud to offer *Casenote® Legal Briefs*—continuing thirty years of publishing America's best-selling legal briefs.

Casenote® Legal Briefs are designed to help you save time when briefing assigned cases. Organized under convenient headings, they show you how to abstract the basic facts and holdings from the text of the actual opinions handed down by the courts. Used as part of a rigorous study regimen, they can help you spend more time analyzing and critiquing points of law than on copying bits and pieces of judicial opinions into your notebook or outline.

Casenote® Legal Briefs should never be used as a substitute for assigned casebook readings. They work best when read as a follow-up to reviewing the underlying opinions themselves. Students who try to avoid reading and digesting the judicial opinions in their casebooks or online sources will end up shortchanging themselves in the long run. The ability to absorb, critique, and restate the dynamic and complex elements of case law decisions is crucial to your success in law school and beyond. It cannot be developed vicariously.

Casenote® Legal Briefs represents but one of the many offerings in Legal Education's Study Aid Timeline, which includes:

- *Casenote® Legal Briefs*
- *Emanuel® Law Outlines*
- Emanuel® *Law in a Flash* Flash Cards
- Emanuel® *CrunchTime®* Series
- *Siegel's Essay and Multiple-Choice Questions and Answers Series*

Each of these series is designed to provide you with easy-to-understand explanations of complex points of law. Each volume offers guidance on the principles of legal analysis and, consulted regularly, will hone your ability to spot relevant issues. We have titles that will help you prepare for class, prepare for your exams, and enhance your general comprehension of the law along the way.

To find out more about Wolters Kluwer Law & Business' study aid publications, visit us online at *www.wolterskluwerlb.com* or email us at *legaledu@wolterskluwer.com*. We'll be happy to assist you.

A. Decide on a Format and Stick to It

Structure is essential to a good brief. It enables you to arrange systematically the related parts that are scattered throughout most cases, thus making manageable and understandable what might otherwise seem to be an endless and unfathomable sea of information. There are, of course, an unlimited number of formats that can be utilized. However, it is best to find one that suits your needs and stick to it. Consistency breeds both efficiency and the security that when called upon you will know where to look in your brief for the information you are asked to give.

Any format, as long as it presents the essential elements of a case in an organized fashion, can be used. Experience, however, has led *Casenote*® *Legal Briefs* to develop and utilize the following format because of its logical flow and universal applicability.

NATURE OF CASE: This is a brief statement of the legal character and procedural status of the case (e.g., "Appeal of a burglary conviction").

There are many different alternatives open to a litigant dissatisfied with a court ruling. The key to determining which one has been used is to discover *who is asking this court for what.*

This first entry in the brief should be kept as *short as possible.* Use the court's terminology if you understand it. But since jurisdictions vary as to the titles of pleadings, the best entry is the one that addresses who wants what in this proceeding, not the one that sounds most like the court's language.

RULE OF LAW: A statement of the general principle of law that the case illustrates (e.g., "An acceptance that varies any term of the offer is considered a rejection and counteroffer").

Determining the rule of law of a case is a procedure similar to determining the issue of the case. Avoid being fooled by red herrings; there may be a few rules of law mentioned in the case excerpt, but usually only one is *the* rule with which the casebook editor is concerned. The techniques used to locate the issue, described below, may also be utilized to find the rule of law. Generally, your best guide is simply the chapter heading. It is a clue to the point the casebook editor seeks to make and should be kept in mind when reading every case in the respective section.

FACTS: A synopsis of only the essential facts of the case, i.e., those bearing upon or leading up to the issue.

The facts entry should be a short statement of the events and transactions that led one party to initiate legal proceedings against another in the first place. While some cases conveniently state the salient facts at the beginning of the decision, in other instances they will have to be culled from hiding places throughout the text, even from concurring and dissenting opinions. Some of the "facts" will often be in dispute and should be so noted. Conflicting evidence may be briefly pointed up. "Hard" facts must be included. Both must be *relevant* in order to be listed in the facts entry. It is impossible to tell what is relevant until the entire case is read, as the ultimate determination of the rights and liabilities of the parties may turn on something buried deep in the opinion.

Generally, the facts entry should not be longer than three to five *short* sentences.

It is often helpful to identify the role played by a party in a given context. For example, in a construction contract case the identification of a party as the "contractor" or "builder" alleviates the need to tell that that party was the one who was supposed to have built the house.

It is always helpful, and a good general practice, to identify the "plaintiff" and the "defendant." This may seem elementary and uncomplicated, but, especially in view of the creative editing practiced by some casebook editors, it is sometimes a difficult or even impossible task. Bear in mind that the *party presently* seeking something from this court may not be the plaintiff, and that sometimes only the cross-claim of a defendant is treated in the excerpt. Confusing or misaligning the parties can ruin your analysis and understanding of the case.

ISSUE: A statement of the general legal question answered by or illustrated in the case. For clarity, the issue is best put in the form of a question capable of a "yes" or "no" answer. In reality, the issue is simply the Rule of Law put in the form of a question (e.g., "May an offer be accepted by performance?").

The major problem presented in discerning what is *the* issue in the case is that an opinion usually purports to raise and answer several questions. However, except for rare cases, only one such question is really the issue in the case. Collateral issues not necessary to the resolution of the matter in controversy are handled by the court by language known as *"obiter dictum"* or merely *"dictum."* While dicta may be included later in the brief, they have no place under the issue heading.

To find the issue, ask *who wants what* and then go on to ask *why did that party succeed or fail in getting it.* Once this is determined, the "why" should be turned into a question.

The complexity of the issues in the cases will vary, but in all cases a single-sentence question should sum up the issue. *In a few cases,* there will be two, or even more rarely, three issues of equal importance to the resolution of the case. Each should be expressed in a single-sentence question.

Since many issues are resolved by a court in coming to a final disposition of a case, the casebook editor will reproduce the portion of the opinion containing the issue or issues most relevant to the area of law under scrutiny. A noted law professor gave this advice: "Close the book; look at the title on the cover." Chances are, if it is Property, you need not concern yourself with whether, for example, the federal government's treatment of the plaintiff's land really raises a federal question sufficient to support jurisdiction on this ground in federal court.

The same rule applies to chapter headings designating sub-areas within the subjects. They tip you off as to what the text is designed to teach. The cases are arranged in a casebook to show a progression or development of the law, so that the preceding cases may also help.

It is also most important to remember to *read the notes and questions* at the end of a case to determine what the editors wanted you to have gleaned from it.

HOLDING AND DECISION: This section should succinctly explain the rationale of the court in arriving at its decision. In capsulizing the "reasoning" of the court, it should always include an application of the general rule or rules of law to the specific facts of the case. Hidden justifications come to light in this entry: the reasons for the state of the law, the public policies, the biases and prejudices, those considerations that influence the justices' thinking and, ultimately, the outcome of the case. At the end, there should be a short indication of the disposition or procedural resolution of the case (e.g., "Decision of the trial court for Mr. Smith (P) reversed").

The foregoing format is designed to help you "digest" the reams of case material with which you will be faced in your law school career. Once mastered by practice, it will place at your fingertips the information the authors of your casebooks have sought to impart to you in case-by-case illustration and analysis.

B. Be as Economical as Possible in Briefing Cases

Once armed with a format that encourages succinctness, it is as important to be economical with regard to the time spent on the actual reading of the case as it is to be economical in the writing of the brief itself. This does not mean "skimming" a case. Rather, it means reading the case with an "eye" trained to recognize into which "section" of your brief a particular passage or line fits and having a system for quickly and precisely marking the case so that the passages fitting any one particular part of

the brief can be easily identified and brought together in a concise and accurate manner when the brief is actually written.

It is of no use to simply repeat everything in the opinion of the court; record only enough information to trigger your recollection of what the court said. Nevertheless, an accurate statement of the "law of the case," i.e., the legal principle applied to the facts, is absolutely essential to class preparation and to learning the law under the case method.

To that end, it is important to develop a "shorthand" that you can use to make marginal notations. These notations will tell you at a glance in which section of the brief you will be placing that particular passage or portion of the opinion.

Some students prefer to underline all the salient portions of the opinion (with a pencil or colored underliner marker), making marginal notations as they go along. Others prefer the color-coded method of underlining, utilizing different colors of markers to underline the salient portions of the case, each separate color being used to represent a different section of the brief. For example, blue underlining could be used for passages relating to the rule of law, yellow for those relating to the issue, and green for those relating to the holding and decision, etc. While it has its advocates, the color-coded method can be confusing and time-consuming (all that time spent on changing colored markers). Furthermore, it can interfere with the continuity and concentration many students deem essential to the reading of a case for maximum comprehension. In the end, however, it is a matter of personal preference and style. Just remember, whatever method you use, underlining must be used sparingly or its value is lost.

If you take the marginal notation route, an efficient and easy method is to go along underlining the key portions of the case and placing in the margin alongside them the following "markers" to indicate where a particular passage or line "belongs" in the brief you will write:

N   (NATURE OF CASE)
RL   (RULE OF LAW)
I   (ISSUE)
HL   (HOLDING AND DECISION, relates to the RULE OF LAW behind the decision)
HR   (HOLDING AND DECISION, gives the RATIONALE or reasoning behind the decision)
HA   (HOLDING AND DECISION, applies the general principle(s) of law to the facts of the case to arrive at the decision)

Remember that a particular passage may well contain information necessary to more than one part of your brief, in which case you simply note that in the margin. If you are using the color-coded underlining method instead of marginal notation, simply make asterisks or checks in the margin next to the passage in question in the colors that indicate the additional sections of the brief where it might be utilized.

The economy of utilizing "shorthand" in marking cases for briefing can be maintained in the actual brief writing process itself by utilizing "law student shorthand" within the brief. There are many commonly used words and phrases for which abbreviations can be substituted in your briefs (and in your class notes also). You can develop abbreviations that are personal to you and which will save you a lot of time. A reference list of briefing abbreviations can be found on page x of this book.

C. Use Both the Briefing Process and the Brief as a Learning Tool

Now that you have a format and the tools for briefing cases efficiently, the most important thing is to make the time spent in briefing profitable to you and to make the most advantageous use of the briefs you create. Of course, the briefs are invaluable for classroom reference when you are called upon to explain or analyze a particular case. However, they are also useful in reviewing for exams. A quick glance at the fact summary should bring the case to mind, and a rereading of the rule of law should enable you to go over the underlying legal concept in your mind, how it was applied in that particular case, and how it might apply in other factual settings.

As to the value to be derived from engaging in the briefing process itself, there is an immediate benefit that arises from being forced to sift through the essential facts and reasoning from the court's opinion and to succinctly express them in your own words in your brief. The process ensures that you understand the case and the point that it illustrates, and that means you will be ready to absorb further analysis and information brought forth in class. It also ensures you will have something to say when called upon in class. The briefing process helps develop a mental agility for getting to the *gist* of a case and for identifying, expounding on, and applying the legal concepts and issues found there. The briefing process is the mental process on which you must rely in taking law school examinations; it is also the mental process upon which a lawyer relies in serving his clients and in making his living.

Abbreviations for Briefs

acceptance	acp
affirmed	aff
answer	ans
assumption of risk	a/r
attorney	atty
beyond a reasonable doubt	b/r/d
bona fide purchaser	BFP
breach of contract	br/k
cause of action	c/a
common law	c/l
Constitution	Con
constitutional	con
contract	K
contributory negligence	c/n
cross	x
cross-complaint	x/c
cross-examination	x/ex
cruel and unusual punishment	c/u/p
defendant	D
dismissed	dis
double jeopardy	d/j
due process	d/p
equal protection	e/p
equity	eq
evidence	ev
exclude	exc
exclusionary rule	exc/r
felony	f/n
freedom of speech	f/s
good faith	g/f
habeas corpus	h/c
hearsay	hr
husband	H
injunction	inj
in loco parentis	ILP
inter vivos	I/v
joint tenancy	j/t
judgment	judgt
jurisdiction	jur
last clear chance	LCC
long-arm statute	LAS
majority view	maj
meeting of minds	MOM
minority view	min
Miranda rule	Mir/r
Miranda warnings	Mir/w
negligence	neg
notice	ntc
nuisance	nus
obligation	ob
obscene	obs
offer	O
offeree	OE
offeror	OR
ordinance	ord
pain and suffering	p/s
parol evidence	p/e
plaintiff	P
prima facie	p/f
probable cause	p/c
proximate cause	px/c
real property	r/p
reasonable doubt	r/d
reasonable man	r/m
rebuttable presumption	rb/p
remanded	rem
res ipsa loquitur	RIL
respondeat superior	r/s
Restatement	RS
reversed	rev
Rule Against Perpetuities	RAP
search and seizure	s/s
search warrant	s/w
self-defense	s/d
specific performance	s/p
statute	S
statute of frauds	S/F
statute of limitations	S/L
summary judgment	s/j
tenancy at will	t/w
tenancy in common	t/c
tenant	t
third party	TP
third party beneficiary	TPB
transferred intent	TI
unconscionable	uncon
unconstitutional	unconst
undue influence	u/e
Uniform Commercial Code	UCC
unilateral	uni
vendee	VE
vendor	VR
versus	v
void for vagueness	VFV
weight of authority	w/a
weight of the evidence	w/e
wife	W
with	w/
within	w/i
without	w/o
without prejudice	w/o/p
wrongful death	wr/d

Table of Cases

Evidence

Quick Reference Rules of Law

Tanner v. United States

Convicted felon (D) v. Federal government (P)

483 U.S. 107 (1987).

NATURE OF CASE: Review of order denying post-conviction hearing and new trial.

FACT SUMMARY: Following his conviction, defendant attempted to demonstrate juror misconduct involving drug and alcohol consumption.

🏛 RULE OF LAW
Following a verdict in a criminal action a court is not required to consider evidence of juror intoxication in a motion for new trial.

FACTS: Tanner (D) was convicted of mail fraud. After the conviction, a pair of jurors made it known to his attorney that, for much of the trial, some of the jurors ingested significant amounts of alcohol, cocaine, and marijuana. Tanner (D) submitted a declaration concerning this from a juror in support of a motion for a new trial. The district court held the declaration inadmissible under Fed. R. Evid. 606, and denied the motion. The Eleventh Circuit affirmed. Tanner (D) obtained certiorari in the Supreme Court.

ISSUE: Is a court required, following a verdict in a criminal action, to consider evidence of juror intoxication in a motion for new trial?

HOLDING AND DECISION: (O'Connor, J.) No. Following a verdict in a criminal action, a court is not required to consider evidence of juror intoxication in a motion for new trial. It has long been the rule that, in order to guard the admittedly imperfect jury systems from a barrage of assaults, from which it possibly could not survive, juror testimony may not be admitted to impeach a jury verdict unless the testimony concerns some sort of extraneous influence, such as a bribe. This common law rule was codified in Fed. R. Evid. 606. Allegations of mental or physical incompetence have always been treated as internal rather than external matters, and the conduct called into question here fits into that category. It is clear that Congress intended that juror testimony not be admissible to impeach a jury verdict, as it specifically rejected a bill that would have so permitted. This being so, the district court was correct in refusing to consider the juror's declaration and denying the motion. Affirmed.

CONCURRENCE AND DISSENT: (Marshall, J.) A criminal defendant has a right, under the Sixth Amendment, to trial by a competent jury. Where evidence sufficient to raise a question whether a jury was competent exists, the court should be compelled to consider the evidence.

▶ ANALYSIS

Fed. R. Evid. 606 originally differed in its versions in the House of Representatives and the Senate. The House bill would have permitted juror testimony to be considered; the Senate bill did not. The Conference Committee eventually took the Senate side of the issue. Thus, in this instance the legislative history made the intent of Congress quite clear.

■■■

Quicknotes

CERTIORARI A discretionary writ issued by a superior court to an inferior court in order to review the lower court's decisions; the Supreme Court's writ ordering such review.

SIXTH AMENDMENT Provides the right to a speedy and public trial by impartial jury, the right to be informed of the accusation, the right to confront witnesses, and the right to have the assistance of counsel in all criminal prosecutions.

General Principles of Relevance

Quick Reference Rules of Law

United States v. James

Federal government (P) v. Alleged aider and abettor (D)

169 F.3d 1210, *en banc* (9th Cir. 1999).

NATURE OF CASE: Appeal from conviction for aiding and abetting manslaughter.

FACT SUMMARY: Defendant was convicted of aiding and abetting her daughter in the manslaughter of defendant's boyfriend. The trial judge excluded evidence demonstrating boyfriend's violent criminal past and defendant appealed.

🏛 RULE OF LAW
Documentary records are admissible to corroborate testimony and bolster credibility even when the testifying witness being corroborated and bolstered did not know the contents of the records.

FACTS: Ernestine Audrey James's (D) boyfriend, David Ogden, became quite violent when drunk. Ogden had bragged to James (D) about stabbing a man in the neck with a ballpoint pen and about robbing an elderly man by threatening to cut out the man's eyes with a knife. After a party, Ogden knocked a man unconscious and got into an altercation with James's (D) daughter, Jaylene Jeffries. James (D) was in the driver's seat of her van when Jaylene ran to her and asked for a gun. James (D) pulled a gun from her handbag and gave it to Jaylene, who shot and killed Ogden. At James's (D) trial for aiding and abetting manslaughter, James (D) testified that she gave Jaylene the gun so that she could protect herself and the family members because she knew how violent Ogden could be. The defense's stance that the manslaughter was self-defense meant that the jury could only consider what James (D) knew and felt at the time of the shooting. At the pre-trial conference, the trial judge excluded extrinsic evidence of Ogden's violent criminal past because James (D) would not have known about the extrinsic records at the time she gave Jaylene the gun. During jury deliberations, the jury sent the judge a question about the veracity of the stories about Ogden's violent past, but the judge did not answer because that would have meant admitting the criminal records to verify the testimony. The jury convicted James (D) of aiding and abetting in the manslaughter of Ogden. James (D) appealed and a divided panel of the Ninth Circuit affirmed. The court then took the case en banc.

ISSUE: Are documentary records admissible to corroborate testimony and bolster credibility even when the testifying witness being corroborated and bolstered did not know the contents of the records?

HOLDING AND DECISION: (Noonan, J.) Yes. Documentary records are admissible to corroborate testimony and bolster credibility even when the testifying

witness being corroborated and bolstered did not know the contents of the records. James (D) testified to the stories Ogden had told her of his criminal, violent past. The trial judge did not allow the admission of documentary records which would have corroborated James's (D) testimony and validated her fears of Ogden's violent nature. James (D) argued she feared she and her daughter were in danger of grievous bodily harm or death from Ogden. The jury may have accepted James's (D) self-defense theory if they had been convinced that her knowledge of Ogden's violent nature justified her fears at the time of the shooting. The trial court did not admit the records because James (D) would not have known the contents of the records at the time of the shooting, but only knew what Ogden had told her. Therefore, the court reasoned, the jury should only hear what Ogden in fact knew at that time. This is too narrow a holding, however, and the trial court should have admitted the extrinsic documentary records, especially because James's (D) defense rested on her credibility. Reversed.

DISSENT: (Kleinfeld, J.) James (D) received a fair trial because the evidence offered went less to her credibility and more to the character of the victim. There were good reasons to keep the documents out. The documents were somewhat remote corroboration, not direct evidence of anything relevant. They showed nothing directly about James's state of mind, because she had never seen them. And the risk of unfair prejudice to the prosecution was consideration. Some people, maybe even the jurors, may have felt Ogden deserved to die for stabbing someone in the neck with a pen and killing a man, but that does not create self-defense in James's (D) case. Rather than following *United States v. Burks*, 470 F.2d 432 (1972), as the majority does, the court should have followed *United States v. Driver*, 945 F.2d 1410 (8th Cir. 1991). In *Driver*, defendant argued self-defense and wanted to admit evidence that the victim had been under investigation for child abuse, thus implying he was a bad man "deserving" of death. That evidence was deemed inadmissible because it was not relevant to the theory of self-defense. The prior history of Ogden, without a showing that James (D) knew of it and feared him at the time of the shooting because of it, similarly did not support the defense's current claim of self-defense.

▶ ANALYSIS

Courts must consider the materiality and probative value of evidence to determine its overall admissibility and

Continued on next page.

relevance to the issue at hand. It is difficult to see how the records in the *James* case would be material to James's (D) fear of Ogden when she did not know of the records' existence, but the exclusion of the records certainly hindered James's (D) credibility. The point to consider is whether Ogden's past acts should be admissible to prove that he was violent enough in this situation to justify the actions of James (D) and her daughter. On the other hand, the dissent points out, showing that Ogden was a "bad man" is more likely to be a showing that he "deserved to die" rather than that James (D) had a justifiable reason for contributing to his death.

■═■

Quicknotes

AIDING AND ABETTING Assistance given in order to facilitate the commission of a criminal act.

EXTRINSIC EVIDENCE Evidence that is not contained within the text of a document or contract, but which is derived from the parties' statements or the circumstances under which the agreement was made.

FED. R. EVID. 403 Discretionary rule that allows a trial judge to exclude evidence if the danger of unfair prejudice to defendant outweighs its probative value.

MANSLAUGHTER The killing of another person without premeditation, deliberation or with the intent to kill or to commit a felony, which may be reasonably expected to result in death or serious bodily injury; manslaughter is characterized by reckless conduct or by some adequate provocation on the part of the actor, as determined by a subjective standard.

SELF-DEFENSE The right to protect an individual's person, family or property against attempted injury by another.

■═■

Cox v. State

Convicted murderer (D) v. State (P)

Ind. Sup. Ct., 696 N.E.2d 853 (1998).

NATURE OF CASE: Appeal from murder conviction.

FACT SUMMARY: At defendant's trial for murder, the prosecution introduced evidence relevant only if defendant knew of its existence prior to the murder. Defendant appealed his conviction, contending the prosecution did not prove he knew of the evidence prior to the murder, thus the evidence was inadmissible and highly prejudicial.

🏛 RULE OF LAW
Conditionally relevant evidence is admissible if a judge determines that a reasonable jury could make the requisite factual finding based on the evidence before it.

FACTS: Jamie Hammer was arrested for the molestation of the young daughter of James and Patricia Leonard. Patrick Cox (D) was a close friend of Hammer and spent nearly every day at Hammer's house with Hammer's mother, even after Hammer went to prison awaiting trial. Late one night, Cox (D) shot into the Leonard's bedroom killing James Leonard. At Cox's (D) trial for murder, the prosecution's theory was that Cox (D) killed Leonard in retaliation for the charges against Hammer. To support this theory, the prosecutor in Hammer's case testified at Cox's (D) trial that Hammer had a bond reduction hearing four days before the murder, which Hammer's mother attended and where Hammer's bond was not reduced. The trial court admitted the evidence on the basis that Cox (D) was likely aware of the hearing's outcome because Hammer's mother was aware. The jury convicted Cox (D) of murder and Cox (D) appealed. Cox (D) claimed the prosecution first had to prove he knew the outcome of Hammer's hearing before introducing the evidence as his motive. If Cox (D) had not known of the outcome, the evidence was irrelevant and prejudicial.

ISSUE: Is conditionally relevant evidence admissible if a judge determines that a reasonable jury could make the requisite factual finding based on the evidence before it?

HOLDING AND DECISION: (Boehm, J.) Yes. Conditionally relevant evidence is admissible if a judge determines that a reasonable jury could make the requisite factual finding based on the evidence before it. This standard for questions under Indiana Evidence Rule 104(b), "Relevancy Conditioned on Fact," is identical to the federal standard for the equivalent Federal Rule 104(b). The trial court does not have to weigh the credibility of the evidence or make a finding, but rather determine if a reasonable jury could make the finding. Here, the jury was told that

Cox (D) spent all his time at Hammer's house with Hammer's mother before and after the bond reduction hearing. A reasonable jury could find that Cox (D) knew of the hearing's outcome. Affirmed.

▶ ANALYSIS

The conditional relevance of evidence could become a never-ending hunt for additional facts as each new fact is required to make the fact before it relevant. Assumptions of basic human traits (e.g., that Hammer's mother would share the outcome of the hearing with her son's closest friend) are usually made somewhere along the evidentiary trail. If a sharp lawyer can detect the assumptions made and put forth a Rule 104(b) question, the judge must consider the sufficiency of the supporting evidence. The U.S. Supreme Court in *Huddleston v. United States*, 485 U.S. 681 (1988), held that there must be a preponderance of the evidence that supports the finding of the conditional fact.

■=■

Quicknotes

FED. R. EVID. 104 Permits a court to consider all non-privileged matters, whether independently admissible or not, when determining preliminary issues of admissibility.

PREPONDERANCE OF THE EVIDENCE A standard of proof requiring the trier of fact to determine whether the fact sought to be established is more probable than not.

■=■

State v. Bocharski

State (P) v. Convicted murderer and burglar (D)

Ariz. Sup. Ct., 22 P.3d 43 (2001).

NATURE OF CASE: Appeal from burglary and murder convictions and a capital sentence.

FACT SUMMARY: At defendant's trial for murder and burglary, the prosecution introduced several grisly photographs of the victim's decomposed body and the fatal stab wounds. On appeal, defendant argued that the photographs were highly prejudicial, not particularly probative, and should not have been admissible under Ariz. R. Evid. 403.

🏛 **RULE OF LAW**
While gruesome photographs of victims and the manner of death may certainly be relevant in a murder trial, not every photograph is admissible if its purpose is merely to inflame or outrage the jury and prejudice the defense.

FACTS: Phillip Alan Bocharski (D) lived in an Arizona campsite next to eighty-four year old Freeda Brown and near his friend, Frank Sukis. Sukis and Bocharski (D) were longtime friends and Bocharski (D) was quite proud of a Kabar knife that he always carried, which had been a gift from Sukis. One day in May, Bocharski (D) and Sukis had a discussion about Brown's complaints about constant pain from arthritis and her wish that God would end her suffering. Three days later, Brown was found dead in her trailer by Sukis and another neighbor. Although the body was in advanced decomposition, an autopsy confirmed that Brown died as a result of sixteen stab wounds to her head. Police could not locate Bocharski's (D) knife and never found a murder weapon, but arrested Bocharski (D) for the murder and burglary of Brown's trailer. A jury convicted Bocharski (D) of felony murder and burglary and Bocharski (D) received a capital sentence. The Arizona Supreme Court took the case on direct, automatic appeal. On appeal, Bocharski (D) contended that six grisly photographs of Brown's decomposing body and the fatal stab wounds were overly prejudicial and should not have been admitted under Ariz. R. Evid. 403.

ISSUE: Is every photograph of a murder victim and manner of death admissible in a murder trial?

HOLDING AND DECISION: (Zlaket, C.J.) No. While gruesome photographs of victims and manner of death may certainly be relevant in a murder trial, not every photograph is admissible if its purpose is merely to inflame or outrage the jury and prejudice the defense. The trial court must conduct a Rule 403 review of the offered photographs to determine if the photos are more prejudicial than probative in value. Here, the photographs' probative value is suspect because Bocharski (D) was not contesting the fact or manner of Brown's death or the extent of her injuries. The photographs depicting the advanced state of decomposition did not add much to the prosecution's case, but the prosecution is allowed to admit relevant, however minimally relevant, evidence. The photographs of the fatal stab wounds, however, did not prove that Bocharski's (D) knife caused them nor did the prosecution elicit testimony that the angle of the wounds supported its theory of Bocharski (D) as the murderer. The only purpose in admitting the photographs then seems to be to inflame and outrage the jury, which is not allowed under Rule 403. Those photographs should have been inadmissible. In this case, however, the trial judge noted that the jury did not seem to be disturbed when viewing the photographs of the knife wounds. Therefore, the defendant was not prejudiced by their admission. Affirmed.

CONCURRENCE AND DISSENT: (Martone, J.) The convictions should be affirmed, but the majority takes a condescending view towards the jury's ability to distinguish between inflammatory photographs and relevant evidence. The trial court conducted a Rule 403 examination and those findings should not be disturbed by an appellate court's second-guessing. The trial court did not err in admitting all six photographs.

▶ **ANALYSIS**

A strong prosecutorial tool is a grisly, gruesome photograph of a murder victim. While likely probative to the fact and manner of death, the average juror is still going to be disturbed by pictorial evidence of another human being's pain and death. Then that average juror may look to the person sitting in the defense chair and direct understandable outrage toward that defendant prior to hearing all of the facts of the case. On the other hand, the judicial system relies on the fact that the average juror, while upset or even horrified, will still listen to all of the facts, separate the horror of a grisly photograph from the evidence placed before her, and arrive at an appropriate verdict. Trial courts conducting Rule 403 examinations of offered evidence must consider whether the photograph offered is merely to elicit the emotional response of a juror or has probative value beyond its gruesomeness, and then the court must trust that the jurors will abide by their duties. It is not fair to expect a prosecutor to try a case with all emotion removed, but a proper trial court will ensure that evidence, rather than emotion, carries the day.

■▬■

Continued on next page.

Quicknotes

FED. R. EVID. 401 Defines relevant evidence.

FED. R. EVID. 403 Discretionary rule that allows a trial judge to exclude evidence if the danger of unfair prejudice to defendant outweighs its probative value.

PREJUDICIAL ERROR An error that affects the outcome of a trial, the judgment of which may be reversed, establishing a basis for a new trial.

RELEVANT EVIDENCE Evidence having any tendency to prove or disprove a disputed fact.

■━━■

Commonwealth v. Serge

State (P) v. Convicted murderer (D)

Pa. Sup. Ct., 586 Pa. 671, 896 A.2d 1170, *cert. denied*, 549 U.S. 920 (2006).

NATURE OF CASE: Appeal of murder conviction and life sentence.

FACT SUMMARY: Michael Serge (D) shot and killed his wife in their home. He was arrested and charged with murder. The Commonwealth (P) sought to present its theory of the shooting through a computer-generated animation based on forensic and physical evidence.

🏛 RULE OF LAW
Computer-generated animations illustrating a theory of a homicide are admissible if they are authenticated, relevant, their relevance outweighs any potential prejudice, and the judge instructs the jury about their role as demonstrative, and not substantive, evidence.

FACTS: Michael Serge (D) shot and killed his wife in their home. He was arrested and charged with murder. The State (P) sought to present its theory of the shooting through a computer-generated animation based on forensic and physical evidence. At his trial, he (D) claimed he acted in self-defense, as his wife attacked him with a knife. He (D) argued alternatively that his extreme intoxication at the time of the shooting rendered him incapable of formulating the specific intent to kill. The Commonwealth (P) used a computer-generated animation to show its theory that Serge (D), who was at one time a police officer, shot his wife first in the lower back, then through the heart as she knelt on the living room floor. The animation also showed the location of Serge (D) and his wife in the living room, the positioning of their bodies, and the sequence, path, trajectory, and impact sites of the bullets fired from the handgun. The court informed the jury that the animation was purely demonstrative, and that they should not view the animation as a definitive re-creation of the actual incident. Serge (D) was convicted of first-degree murder and sentenced to life imprisonment.

ISSUE: Are computer-generated animations illustrating a theory of a homicide admissible if they are authenticated, relevant, their relevance outweighs any potential prejudice, and the judge instructs the jury about their role as demonstrative, and not substantive, evidence?

HOLDING AND DECISION: (Newman, J.) Yes. Computer-generated animations illustrating a theory of a homicide are admissible if they are authenticated, relevant, their relevance outweighs any potential prejudice, and the judge instructs the jury about their role as demonstrative, and not substantive, evidence. Computer-generated anima-

tions should be treated equivalently to any other demonstrative exhibit or graphic representation, and should therefore be admissible if they are authenticated, relevant, and their relevance outweighs any potential prejudice, but with the added safeguard that prior to viewing an animation, the jury should be instructed about the nature and role of the animation, to protect against the possibility of jury confusion over its role or potential prejudice. In this case, the animation evidence was authenticated by the testimony of many individuals, including the creator of the animation who testified that the animation was a graphical presentation of an expert's opinion, not the conclusions or calculations of a computer or himself, and that it was a strict depiction of the Commonwealth's (P) forensic evidence and expert opinions. It was relevant, because it clearly, concisely, and accurately depicted the Commonwealth's (P) theory of the case and helped the jury understand the testimony of the witnesses. And, finally, while animations have potentially powerful impact based on their visual nature, the one used in this case was neither inflammatory nor unfairly prejudicial, and the court issued cautionary instructions before playing the animation to educate the jury on the exact nature and role of the animation, in order to safeguard against the possibility of jury confusion over the animation or potential prejudice. Affirmed.

CONCURRENCE: (Cappy, C.J.) The trial court will need to consider whether giving the defendant the opportunity to present his own computer-generated animation will mitigate the prejudicial impact of the evidence when reviewing the probative/prejudice prong of admissibility.

CONCURRENCE: (Castille, J.) Where both parties have the means to hire the computer professionals necessary to challenge the accuracy of a proffered computer-generated animation, manipulation of the end-product of one party can be mitigated. Where one of the parties does not have the resources to produce a competing computer-generated animation or evaluate the accuracy of the opposing party, a judge might consider excluding such evidence entirely, assuming it is of limited value anyway.

CONCURRENCE: (Eakin, J.) The admissibility of evidence cannot rest on the relative resources of the other party. One side should not be precluded from introducing relevant evidence because the opposing party cannot afford similar evidence. Social sensitivity should not trump legal reasoning.

Continued on next page.

▶ *ANALYSIS*

Pennsylvania is one of only a few courts to rule on the admissibility of computer-generated animations (CGAs). CGAs are, as the court indicates, distinct from computer-generated simulations, which use software to analyze data and reach a conclusion. A CGA, on the other hand, represents other testimony, and the computer itself plays no part in calculating an outcome.

■══■

Quicknotes

DEMONSTRATIVE EVIDENCE Evidence that is presented in a form other than testimony and that takes the form of tangible evidence, e.g., chart, model, etc.

FIRST-DEGREE MURDER The willful killing of another person with deliberation and premeditation; first-degree murder also encompasses those situations in which a person is killed within the perpetration of, or attempt to perpetrate, specified felonies.

■══■

United States v. Myers

Federal government (P) v. Convicted bank robber (D)

550 F.2d 1036 (5th Cir. 1977), *cert. denied*, 439 U.S. 847 (1978).

NATURE OF CASE: Appeal from robbery conviction.

FACT SUMMARY: At defendant's trial for bank robbery, the trial court instructed the jury on the proper use of evidence of defendant's flight from law enforcement. On appeal, defendant contended the evidence did not support giving an instruction because there was insufficient evidence of his flight.

🏛 RULE OF LAW

Evidence of flight may be probative of circumstantial evidence of guilt if four enumerated inferences may be drawn from the act of flight; otherwise, the act of fleeing is too prejudicial to be admitted.

FACTS: Larry Allen Myers (D) was charged with robbing a Florida bank, but he declared his innocence and his friend, Dennis Coffie, later confessed to being the lone robber. At approximately the same time, Myers (D) and Coffie were charged with robbing a Pennsylvania bank. Coffie confessed to that robbery as well and Myers (D) was convicted at trial. At Myers's (D) first trial for the Florida robbery, the jury could not reach a verdict and a mistrial was declared. At Myers's (D) second trial, the trial court instructed the jury on the proper use of evidence that Myers (D) fled from FBI agents in Florida and California. The evidence of flight in Florida consisted of the testimony of Debra Dunn, with whom Myers (D) lived for a few months prior to the robbery. Dunn testified that Myers was avoiding two FBI agents trying to contact him through her, and that the agents followed her to a shopping center one day where she was to meet Myers (D). When Dunn's daughter identified Myers (D), one of the agents, in plain clothes and without identifying himself in any way, ran toward Myers (D) who ran into the mall. Approximately two weeks later, Myers (D) traveled to California. The evidence of flight in California came in the form of testimony of an FBI agent who testified that plainclothes agents in an unmarked car swerved at Myers (D) and Coffie who were traveling on a motorcycle. The agent then testified that Myers (D) and Coffie got off the motorcycle and traveled approximately 50 feet in opposite directions before being arrested. The agent's testimony was contradicted, however, by his testimony from Myers's (D) trial for the Pennsylvania robbery where the agent had testified that he did not believe Myers (D) was trying to flee in California. The jury convicted Myers (D) and Myers (D) appealed, contending that there was insufficient evidence that he fled, thus the trial court erred in instructing the jury on the proper use of flight evidence.

ISSUE: Is evidence of flight probative of circumstantial evidence of guilt?

HOLDING AND DECISION: (Clark, J.) Yes. Evidence of flight may be probative of circumstantial evidence of guilt if four enumerated inferences may be drawn from the act of flight; otherwise, the act of fleeing is too prejudicial to be admitted. The four inferences from which circumstantial evidence of guilt is drawn are: "(1) from the defendant's behavior to flight; (2) from flight to consciousness of guilt; (3) from consciousness of guilt to consciousness of guilt concerning the crime charged; and (4) from consciousness of guilt concerning the crime charged to actual guilt of the crime charged." The California evidence of flight is too weak to be at all probative. The agent's testimony was contradictory. It is unlikely that Myers (D) would have gotten off the motorcycle had he truly been attempting flight, and it is understandable that Myers (D) would attempt to get away from unidentified persons in plain clothes swerving at his motorcycle in an unmarked car. The first inference cannot be drawn here. Additionally, the third inference cannot be drawn because Myers (D) was arguably conscious of his guilt for the Pennsylvania robbery and was not reacting to the Florida robbery at all. Therefore, the evidence of flight should not be admitted in the Florida proceedings. The Florida evidence of flight is slightly stronger, but still not sufficient to support an instruction. Myers (D) was running away from an unidentified person running at him in a shopping center, and then left for California weeks after the robbery. The more remote in time the flight occurs, the less probative it is of guilt. The trial court's error in giving the instruction was too prejudicial due to the even balance of evidence in this case; therefore, the conviction must be reversed.

▶ ANALYSIS

The court did not allow the FBI agent's testimony of the alleged California flight to be admitted on remand because it was too prejudicial to the defense. Prejudicial evidence is not on its face inadmissible unless it is unfairly prejudicial. Here, the unfairness was overwhelming because of the little evidence of actual flight versus the implication that Myers (D) was running from law enforcement due to acknowledged guilt over the specific robbery.

■=■

Continued on next page.

Quicknotes

FLIGHT FROM JUSTICE Avoiding the course of justice by fleeing from arrest or detention or other criminal proceedings, whether or not one leaves the jurisdiction.

■▬■

People v. Collins

State (P) v. Convicted robber (D)

Cal. Sup. Ct., 68 Cal.2d 319, 438 P.2d 33 (1968).

NATURE OF CASE: Appeal from conviction of second-degree robbery.

FACT SUMMARY: In the People's (P) suit against Collins (D) for second-degree armed robbery, Collins (D) contended that testimony admitted into evidence at trial as to the mathematical probability that Collins (D) committed the crime unduly influenced the jury and infected the case with fatal error.

🏛 RULE OF LAW
Applications of mathematical techniques in the proof of facts in a criminal case must be critically examined in view of the substantial unfairness to the defendant which may result.

FACTS: In the People's (P) suit against Collins (D) for second-degree robbery, the prosecution experienced some difficulty in establishing the perpetrators of the robbery. In order to bolster the identification of Collins (D) as the perpetrator, the prosecutor called a mathematics instructor from a state college who testified about the mathematical probability that persons who possessed the various characteristics possessed by Collins (D) and his wife, a co-defendant, existed. The witness inferred that there could be but one chance in twelve million that Collins (D) and his wife were innocent and that another equally distinctive couple actually committed the robbery. Collins (D) objected to the witness's testimony on the grounds that it was based on unfounded assumptions. Collins (D) was convicted and appealed on the grounds the mathematician's testimony infected the case with fatal error.

ISSUE: Must applications of mathematical techniques in the proof of facts in a criminal case be critically examined in view of the substantial unfairness to the defendant which may result?

HOLDING AND DECISION: (Sullivan, J.) Yes. Application of mathematical techniques in the proof of facts in a criminal case must be critically examined in view of the substantial unfairness to the defendant which may result. Here, the prosecution's theory of probability rested on the assumption that the witness called by the People (P) had conclusively established that the guilty couple possessed the precise characteristics relied upon by the prosecution. But no mathematical formula could ever establish beyond a reasonable doubt that the prosecution's witness correctly observed and accurately described the distinctive features which were employed to link the Collinses (D) to the crime. The most a mathematical computation could ever yield would be a measure of the probability that a random couple would possess the distinctive features in question. Reversed.

▶ ANALYSIS

It appears that the explicit use of theories of probability and statistical inference remains controversial. This is true whether the theories serve either as a basis for the opinions of the experts themselves or as a course of education for jurors in how to think about scientific identification evidence. However, so long as counsel and the experts do not try to place a scientific seal of approval on results not shown to be grounded in science, there is probably room for judicious use of these theories to put identification evidence in perspective.

Quicknotes

ROBBERY The unlawful taking of property from the person of another through the use of force or fear.

United States v. Jackson

Federal government (P) v. Alleged bank robber (D)

405 F. Supp. 938 (E.D.N.Y. 1975).

NATURE OF CASE: Pretrial motion to exclude evidence.

FACT SUMMARY: Defendant is charged with a New York bank robbery at gunpoint. Subsequent to the date of the robbery but prior to his arrest, defendant was arrested in Georgia on an unrelated charge and gave false identification. Defendant filed a pretrial motion to exclude the evidence of the Georgia arrest and false ID on the grounds that it would be overly prejudicial.

🏛 RULE OF LAW

Conditional exclusion of evidence upon entry of a stipulation is an appropriate solution to a complex Rule 403 analysis where both highly prejudicial and yet probative evidence exists.

FACTS: Jackson (D) allegedly robbed a New York bank and then fled to Georgia. While New York police were searching for Jackson (D), a Georgia patrolman arrested Jackson (D) after a traffic stop because he was acting suspiciously in an area near a recent bank robbery. Upon arrest, Jackson (D) gave false identification. Jackson (D) escaped from the Georgia jail and was subsequently arrested and charged with the New York robbery. Jackson (D) filed this pretrial motion to exclude the evidence of the Georgia arrest and false identification, contending it would be too prejudicial to his present defense.

ISSUE: Is conditional exclusion of evidence upon entry of a stipulation an appropriate solution to a complex Rule 403 analysis where both highly prejudicial and yet probative evidence exists?

HOLDING AND DECISION: (Weinstein, J.) Yes. Conditional exclusion of evidence upon entry of a stipulation is an appropriate solution to a complex Rule 403 analysis where both highly prejudicial and yet probative evidence exists. Admission of the Georgia evidence would likely violate Fed. R. Evid. 404(b), which prohibits admission of evidence of other crimes when offered to show a general propensity to violate the law. Evidence of flight to another jurisdiction and use of a false identification to possibly avoid detection is highly probative. A proper response to this difficult Rule 403 analysis is to exclude the evidence in exchange for a stipulation from the defense. This is proper under Fed. R. Evid. 102, which encourages minimizing evidentiary costs when protecting parties against prejudice. It is a frustrating but necessary fact that juries will only hear partial truths and constructed stories, but the justice system does not require disclosure of the entire truth when decisions should only be made about limited questions of law

and fact. Jackson (D) will stipulate that he was in Georgia and provided false identification, but the reason he provided false identification and the arrest for the Georgia bank robbery will be excluded. Motion granted.

▶ ANALYSIS

The court points out that juries only hear a carefully crafted version of events rather than the entire "mystery" laid out before them. Perhaps not enough faith is placed in juries to separate the relevance of prior crimes from the evidence of the crime at issue. The court assumes that the jury will use the Georgia charges against Jackson when considering his guilt of the New York charge, but the Federal Rules of Evidence also assume this in providing the noted protections against prejudice to the defense. The compromise ruling here with the stipulation may provide the best of both worlds.

■=■

Quicknotes

FED. R. EVID. 403 Discretionary rule that allows a trial judge to exclude evidence if the danger of unfair prejudice to defendant outweighs its probative value.

FED. R. EVID. 404 Sets forth the general rule that evidence of a person's character is inadmissible to prove his conduct, with certain exceptions.

■=■

Old Chief v. United States

Convicted criminal (D) v. Federal government (P)

519 U.S. 172 (1997).

NATURE OF CASE: Appeal of conviction for assault with a deadly weapon and for being a felon in possession of a firearm.

FACT SUMMARY: Defendant, on trial for violating 18 U.S.C. § 922(g)(1), which prohibits possession of a firearm by anyone with a felony conviction, sought to concede the fact of his prior conviction and prevent the Government (P) from identifying or mentioning the prior conviction aside from the fact that it existed.

🏛 RULE OF LAW
During a prosecution for violation of 18 U.S.C. § 922(g)(1), which prohibits possession of a firearm by anyone with a felony conviction, a court may permit a defendant to concede the fact of a prior conviction before the government has the opportunity to offer evidence identifying the previous offense.

FACTS: Old Chief (D) was arrested after a scuffle involving at least one gunshot. Federal charges were filed against him, including assault with a deadly weapon and violation of 18 U.S.C. § 922(g)(1). He had previously been convicted of assault causing serious bodily injury. Before trial, Old Chief (D) filed a motion for an order requiring the Government (P) to refrain from making any reference to his prior conviction other than the fact that it was a crime punishable by imprisonment exceeding one year. Old Chief (D) argued that the Government (P) was prohibited from revealing the name and nature of the prior conviction under Fed. R. Evid. 403, which prevents the introduction of evidence where its probative value is substantially outweighed by prejudicial nature. The Government (P) refused to join in Old Chief's (D) requested stipulation, and the trial court permitted the Government (P) to introduce the nature of Old Chief's (D) prior conviction. Old Chief (D) was found guilty on all counts and appealed. The circuit court affirmed, Old Chief (D) appealed again, and the Supreme Court granted certiorari.

ISSUE: During a prosecution for violation of 18 U.S.C. § 922(g)(1), may a court permit a defendant to concede the fact of a prior conviction before the government has the opportunity to offer evidence identifying the previous offense?

HOLDING AND DECISION: (Souter, J.) Yes. During a prosecution for violation of 18 U.S.C. § 922(g)(1), which prohibits possession of a firearm by anyone with a felony conviction, a court may permit a defendant to concede the fact of a prior conviction before the government has the opportunity to offer evidence identifying the previ-

ous offense. Rule 403 authorizes the exclusion of relevant evidence when its probative value is substantially outweighed by the danger of unfair prejudice, confusion of the issues, or misleading the jury, or by concerns of undue delay, waste of time, or needless presentation of cumulative evidence. This Rule serves to prevent the admission of evidence which, although concededly may be relevant, is likely to lure a fact-finder to declare guilt on a ground different from that at issue in the present case. Rule 403 requires a balancing of interests, and 18 U.S.C. § 922(g)(1) raises a unique and specific problem. Examining the statutory language of 18 U.S.C. § 922(g)(1) reveals that the prior-conviction requirement indicates no congressional concern for the specific name or nature of the offense beyond what is necessary to place it within the broad category of qualifying felonies. The Government (P) also argues that any stipulation should not be allowed to diminish the "full evidentiary force" of the Government's (P) case. The storytelling aspect of a trial and the force of a witness relating events as they occur are legitimate tools of the prosecution and a naked admission of the defense can neutralize the effectiveness of that tool. Acknowledging the Government's (P) right to choose its method of prosecution is not relevant here, however, when the defendant's legal status is the sole issue and not anything with a narrative. Therefore, Old Chief (D) was correct in arguing the most the jury needs to know about the conviction was that it falls within the class of crimes that Congress thought should bar a convict from possessing a gun. Any further mention of the previous crime should be prohibited. Reversed and remanded.

DISSENT: (O'Connor, J.) The majority misapplies Rule 403 and upsets longstanding precedent regarding criminal convictions. The Court is incorrect in stating that Congress did not intend for the name and nature of the crime under 18 U.S.C. § 922(g)(1) to be revealed. Furthermore, the Court never precisely explains why it constitutes unfair prejudice for the Government (P) to directly prove an essential element of the offense under 18 U.S.C. § 922(g)(1). The Court manufactures a new rule which precludes the Government (P) from proving all of the required elements of the charged offense, as is required by the Constitution.

▶ ANALYSIS

As the majority argues, it would seem as if the fact of the prior conviction would be sufficient since the jury would know that it was a felony punishable by more than one

Continued on next page.

year in prison. To many, this alone would be prejudicial. Despite the dissent's objections, it is important to keep in mind that this ruling is limited to the statute at hand, 18 U.S.C. § 922(g)(1), and is therefore quite a narrow holding.

■═■

Quicknotes

CERTIORARI A discretionary writ issued by a superior court to an inferior court in order to review the lower court's decisions; the Supreme Court's writ ordering such review.

FED. R. EVID. 403 Discretionary rule that allows a trial judge to exclude evidence if the danger of unfair prejudice to defendant outweighs its probative value.

FELONY A criminal offense of greater seriousness than a misdemeanor; felonies are generally defined pursuant to statute as any crime that is punishable by death or by a term of imprisonment exceeding one year.

UNFAIR PREJUDICE Risk that a defendant will be convicted based on an improper reason.

■═■

The Specialized Relevance Rules

Quick Reference Rules of Law

Tuer v. McDonald

Patient's widow (P) v. Doctor (D)

Md. Ct. App., 347 Md. 507, 701 A.2d 1101 (1997).

NATURE OF CASE: Medical malpractice suit.

FACT SUMMARY: Plaintiff brought suit against St. Joseph's Hospital (D) and two surgeons alleging medical malpractice based on their failure to readminister Heparin, an anticoagulant, to her husband after his surgery was postponed, allegedly leading to his suffering from cardiac arrest and subsequent death.

RULE OF LAW

Subsequent remedial measure evidence is not generally admissible for impeachment purposes if it is merely offered to contradict a defense witness's testimony.

FACTS: Mary Tuer (P) brought a medical malpractice suit against St. Joseph's Hospital ("the hospital") (D) and doctors McDonald (D) and Brawley (D) after her husband, Eugene, died of cardiac arrest while awaiting coronary artery bypass graft surgery (CABG). Eugene was admitted to the hospital (D) and scheduled for surgery. He was placed on Atenolol and Heparin. Following hospital (D) procedure, the anesthesiologist stopped the Heparin Monday morning so that Eugene would not have an anticoagulant in his system during surgery. Eugene was prepared for surgery, but an emergency involving another patient required Eugene's surgery to be postponed. Shortly thereafter, Eugene went into cardiac arrest and died the next day. After Eugene's death, the hospital (D) changed its procedure with respect to discontinuing Heparin for patients with stable angina. Heparin is now continued until the patient is taken into the operating room. The defendants made a motion in limine to exclude reference to the change in procedure. Tuer (P) argued the evidence was admissible since the change was not a remedial measure because the hospital claimed the prior procedure was correct and she was entitled to prove the change to show that continuing Heparin was "feasible." The trial court rejected the first argument but stated that it would admit the evidence if the hospital (D) denied feasibility.

ISSUE: Is subsequent remedial measure evidence generally admissible for impeachment purposes if it is merely offered to contradict a defense witness's testimony?

HOLDING AND DECISION: (Wilner, J.) No. Subsequent remedial measure evidence is not generally admissible for impeachment purposes if it is merely offered to contradict a defense witness's testimony. Maryland Rule 5-407 exempts evidence of subsequent remedial measures when it is offered to prove feasibility, if feasibility has been controverted. This requires the court to determine what is meant by the term "feasibility" and whether feasibility was in fact controverted. Jurisdictions are divided in construing the feasibility exception. One view is that the term "feasibility" should be defined narrowly, excluding evidence of subsequent remedial measures unless the defendant specifically argues the measures were not possible under the prevailing circumstances. This view states that feasibility is not controverted (and subsequent remedial evidence not admissible) if a defendant contends the design or practice was chosen due to its perceived advantage over the alternative design or practice; if the defendant claims the instructions or warnings were adequate and additional or different warnings or instructions could not have been given; or the defendant claims the alternative would not have prevented the type of injury sustained in the present case. The other, more expansive view concludes that "feasible" applies not only to that which is possible but also to that which is capable of being utilized successfully. Here, the expert testimony did not suggest that the Heparin could not have been readministered following the postponement of Eugene's surgery; instead they contend there were no signs of renewed unstable angina. McDonald (D) stated that the Heparin was not continued because he regarded it as unsafe is equal to a statement that it was unfeasible. This statement suffices to controvert the feasibility of the measure. Affirmed.

ANALYSIS

The exclusion of evidence for subsequent remedial measures is based primarily on public policy reasons. The legislature seeks to encourage businesses and persons to adopt improved procedures or designs. If evidence of such improvements were admissible, the fear is that this evidence would lead to a presumption of negligence or admission of guilt with respect to the prior procedure.

Quicknotes

MEDICAL MALPRACTICE Conduct on the part of a doctor falling below that demonstrated by other doctors of ordinary skill and competency under the circumstances, resulting in damages.

MOTION IN LIMINE Motion by one party brought prior to trial to exclude the potential introduction of prejudicial evidence.

PUBLIC POLICY Policy administered by the state with respect to the health, safety and morals of its people

Continued on next page.

CASENOTE® LEGAL BRIEFS | **19**
Evidence

in accordance with common notions of fairness and decency.

SUBSEQUENT REMEDIAL MEASURES Actions taken by a defendant to correct the instrumentality that caused an injury; inadmissible to show any liability or culpability on the part of the defendant.

■≡■

Bankcard America, Inc. v. Universal Bancard Systems, Inc.

Independent sales organization (P) v. Alleged contract breacher (D)

203 F.3d 477 (7th Cir.), *cert. denied*, 531 U.S. 877 (2000).

NATURE OF CASE: Appeal from order for new trial and entry of judgment for plaintiff.

FACT SUMMARY: A trial judge threw out the jury verdict for defendant and ordered a new trial, citing error of the first trial judge in admitting evidence of settlement discussions. The new trial also resulted in a jury verdict for defendant, but the trial judge threw out that verdict as well for insufficient evidentiary support. Defendant appealed the award of the new trial and the subsequent override of the jury verdicts.

RULE OF LAW

Evidence of settlement negotiations is admissible if offered for a purpose other than to establish liability.

FACTS: Bankcard America, Inc. (Bankcard) (P), an independent sales organization (ISO), subcontracted with Universal Bancard Systems, Inc. (Universal) (D) to sign up merchants for credit card transactions. Universal (D) agreed to refrain from recruiting merchants for any Bankcard competitor ISO for one year after termination of the contract with Bankcard (P). Bankcard (P) subsequently terminated the contract, sued Universal (D) for breach of contract, and Universal (D) counterclaimed against Bankcard (P) for breach of contract. After approximately three months, Universal (D) began turning merchant accounts over to a Bankcard (P) competitor. Universal (D) contended that it did so because it believed it was allowed to do so under a settlement with Bankcard (P). At trial, the judge conducted a Fed. R. Evid. 408 review to determine if that reason was admissible because it involved settlement negotiations. The trial judge allowed the evidence and the jury returned a verdict for Universal (D). The presiding judge became a senior judge and Judge Posner took the case. Judge Posner threw out the jury verdict and ordered a new trial, citing, inter alia, that the trial judge erred in allowing in the evidence of settlement negotiations. The second jury also returned a verdict for Universal (D), but Judge Posner threw that verdict out as well, citing insufficient evidentiary support for the verdict. Universal (D) appealed, claiming the second trial should not have been ordered because the settlement negotiation evidence was properly admitted.

ISSUE: Is evidence of settlement negotiations admissible if offered for a purpose other than to establish liability?

HOLDING AND DECISION: (Evans, J.) Yes. Evidence of settlement negotiations is admissible if offered for a purpose other than to establish liability. Universal (D)

needed to explain to the jury why it thought it was allowed to convert the merchant accounts prior to the expiration of the one year contract deadline. Simply because the discussions that led to that decision occurred around a settlement table does not automatically exclude them under Rule 408. That rule only excludes evidence of settlement negotiations if offered to show the liability of one party. Rule 408 is not meant to allow one party to encourage the other into breaching a contract and then preventing an explanation of that breach because the encouragement occurred during settlement discussions. Judge Posner erred in ordering the second trial and the first verdict should be reinstated. The second verdict is thus a nullity. Remanded for entry of an amended judgment.

ANALYSIS

Fed. R. Evid. 408 is intended to protect open communication between parties in hopes of encouraging settlements. Admitting all settlement discussions would have a chilling effect on such negotiations. The protection, however, is not intended to extend to unscrupulous companies encouraging damaging behavior and then later benefiting from the inability to justify that behavior. Allowing evidence of settlement discussions that range outside of liability is appropriate.

Quicknotes

FED. R. EVID. 408 Evidence of compromise or offers to compromise may not be admitted to prove liability for or invalidity of a claim of its amount. The evidence may, however, be admitted for other purposes.

INTER ALIA Among other things.

Williams v. McCoy

Motor vehicle driver (P) v. Motor vehicle driver (D)

N.C. Ct. App., 145 N.C. 111, 550 S.E.2d 796 (2001).

NATURE OF CASE: Appeal from judgment for plaintiff in motor vehicle case.

FACT SUMMARY: Plaintiff and defendant were in a motor vehicle accident and plaintiff sought damages. At trial, plaintiff was prohibited from mentioning insurance in any fashion and defendant used that to imply that plaintiff was litigious. Plaintiff appealed, contending she should have been allowed to discuss insurance outside of a liability context.

🏛 RULE OF LAW
Evidence related to insurance is admissible so long as it is offered other than to show the mere existence or non-existence of insurance as evidence of negligence or wrongdoing.

FACTS: Joanne Williams (P) sought damages from Mia McCoy (D) arising from a motor vehicle accident involving them both. Williams (P) hired an attorney after McCoy's (D) insurance adjuster pressured Williams (P) to settle because she had a prior injury and she was "wasting [her] time." After meeting with the attorney, Williams (P) visited her chiropractor to address her injuries. At trial, however, Williams (P) was not allowed to explain why she hired the attorney prior to visiting her chiropractor because the trial court prohibited any mention of insurance. The trial court relied on Fed. R. Evid. 411, which prohibits testimony concerning the existence or non-existence of liability insurance as evidence of negligence or wrongdoing. The defense attorney elicited a confusing response from Williams (P) as to why she hired her attorney when she did, and then implied that she hired the attorney because she was litigious and greedy. Williams (P) could not correct the confusion because she was prohibited from mentioning the insurance claims adjuster. The jury returned a verdict for Williams (P) in the amount of $3,000 and the judge assessed the costs of the action against Williams (P). Williams (P) appealed, claiming her testimony about the claims adjuster would not fall under Rule 411 and should have been admitted.

ISSUE: Is evidence related to insurance admissible so long as it is offered other than to show the mere existence or non-existence of insurance as evidence of negligence or wrongdoing?

HOLDING AND DECISION: (Timmons-Goodson, J.) Yes. Evidence related to insurance is admissible so long as it is offered other than to show the mere existence or non-existence of insurance as evidence of negligence or wrongdoing. Williams (P) was not testifying to the fact that McCoy (D) had liability insurance and therefore was negligent. Williams (P) wanted to testify that a negative experience with McCoy's (D) claims adjuster led to Williams (P) hiring an attorney prior to visiting her chiropractor. This testimony would have rehabilitated Williams's (P) character after the defense attorney painted her as litigious and greedy in hiring an attorney for no apparent reason prior to visiting her chiropractor. The trial court erred in holding that this testimony fell under Rule 411. The prejudice to defendant is slight when compared to the prejudice to plaintiff if the evidence is not admitted. Reversed and remanded.

▶ ANALYSIS

The trial judge was taking Rule 411 to literally exclude any mention of even the word "insurance." The intent of Rule 411 is to prevent jurors from assuming that the existence of liability insurance means the insurance holder was negligent. The rule was not intended to bar any discussion of insurance no matter how relevant. Additionally, most jurors are going to be aware that most drivers of motor vehicles have liability insurance anyway. Mentioning the existence of the insurance in another context will have no overtly prejudicial effect.

Quicknotes

FED. R. EVID. 105 Defines the limited admissibility of some evidence.

FED. R. EVID. 411 Evidence one was insured or not insured against liability may not be admitted upon the issue of whether the person acted negligently or wrongfully.

REVERSIBLE ERROR A substantial error that might reasonably have prejudiced the party complaining.

United States v. Biaggi

Federal government (P) v. Convicted former Congressman (D)

909 F.2d 662 (2d Cir. 1990), *cert. denied sub nom. Simon v. United States*, 499 U.S. 904 (1991).

NATURE OF CASE: Appeal from criminal conviction.

FACT SUMMARY: Defendant refused an offer of immunity from the government because he claimed he had no inside knowledge of wrongdoing to offer in exchange for immunity. At trial, defendant sought to introduce this refusal as further proof of his innocence, but the trial judge excluded it. Defendant appealed, contending the evidence should have been admissible under Fed. R. Evid. 403 as more probative than prejudicial.

🏛 RULE OF LAW
A rejected immunity offer is significantly more probative than prejudicial and should be admissible as evidence of innocence.

FACTS: Congressman Mario Biaggi (D) was indicted with several others, including John Mariotta (D), former chief executive officer of Wedtech, in connection with a New York corporation illegally receiving Defense Department contracts. The Government (P) offered Mariotta (D) immunity in exchange for testimony of wrongdoing on the part of the others, but Mariotta (D) claimed to have no such knowledge of wrongdoing. At trial, Mariotta (D) sought to introduce his rejection of immunity as further evidence that he had no knowledge of any wrongdoing and was not guilty of the charges. The Government (P) claimed the Fed. R. Evid. 410 prevented admission of such evidence, much as evidence of plea negotiations is not admissible. The trial judge weighed the evidence against Fed. R. Evid. 403 for its prejudicial and probative value and held that the evidence was not probative of anything more than Mariotta's (D) not guilty plea. The jury convicted Mariotta (D) and he appealed, contending the evidence of his immunity rejection did not fall under Rule 410, was more probative than prejudicial under Rule 403, and should have been admitted.

ISSUE: Is a rejected immunity offer significantly more probative than prejudicial and admissible as evidence of innocence?

HOLDING AND DECISION: (Newman, J.) Yes. A rejected immunity offer is significantly more probative than prejudicial and should be admissible as evidence of innocence. Rule 410 prohibits admission of evidence of plea negotiations against the defendant. The government is not necessarily entitled to the same protection, and an immunity rejection is not the same as a plea agreement rejection. Immunity would protect a person from all con-

sequences and most people would take that opportunity. Rejection of such an opportunity certainly supports a defendant's contention that he had nothing to offer in exchange for the immunity and was innocent of any knowledge of wrongdoing. The admission of such evidence of consciousness of innocence is very probative to the defendant's theory and not particularly prejudicial to the Government (P) which is presenting evidence of defendant's consciousness of guilt. Admission of such evidence provides a fair presentation of defendant's case. New trial ordered.

▶ ANALYSIS

Rejection of immunity is significantly different from rejection of a plea agreement. A defendant may simply prefer to take her chances at trial and gain an acquittal rather than accepting certain punishment under a plea agreement. Immunity offers complete protection, so a person conscious of her guilt would most likely accept such an offer. Where relevance of evidence so highly outweighs its prejudice, the evidence should be admitted.

■══■

Quicknotes

FED. R. EVID. 403 Discretionary rule that allows a trial judge to exclude evidence if the danger of unfair prejudice to defendant outweighs its probative value.

FED. R. EVID. 410 Addresses the inadmissibility of pleas, plea discussions and other related statements, except in limited exceptions.

IMMUNITY FROM PROSECUTION Statutory protection from prosecution afforded to a witness in exchange for his testimony.

■══■

Character Evidence

Quick Reference Rules of Law

People v. Zackowitz

State of New York (P) v. Convicted murderer (D)

N.Y. Ct. App., 254 N.Y. 192, 172 N.E. 466 (1930).

NATURE OF CASE: Appeal of first-degree murder conviction.

FACT SUMMARY: Coppola, the decedent, insulted Zackowitz's (D) wife, and Zackowitz (D) later, while in a rage and under the influence of alcohol, shot and killed him.

🏛 RULE OF LAW
Character is never an issue in a criminal prosecution unless the defendant chooses to make it one.

FACTS: Coppola, the decedent, was one of four men who insulted Zackowitz's (D) wife. Zackowitz (D) threatened to kill them if they did not leave within five minutes. Zackowitz (D) walked his wife home, where she told him that the men had propositioned her. Zackowitz (D) had been drinking and went into a rage. He either armed himself with a pistol or had previously been carrying one (he offered two different stories, the latter one at trial) and went back to see if the men were still there. There were words and a fight, during which Zackowitz (D) shot Coppola. Zackowitz (D) left the scene and was subsequently arrested about two months later. The question at trial was Zackowitz's (D) state of mind. Was the murder premeditated or was it done in the heat of a liquor-induced rage (second-degree murder)? The prosecution was allowed to introduce, over Zackowitz's (D) objection, testimony showing that Zackowitz (D) owned three other pistols and a tear gas gun. These weapons had been obtained prior to the shooting, and there was no claim made that they were carried by Zackowitz (D) when he shot Coppola. The evidence was introduced to show that Zackowitz (D) was "a desperate type of criminal," a "person criminally inclined." Zackowitz (D) was convicted of first-degree murder.

ISSUE: Should a defendant's guilt of a specific crime be inferable from his general character?

HOLDING AND DECISION: (Cardozo, J.) No. It is a fundamental rule that character is never an issue in a criminal prosecution unless the defendant chooses to make it one. In a very real sense, a defendant starts his life anew. His guilt must be established with regard to the particular crime with which he is charged. The law has made a policy decision to exclude evidence of this nature in order to protect the innocent. "The natural and inevitable tendency of the tribunal—whether judge or jury—is to give excessive weight to the vicious record of crime thus exhibited, and either to allow it to bear too strongly on the present charge, or to take the proof of it as justifying a condemnation

irrespective of guilt of the present charge." (Wigmore, *Evidence*, vol. 1, § 194, and cases cited.) The evidence of the hidden guns would be admissible if they had been purchased subsequent to Zackowitz's (D) wife being insulted in order to show motive or design or if Zackowitz (D) had been carrying all of them (act of preparation). However, the fact that Zackowitz (D) had the guns at home does not tend to prove, even inferentially, his murder of Coppola was premeditated. Ownership of weapons was not relevant to the charge. Reversed. New trial ordered.

DISSENT: (Pound, J.) The real question here is whether the matter relied on has such a connection with the crime charged as to be admissible on any ground. If so, the fact that it constitutes another distinct crime does not render it inadmissible. The defendant was presented to the jury not as a man of a dangerous disposition in general, but as one who, having an opportunity to select a weapon to carry out his threats, proceeded to do so. The judgment of conviction should be affirmed.

▶ ANALYSIS

Aside from the prejudicial nature of character evidence in criminal prosecutions is the question of its probative value. If its introduction will not prove one of the elements of the crime charged, is it really relevant? Does the fact that Zackowitz (D) had weapons available prove, either directly or inferentially, that the killing was premeditated? If it does, why can't the same reasoning apply to anyone owning a single handgun, switchblade, etc.? The question here is whether Zackowitz (D) had a rational intent to murder Coppola prior to the commission of the killing. Does the fact that he had a weapon or weapons at home bear any relevance to intent? The law has made it a general policy that what a party was or had previously done is not relevant to the current charges against him. If the defendant introduces testimony as to his good character, the prosecution may rebut by introducing evidence as to his past crimes, misconduct, or reputation. The rationale is that the prosecution always has the right to rebut direct testimony and the fact that this would prejudice the defendant is irrelevant.

■=■

Quicknotes

ADMISSIBILITY OF EVIDENCE Refers to whether particular evidence may be received by the court to aid the jury in determining the resolution of a controversy.

Continued on next page.

CHARACTER EVIDENCE Evidence of someone's moral standing in a community based on reputation.

PREMEDITATION The contemplation of undertaking an activity prior to action.

■■■

United States v. Trenkler

2/5

Federal government (P) v. Alleged bomb builder (D)

61 F.3d 45 (1st Cir. 1995).

NATURE OF CASE: Appeal from criminal convictions related to a bombing.

FACT SUMMARY: At defendant's trial for building a bomb that killed a police officer, evidence of a prior bomb constructed by defendant was admitted to show identity, skill, and knowledge for the present bomb. Defendant was convicted and appealed, contending the prior bomb was not sufficiently similar for admissibility.

RULE OF LAW
Evidence of other crimes is admissible if there is a showing of "special relevance" beyond demonstrating criminal propensity and the evidence is more probative than prejudicial.

FACTS: Thomas Shay, Jr. allegedly approached Alfred Trenkler (D) about constructing a bomb to use against Thomas Shay, Sr. in Roslindale, Massachusetts. Subsequently, a bomb was attached underneath Shay, Sr.'s car using a heavy magnet and Shay, Sr. called the Boston Police Department Bomb Squad. The bomb detonated, killing one officer and seriously injuring another. Trenkler (D) was indicted for constructing the bomb. At trial, the Government (P) sought to introduce evidence that Trenkler (D) constructed a similar bomb in Quincy years before and had confessed to making that bomb. The trial judge weighed the relevance of the evidence and its probative value and then ruled it was admissible. Experts testified for both sides as to the similarity of the bombs with the Government (P) offering expert testimony from the person responsible for maintaining the EXIS database that identified several characteristics common to both the Quincy and the Roslindale bombs. A jury convicted Trenkler (D) and he appealed, claiming the Quincy bomb was not sufficiently similar for admissibility.

ISSUE: Is evidence of other crimes admissible if there is a showing of "special relevance" beyond demonstrating criminal propensity and the evidence is more probative than prejudicial?

HOLDING AND DECISION: (Stahl, J.) Yes. Evidence of other crimes is admissible if there is a showing of "special relevance" beyond demonstrating criminal propensity and the evidence is more probative than prejudicial. The expert evidence on either side weighed relatively evenly as to the potential similarity or dissimilarity of the two bombs. Fed. R. Evid. 404(a) allows evidence of other crimes only if offered to show something other than a propensity of the defendant to criminal behavior. The Government (P) here was offering the evidence to show that the identity of the bomb maker was likely the same for the Roslindale bomb as for the Quincy bomb because the characteristics of the two bombs were so similar. Also, the evidence was offered to show that Trenkler (D) had the skill and the knowledge to make such a bomb. Thus, the evidence had "special relevance" under Rule 404(a) beyond showing criminal propensity. The next step is to consider the evidence under Rule 404(b). The defendant was not unfairly prejudiced here because the Quincy bombing did not result in loss of life or major property destruction and the trial judge accurately instructed the jury as to the weight of that evidence. Affirmed.

DISSENT: (Torruella, C.J.) The expert testifying about the EXIS data neglected to explain why he input only certain characteristics of the two bombs rather than comparing all characteristics. The majority does not point out this inconsistency, but it is vital to understand that the expert was specifically looking to connect the two incidents.

ANALYSIS

The "special relevance" rule does not require that the two bombs be exactly identical in order to be admissible under Rule 404. The battle of the experts on the similarities allows the jury to determine the significance of the similarity of the bombs as it relates to the identity of the bomb maker.

■=■

Quicknotes

FED. R. EVID. 404 Sets forth the general rule that evidence of a person's character is inadmissible to prove his conduct, with certain exceptions.

■=■

United States v. Stevens

Federal government (P) v. Convicted felon (D)

935 F.2d 1380 (3d Cir. 1991).

NATURE OF CASE: Appeal from convictions for robbery and sexual assault.

FACT SUMMARY: At defendant's trial for robbery and sexual assault of two military personnel, the defendant sought to introduce evidence of a similar crime occurring just a few days later where he was identified as one who was not the perpetrator. That evidence was deemed inadmissible and defendant appealed.

🏛 RULE OF LAW
A defendant may introduce other crimes' evidence so long as the evidence tends to negate his guilt and is more probative than prejudicial.

FACTS: A black male robbed two white Air Force police officers at gunpoint and sexually assaulted the female. At the police department, both officers identified a photograph of Richard Stevens (D), a black male, as that of their attacker. Stevens (D) was charged with the robbery and sexual assault, but the first trial ended in a mistrial due to a deadlocked jury. At the second trial, Stevens (D) sought to admit evidence of a similar robbery occurring days after the first because the black victim in that robbery, Tyrone Mitchell, did not identify Stevens (D) as his attacker. Stevens (D) claimed that this lent credence to his theory that the first two victims misidentified him, in part because of his race. The evidence was not allowed and the jury convicted Stevens (D) of robbery and sexual assault. Stevens (D) appealed, contending that the "reverse 404(b)" evidence of other crimes should have been admissible.

ISSUE: May a defendant introduce other crimes' evidence so long as the evidence tends to negate his guilt and is more probative than prejudicial?

HOLDING AND DECISION: (Becker, J.) Yes. A defendant may introduce other crimes' evidence so long as the evidence tends to negate his guilt and is more probative than prejudicial. Other crimes' evidence introduced under Fed. R. Evid. 404(b) is usually introduced against a defendant, but "reverse 404(b)" is introduced to exonerate defendants. Stevens (D) claimed that the victims misidentified him because he is black and they are white. He wanted to introduce further proof of the alleged misidentification by offering the evidence of the Mitchell robbery to show the similarities between the robberies and the fact that Mitchell, another black man, did not believe Stevens (D) to be his attacker. The similarities between the robberies are significant and the lack of sexual assault in the Mitchell robbery can be attributed to the fact that Mitchell did not have a female companion with him. The Government (P) argued

that Stevens (D) should have to show more than one similar crime, misidentification as the perpetrator in a similar crime, or that the other crime was a "signature" crime attributable to someone else's crime pattern. Stevens (D) was asserting none of those things, but they are not necessary requirements for "reverse 404(b)." A defendant must simply demonstrate that the evidence offered tends to negate his guilt, and that it survives a Rule 403 analysis of probative versus prejudicial value. As no real risk existed that the trial would become a mini-trial of whether or not Stevens (D) robbed Mitchell, the evidence was highly probative for Stevens (D) and minimally prejudicial to the Government (P). The first jury ended in a deadlock, so the evidence against Stevens (D) was clearly relatively level on both sides and the error in not admitting the evidence was not harmless. Reversed and remanded.

▶ ANALYSIS

The Government (P) was in no danger of suffering unfair prejudice from the admission of Stevens's (D) evidence, so that aspect of Rule 403 was not a consideration. Rather, considerations of waste of resources and confusion of the issues were paramount. The danger here still lies with the defendant because his offer of proof of similarity of the instant crime to another could lead to the possibility of him becoming a suspect in the other crime—as happened in *Stevens* when the military police looked at the defendant for both this robbery/assault and the Mitchell robbery. As with all other crimes' evidence, the trial judge should carefully balance the probative value of the offered evidence with the prejudicial value.

■══■

Quicknotes

FED. R. EVID. 403 Discretionary rule that allows a trial judge to exclude evidence if the danger of unfair prejudice to defendant outweighs its probative value.

FED. R. EVID. 404(b) Evidence of other crimes, wrongs or acts is not admissible to prove the character of a person in order to show that on a particular occasion the person acted in accordance with the character, although it may be admissible for other purposes.

■══■

United States v. DeGeorge

Federal government (P) v. Convicted insurance defrauder (D)

380 F.3d 1203 (9th Cir. 2004).

NATURE OF CASE: Appeal for abuse of discretion in admitting evidence of prior acts.

FACT SUMMARY: An attorney (D) participated in a scheme to defraud an insurance company by purchasing a yacht, inflating its value, purchasing insurance, and trying to sink it to collect the insurance. The judge admitted evidence that he had purchased and lost three other yachts, but did not allow the Government (P) to admit evidence that the attorney collected insurance on those three lost boats.

🏛 RULE OF LAW
Evidence of prior acts may be admitted if necessary to offer a coherent and comprehensible story about the commission of the crime.

FACTS: Rex K. DeGeorge (D), an attorney, participated in a scheme to defraud an insurance company by purchasing a yacht, inflating its value, purchasing insurance, and trying to sink it to collect the insurance. He bought the boat from an Italian builder for $1.9 million. He assigned his rights in it to Continental Pictures Corp., which then sold its interest in the yacht to Polaris Pictures Corp. for $3.6 million. DeGeorge (D) created Polaris, and Paul Ebeling was its President. Polaris financed the purchase of the yacht through notes issued by U.S. Inbanco, Ltd., a corporation formed by DeGeorge (D) and named to sound like a bank. DeGeorge (D) then traded all his shares of Polaris to Tridon Corporation, who's CEO was Ebeling, in exchange for two million shares of Tridon. Tridon, not DeGeorge (D), was now the owner of the yacht. Tridon was made the owner because DeGeorge (D) had lost three other boats, one stolen and two that sank, for which he collected insurance, and that loss history would prevent him from getting insurance in his own name. The district court judge admitted evidence that he had purchased and lost three other yachts, but did not allow the Government (P) to admit details about the losses or evidence that DeGeorge (D) collected insurance on those three lost boats. After insurance was purchased, DeGeorge (D), Ebeling, and a third person left Viareggio, Italy, for the maiden voyage of the yacht, and took turns drilling holes in the boat to sink it. They were unable to sink it, and at dawn, Italian authorities patrolling the coast approached. DeGeorge (D) and his companions made up a story involving a former Russian submarine captain who looked like Robert Redford, and another man, who overpowered DeGeorge (D) and his crew, locked them in the cabin, and began destroying the boat. DeGeorge (D) submitted the insurance claim, and he and the others were indicted for mail fraud, wire fraud, and perjury. DeGeorge (D) was convicted.

ISSUE: May evidence of prior acts be admitted if necessary to offer a coherent and comprehensible story about the commission of the crime?

HOLDING AND DECISION: (Gibson, J.) Yes. Evidence of prior acts may be admitted if necessary to offer a coherent and comprehensible story about the commission of the crime. DeGeorge's (D) concealment of the prior losses was connected to the facts of the current indictment. The Government (P) specifically alleged that DeGeorge's (D) scheme included sham transactions to hide ownership, and the jury could not have understood the relevance of all of the transactions to the fake corporations without hearing some explanation for why DeGeorge (D) couldn't get insurance in his own name. The loss evidence could imply a tendency to defraud insurance companies, and in that sense could be prejudicial, but the district court took precautions against that by not allowing the Government (P) to present evidence that DeGeorge (D) collected under the previous policies, or the details of the loss, and by allowing only as much as was relevant to the specific issues. Affirmed.

▶ ANALYSIS

The prosecution is permitted under the Federal Rules of Evidence to weave together a story that makes sense to a jury. While courts are wary of admitting evidence of prior acts, they will often admit them to the extent necessary to provide the jury with a solid picture of the facts, provided there is no danger of prejudice to the defendant.

■≡■

Quicknotes

MAIL FRAUD A federal offense whereby an individual utilizes the mails with the intent to defraud.

PERJURY The making of false statements under oath.

WIRE FRAUD Use of interstate wire to perpetrate a fraud.

■≡■

2|5

Huddleston v. United States

Seller of stolen goods (D) v. Federal government (P)

485 U.S. 681 (1988).

NATURE OF CASE: Review of conviction based on buying and selling stolen goods.

FACT SUMMARY: In a prosecution based on dealing in stolen goods, the trial court did not make a preliminary finding as to the accuracy of evidence of similar acts introduced to show motive and knowledge, prior to admission of the evidence.

🏛 RULE OF LAW
A court need not make, prior to admitting past acts introduced to show motive or knowledge, a preliminary finding that the acts occurred.

FACTS: Huddleston (D) was indicted on charges of buying and selling stolen goods. At trial, the prosecution sought to introduce evidence of prior similar transactions by Huddleston (D). The court, without making any preliminary findings that the alleged prior acts had occurred, admitted the evidence based on Fed. R. Evid. 404(b), which permits the introduction of evidence of prior acts to show motive or knowledge. Huddleston (D) was convicted, and the court of appeals affirmed. The Supreme Court accepted review.

ISSUE: Must a court make, prior to admitting past acts introduced to show motive or knowledge, a preliminary finding that the acts occurred?

HOLDING AND DECISION: (Rehnquist, C.J.) No. A court need not make, prior to admitting past acts introduced to show motive or knowledge, a preliminary finding that the acts occurred. Fed. R. Evid. 404(b) prohibits the use of evidence of prior acts to prove conduct in conformity therewith, but permits the introduction of such evidence to prove knowledge, motive, opportunity or the like. Huddleston (D) argued the court must preliminarily find that the prior acts did in fact occur. However, this runs contrary to the structure of the Rules of Evidence. Relevant evidence is to be admitted. Evidence of prior conduct, if relevant to show a legitimate item such as motive or knowledge, is equally admissible. It is for the jury to decide whether the prior act occurred. The only determination the court needs to make is that the evidence is relevant, which is to say, that a jury could find that the prior acts do in fact show motive or knowledge. Here, the court appears to have done just that. Affirmed.

▶ ANALYSIS

Fed. R. Evid. 404(b) is essentially an exclusionary section. It prohibits otherwise relevant evidence of prior acts to be introduced to prove conduct in conformity therewith. The rationale behind this is that the possibility of prejudice inherently outweighs whatever probative value exists. However, prior acts introduced to prove other than acts in conformity therewith are admissible.

■=■

Quicknotes

EXTRINSIC EVIDENCE Evidence that is not contained within the text of a document or contract, but which is derived from the parties' statements or the circumstances under which the agreement was made.

FED. R. EVID. 104 Permits a court to consider all non-privileged matters, whether independently admissible or not, when determining preliminary issues of admissibility.

FED. R. EVID. 404(b) Evidence of other crimes, wrongs or acts is not admissible to prove the character of a person in order to show that on a particular occasion the person acted in accordance with the character, although it may be admissible for other purposes.

SUFFICIENCY OF EVIDENCE When all the evidence taken together would warrant a conviction.

■=■

Lannan v. State

Child molester (D) v. State (P)

Ind. Sup. Ct., 600 N.E.2d 1334 (1992).

NATURE OF CASE: Appeal from conviction for child molestation.

FACT SUMMARY: Defendant was convicted of child molestation after testimony regarding prior, uncharged acts of molestation was introduced at trial.

🏛 RULE OF LAW
The depraved sexual instinct exception to the general rule against admissibility of prior bad acts should no longer be recognized.

FACTS: Lannan (D) was charged with molesting a child. At trial the alleged victim also testifed with regard to an act that was not charged. Additionally, another girl testified that Lannan (D) had also molested her in the past. This testimony was admitted pursuant to the depraved sexual instinct exception to the usual rules regarding uncharged misconduct. Lannan (D) was convicted and appealed.

ISSUE: Should the depraved sexual instinct exception to the general rule against admissibility of prior bad acts continue to be recognized?

HOLDING AND DECISION: (Shepard, C.J.) No. The depraved sexual instinct exception to the general rule against admissibility of prior bad acts should no longer be recognized. The exception originated at a time when accusations of child molesting appeared improbable. The exception was thought to be needed in order to bolster the testimony of children. Also, it was thought that sexual predators had a higher recidivism rate than other criminals. Sadly, the first rationale is no longer required and there is no clear and valid evidence supporting the latter justification. However, the general rule prohibiting the introduction of character evidence that shows the defendant was a bad person remains fundamental. The justification for maintaining the exception is outweighed by its very broad nature. The rule does not require any similarity between the prior bad acts and the crime charged. In order for prior bad acts to come into evidence, courts must insist that such evidence be used only to prove an element of the crime. Thus, prior sexual misconduct can be admitted if it proves motive, opportunity, intent, plan, knowledge, or identity. In the present case, the testimony regarding Lannan's (D) misconduct with another girl at a different location has no connection to the charged conduct. Therefore, it should not have been admitted into evidence. However, this was harmless error, and Lannan's (D) conviction is affirmed.

CONCURRENCE: (Givan, J.) The reasons for the depraved sexual instinct exception remain today and the rule should be maintained.

▶ ANALYSIS

Other states have also rejected the depraved sexual instinct exception. Delaware and Tennessee have determined that there are no valid reasons for maintaining different rules for sexual misconduct. Rule 404 governs character evidence and prior bad acts.

Quicknotes

FED. R. EVID. 404 Sets forth the general rule that evidence of a person's character is inadmissible to prove his conduct, with certain exceptions.

State v. Kirsch

State (P) v. Convicted sexual offender (D)

N.H. Sup. Ct., 139 N.H. 647, 662 A.2d 937 (1995).

NATURE OF CASE: Appeal from conviction for sexual assault.

FACT SUMMARY: At defendant's trial for sexual assault, the prosecution introduced evidence in the form of testimony from several other victims that defendant sexually assaulted them in the same manner as he had the victims in this case. Defendant appealed his conviction, claiming that the evidence should not have been admissible under Fed. R. Evid. 404(b).

🏛 RULE OF LAW
The burden is on the prosecution to prove the purpose for which it offers other crimes' evidence and that purpose cannot be merely to show predilection for the crime charged.

FACTS: David Kirsch (D) was charged with sexual assaults on three young girls. At his trial, the prosecution introduced other crimes' evidence under Fed. R. Evid. 404(b) in the form of testimony of three other women with similar stories of assault by the defendant. Kirsch (D) was found guilty and he appealed, claiming that the 404(b) evidence should have been inadmissible because it merely showed his predilection for sexually assaulting young girls in a specific pattern of behavior.

ISSUE: Is the burden on the prosecution to prove the purpose for which it offers other crimes' evidence?

HOLDING AND DECISION: (Batchelder, J.) Yes. The burden is on the prosecution to prove the purpose for which it offers other crimes' evidence and that purpose cannot be merely to show predilection for the crime charged. The Government (P) claimed that it offered the evidence of the prior assaults to show motive, to be probative of Kirsch's (D) intent, and to show common plan. Unfortunately for the Government (P), however, each argument distilled down to simply showing Kirsch's (D) pattern of behavior in molesting young, underprivileged girls lacking a father figure and who were attending Kirsch's (D) church. The evidence was not relevant to show motive, intent, or plan and it should not have been admitted. Its admission was prejudicial to Kirsch (D). Reversed and remanded.

CONCURRENCE AND DISSENT: (Thayer, J.) The majority offers too narrow a reading of the common plan exception. Kirsch's (D) plan was to befriend young, vulnerable girls and then molest them using a common set of criteria.

▶ ANALYSIS

Prosecutors had to be creative to fit past sexual assaults and child molestations into the definitions of intent, motive, and plan for them to become admissible in current trials. Congress responded to this dilemma by enacting Fed. R. Evid. 413–415 allowing evidence of past sexual misconduct in such cases.

■══■

Quicknotes

FED. R. EVID. 404(b) Evidence of other crimes, wrongs or acts is not admissible to prove the character of a person in order to show that on a particular occasion the person acted in accordance with the character, although it may be admissible for other purposes.

■══■

United States v. Guardia

Federal government (P) v. Convicted sexual offender (D)

135 F.3d 1326 (10th Cir. 1998).

NATURE OF CASE: Appeal from grant of motion in limine.

FACT SUMMARY: At defendant's trial for sexual abuse, the prosecution sought to introduce testimony of four other women claiming defendant similarly abused them. Defendant moved in limine to exclude the evidence and the trial court granted the motion. The Government (P) appealed claiming the evidence should have been admitted under Fed. R. Evid. 413.

🏛 RULE OF LAW
Relevant propensity evidence is admissible under Fed. R. Evid. 413 if defendant is accused of a sexual offense, the offered evidence is of defendant's commission of another sexual offense, and the evidence is not unfairly prejudicial.

FACTS: David Guardia (D), a gynecologist, allegedly committed sexual abuse on two patients when his examination crossed the line. At his trial for sexual abuse, the Government (P) offered the testimony under Fed. R. Evid. 413 of four other women with similar stories of abuse by Guardia (D). Guardia (D) filed a motion in limine to exclude the evidence and the trial court held that the risk of jury confusion substantially outweighed the probative value of the evidence. The Government (P) appealed, contending that the evidence was probative and not unfairly prejudicial and should have been admissible.

ISSUE: Is relevant propensity evidence admissible under Fed. R. Evid. 413 if defendant is accused of a sexual offense, the offered evidence is of defendant's commission of another sexual offense, and the evidence is not unfairly prejudicial?

HOLDING AND DECISION: (Tacha, J.) Yes. Relevant propensity evidence is admissible under Fed. R. Evid. 413 if defendant is accused of a sexual offense, the offered evidence is of defendant's commission of another sexual offense, and the evidence is not unfairly prejudicial. The evidence proffered here meets all of the threshold requirements to be admissible under Rule 413. The next step is to consider whether it satisfies the Rule 403 test. Some argue Rule 413 requires automatic admissibility of propensity evidence, while others argue a lenient Rule 403 test is required. Neither approach is correct, although Rule 413 does indeed favor the admissibility of the propensity evidence. The probative value of the propensity evidence will depend on such factors as similarity of the offense, closeness in time, frequency of prior acts, and intervening events. In this case, the additional testimony would in-crease the need for expert witnesses and explanation of the inappropriateness of each woman's exam, which would significantly increase the information presented to the jury. The district court did not abuse its discretion in finding the potential for jury confusion outweighed the probative value of the testimony. Affirmed.

▶ ANALYSIS

Rule 413 does not offer carte blanche to prosecutors seeking to introduce propensity evidence against defendants. Courts must still perform Rule 403 balancing tests and protect against prejudice to the defendant or to the judicial system.

■■■

Quicknotes

FED. R. EVID. 403 Allows a trial judge to exclude evidence if the danger of unfair prejudice to defendant outweighs its probative value.

FED. R. EVID. 413 Permits evidence of a defendant's commission of a similar offense of sexual assault to be admissible and considered for its bearing on any matter to which it is relevant.

MOTION IN LIMINE Motion by one party brought prior to trial to exclude the potential introduction of prejudicial evidence.

RELEVANT EVIDENCE Evidence having any tendency to prove or disprove a disputed fact.

■■■

United States v. Mound

Federal government (P) v. Convicted sexual offender (D)

157 F.3d 1153 (8th Cir. 1998), *cert. denied*, 525 U.S. 1089 (1999).

NATURE OF CASE: Denial of rehearing en banc.

FACT SUMMARY: [Facts not stated in casebook excerpt.]

 RULE OF LAW
[Rule of law not stated in casebook excerpt.]

FACTS: [Facts not stated in casebook excerpt.]

ISSUE: [Issue not stated in casebook excerpt.]

HOLDING AND DECISION: [Holding and decision not stated in casebook excerpt.]

DISSENT: (Arnold, J.) Propensity evidence has historically been excluded out of fear a jury will convict a defendant based on past bad acts rather than true guilt in the crime before them. Considering the strong history of this exclusion and the belief of the forty committee members appointed to study Fed. R. Evid. 413 that the Rule should not be adopted, this court can at least hear the case en banc. Reconsidering and reweighing matters already considered by Congress is inevitable in this type of review, but that is necessary when a change of this magnitude is made in the law.

▶ ANALYSIS

The dissent seeks to reevaluate the decision made by Congress when it passed Rule 413 and allowed propensity evidence in sexual offense cases. The rest of the court obviously did not agree with this level of judicial activism.

■═■

Quicknotes

FED. R. EVID. 413 Permits evidence of a defendant's commission of a similar offense of sexual assault to be admissible and considered for its bearing on any matter to which it is relevant.

■═■

Michelson v. United States

215

Bribery suspect (D) v. Federal government (P)

335 U.S. 469 (1948).

NATURE OF CASE: Appeal from a conviction of bribery.

FACT SUMMARY: Defendant claimed that he had been entrapped by the official he had allegedly bribed. Defendant introduced testimony as to his good reputation.

RULE OF LAW
When a defendant puts his character at issue by calling witnesses to testify as to his good character, the prosecution may ask those witnesses if they have heard of specific acts of bad conduct relating to the defendant.

FACTS: Michelson (D) was accused of bribing an official. Michelson (D) claimed that the official had demanded the money and had threatened to use his official power against Michelson (D) if the money was not paid. Michelson (D) claimed this was entrapment. The outcome of the trial depended upon whom the jury chose to believe, the official or Michelson (D). Michelson (D) introduced reputation evidence as to his own good reputation in the community. The prosecutor asked these witnesses if they had heard that Michelson (D) had been arrested for buying stolen goods some 20 years earlier. These questions were allowed over Michelson's (D) objection. The jury found him guilty.

ISSUE: When a defendant puts his reputation at issue by calling witnesses to testify as to his good character, may the prosecution ask those witnesses if they have heard of specific acts of bad conduct relating to the defendant?

HOLDING AND DECISION: (Jackson, J.) Yes. When a defendant puts his reputation at issue by calling witnesses to testify as to his good character, the prosecution may examine the witnesses as to the extent of their knowledge of the defendant's reputation. This includes specific acts of misconduct. The acts need not be identical to the charges raised against the defendant. It is sufficient that they cast doubt upon his truth, veracity, or reputation in the community. The law in this area is convoluted and archaic. The prosecution may not attempt to prove the defendant's bad character. However, the defendant may introduce evidence as to his good general reputation in the community. No specific acts may be testified to by these witnesses. Once the defendant has placed his reputation in issue the witnesses may be cross-examined as to specific acts of misconduct. These may include arrests where there was no conviction or even an indictment. These questions test the witnesses' knowledge of the defendant's reputation. A twenty-three-year-old conviction may

be excluded at the judge's discretion since the defendant may have been rehabilitated. Here, however, Michelson's (D) attorney mentioned a twenty-year-old conviction of a misdemeanor for trading in counterfeit watch dials. It was within the court's discretion to allow the admission of the earlier crime. The earlier crimes tended to diminish Michelson's (D) reputation evidence. The fact that they were old merely goes to the weight that the jury wishes to place upon these specific acts. Judgment affirmed.

DISSENT: (Rutledge, J.) Questioning of a reputation witness that is intended to "test the standards of the witness" should have been excluded, because it allows the opposing party to convey facts to the jury under the guise of probing the witness's standards by simply asking a question, depending on how it is worded and asked. And the defendant does not have the opportunity to reply. The prosecutor can clearly insinuate that the defendant had committed a crime, as was done in this case, and no instruction to the jury can possibly mitigate the prejudice produced.

ANALYSIS

The prosecution may introduce specific acts of misconduct where they show an ongoing conspiracy, establish a common plan, or establish the defendant's modus operandi. In *Hamilton v. State*, 129 Fla. 219, 17 So. 89 (1937), the Florida Supreme Court allowed the defendant to introduce reputation testimony from her fellow workers, even though she lived in a different area of the city and they never saw her socially.

Quicknotes

BRIBERY The offering, giving, receiving, or soliciting of something of value for the purpose of influencing the action of an official in the discharge of his public or legal duties.

CHARACTER EVIDENCE Evidence of someone's moral standing in a community based on reputation.

CHARACTER WITNESS One who is called to testify to the character and reputation of the defendant.

ENTRAPMENT An act by public officers that induces a defendant into committing a criminal act.

FED. R. EVID. 404 Sets forth the general rule that evidence of a person's character is inadmissible to prove his conduct, with certain exceptions.

Continued on next page.

FED. R. EVID. 405 When character evidence is admissible, proof may be made by testimony as to reputation or in the form of an opinion.

■━━■

Halloran v. Virginia Chemicals, Inc.

Auto mechanic (P) v. Chemical company (D)

N.Y. Ct. App., 361 N.E.2d 991, 41 N.Y.2d 386 (1977).

NATURE OF CASE: Personal injury product liability action.

FACT SUMMARY: The trial judge refused to allow Virginia Chemicals, Inc. (D) to introduce evidence that Halloran (P) had previously used an immersion heating coil to heat cans of refrigerant to show that he was acting in such a negligent fashion when one of the cans blew up and injured him.

🏛 RULE OF LAW
At least where the issue involves proof of a deliberate and repetitive practice, a party should be able to introduce evidence of habit or regular usage to allow the inference of its persistence, and hence negligence, on a particular occasion.

FACTS: Halloran (P), an automobile mechanic, sued Virginia Chemicals, Inc. (D) for the injuries he sustained when a can of refrigerant they produced exploded while he was using it to service the air-conditioning system in a car. The trial judge refused to permit Virginia Chemicals (D) to introduce evidence that Halloran (P) had, on previous occasions, ignored the label warnings on the can by using an immersion coil to heat the can so the refrigerant would flow more easily. The appellate division agreed that evidence of habit or usage was never admissible to establish that one persisted in such habit and hence acted negligently on a particular occasion.

ISSUE: Where the issue involves proof of a deliberate and repetitive practice, may evidence of habit or regular usage be admitted?

HOLDING AND DECISION: (Breitel, C.J.) Yes. At least where the issue involves proof of a deliberate and repetitive practice, a party should be able to introduce evidence of habit or regular usage to allow the inference of its persistence, and hence negligence, on a particular occasion. The statement that evidence of habit or regular usage is never admissible to establish negligence is too broad. Of course, conduct which involves other persons or independently controlled instrumentalities cannot produce a regular usage because of the likely variation of the circumstances in which such conduct will be indulged. However, proof of a deliberate repetitive practice by one in complete control of the circumstances, as in this case, is quite another matter and should be admissible because it is so highly probative. Of course, Virginia Chemicals (D) must be able to show on *voir dire* a sufficient number of instances of the conduct in question to justify introduction of habit or regular usage.

Order of Appellate Division modified by reversing so much of the order as affirmed the award of judgment to plaintiff.

▶ ANALYSIS

Since the days of the common-law reports, habit evidence has generally been admissible to prove conformity on specified occasions. However, where negligence is at issue, many courts have resisted allowing evidence of specific acts of carelessness or carefulness to create an inference that such conduct was repeated when like circumstances were again presented.

Quicknotes

HABIT A practice or custom of repeated behavior in response to a specific set of circumstances.

VOIR DIRE Examination of potential jurors on a case.

Impeachment and Character for Truthfulness

Quick Reference Rules of Law

United States v. Whitmore

Federal government (P) v. Convicted felon (D)

359 F.3d 609 (D.C. Cir. 2004).

NATURE OF CASE: Appeal of conviction for firearm and drug possession.

FACT SUMMARY: The trial court ruled that character witness testimony and the cross-examination of an arresting officer were inadmissible. Without any other evidence for his defense except cross-examining Government (P) witnesses for inconsistencies, Gerald F. Whitmore (D) was convicted for illegal firearm possession and drug possession.

🏛 **RULE OF LAW**
(1) A party may attack the credibility of a witness through reputation evidence of his character for truthfulness if the character witness is qualified by having an acquaintance with the witness, his community, and the circles in which he has moved.
(2) A party may attack the credibility of a witness by cross-examining him on specific instances of past conduct.

FACTS: Two officers of the District of Columbia police department directed a crowd to disperse, and all but Gerald F. Whitmore (D) complied. Officer Efrain Soto started running after Whitmore (D), and in the process saw Whitmore (D) throw a gun toward an apartment building next to an alley. Soto caught Whitmore (D), and when the other officer caught up, Soto found a gun in a window well of a nearby apartment building. The gun seemed to have been thrown against a building, in that it was covered with masonry dust and there were scuffs on it. Nothing was found in Whitmore's (D) right pocket, but cocaine was found in his left. Whitmore (D) argued in court that Soto planted the gun, and wanted to call three character witnesses—Jason Cherkis, Bruce Cooper, and Kenneth Edmonds—to testify as to Soto's character for truthfulness. Cherkis was a reporter, and wrote an article in January 2000 about Soto and three other officers. He would testify that Soto had a reputation as a liar, and his own opinion that Soto was a liar. Cooper was a criminal defense counsel who would testify about Soto's reputation for untruthfulness in the "court community." Edmonds used to live in the neighborhood where Soto worked and would testify as to his opinion that Soto was untruthful. Whitmore (D) also wanted to cross-examine Soto on the suspension of his driver's license and his failure to report the suspension to his supervisors, and on his failure to pay child support. The district court refused to allow the character witness testimony and the cross-examination of Soto. Without any other evidence for his defense except cross-examining

Government (P) witnesses for inconsistencies, Whitmore (D) was convicted for illegal firearm possession and drug possession.

ISSUE:
(1) May a party attack the credibility of a witness through reputation evidence of his character for truthfulness if the character witness is qualified by having an acquaintance with the witness, his community, and the circles in which he has moved?
(2) May a party attack the credibility of a witness by cross-examining him on specific instances of past conduct?

HOLDING AND DECISION: (Henderson, J.)
(1) Yes. A party may attack the credibility of a witness through reputation evidence of his character for truthfulness if the character witness is qualified by having an acquaintance with the witness, his community, and the circles in which he has moved. Fed. R. Evid. 608(a) permits reputation evidence. But Cherkis and Edmonds had no direct contact with Soto or his community for "some time," and the lower court did not abuse its discretion in excluding their testimony as being too remote from the time of trial. The trial court also did not abuse its discretion in excluding Cooper's testimony because it relied on Cooper's conversations with only a few other criminal defense counsels, a subset of the proposed "court community," and the foundation was therefore weak. Opinion evidence is also governed by Fed. R. Evid. 608(a), and even though the foundational requirement for it is easier to meet than that for reputation evidence, the district court did not abuse its discretion in excluding Cooper's and Edmond's opinions, because neither opinion had a reasonable basis, as far as the jury is concerned.
(2) Yes. A party may attack the credibility of a witness by cross-examining him on specific instances of past conduct. Fed. R. Evid. 608(b) permits the cross-examination. The trial court precluded cross-examination because it found that it was based on inadmissible hearsay—the record from the Maryland Motor Vehicle Administration. But a lawyer only needs a reasonable basis for asking questions on cross which tend to incriminate or degrade the witness in order to be permitted to cross-examine under Fed. R. Evid. 608(b), and Soto's Maryland driving record provided such a basis, despite that the record was inadmissible. In addition, because Soto provided the only eyewitness evidence to support the conviction, the district court's error in precluding

Continued on next page.

the cross-examination was not harmless error. Vacated in part, affirmed in part, and remanded.

▶ *ANALYSIS*

This case is very fact-based, but it illustrates courts' approach to the distinction between reputation and opinion evidence, and the higher standard for admission of reputation evidence. To be able to testify authoritatively about another person's reputation, one must know not only the person testified about, but also who he or she consorts with, and what those people think of the person. Reputation testimony requires much more than opinion, even though reputation evidence is, in essence, a form of opinion evidence.

■≡■

Quicknotes

CHARACTER EVIDENCE Evidence of someone's moral standing in a community based on reputation.

CROSS-EXAMINATION The interrogation of a witness by an adverse party either to further inquire as to the subject matter of the direct examination or to call into question the witness's credibility.

OPINION EVIDENCE Evidence pertaining to the beliefs of the witness rather than to the witness's knowledge of the facts.

REPUTATION EVIDENCE Evidence pertaining to an individual's general reputation in the community.

■≡■

United States v. Brewer

Federal government (P) v. Alleged kidnapper (D)

451 F. Supp. 50 (E.D. Tenn. 1978).

NATURE OF CASE: Consideration of motion to exclude evidence.

FACT SUMMARY: Defendant is on trial for kidnapping and seeks to exclude evidence of four prior convictions, which the prosecution seeks to introduce under Fed. R. Evid. 609.

🏛 RULE OF LAW
The probative value of evidence offered under Fed. R. Evid. 609 should be discerned from the nature of the crime, the time of conviction and the witness's subsequent history, the similarity between the past crime and the charged crime, the importance of defendant's testimony, and centrality of the credibility issue.

FACTS: Brewer (D) was charged with kidnapping and transporting a stolen vehicle. In a pretrial motion, Brewer (D) sought to suppress Government (P) evidence of his four prior convictions, including one conviction for kidnapping. The Government (P) sought to introduce the evidence under Rule 609.

ISSUE: Is the probative value of evidence offered under Fed. R. Evid. 609 discerned from the nature of the crime, the time of conviction and the witness's subsequent history, the similarity between the past crime and the charged crime, the importance of defendant's testimony, and centrality of the credibility issue?

HOLDING AND DECISION: (Taylor, J.) Yes. The probative value of evidence offered under Fed. R. Evid. 609 should be discerned from the nature of the crime, the time of conviction and the witness's subsequent history, the similarity between the past crime and the charged crime, the importance of defendant's testimony, and centrality of the credibility issue. The trial court considered the evidence and weighed it against Rule 609. Under Rule 609(b), none of the convictions is over ten years old because the convictions are considered from the date of conviction or the date of release from incarceration. With the earliest conviction, Brewer (D) violated his parole and had to be reincarcerated. That second release date was within the ten-year time frame. Once 609(b) is satisfied, the probative value of the evidence must be considered under 609(a). Looking at the four factors for discerning probative value, the violent nature of the four prior acts should keep them from the jury, the time factor supports admissibility, the similarity supports excluding the kidnapping conviction, and the fourth and fifth factor counterbalance each other. A limiting instruction could cure the similarity of

the prior kidnapping conviction, but the other three prior convictions should be sufficient to impeach the defendant. Motion denied for the three prior convictions and granted as to the kidnapping conviction.

⏵ ANALYSIS

The judge noted that no court had considered whether or not the proper release date to consider under 609(b) was the original release date or the release date after reincarceration for parole violations. The latter seems to be more appropriate as the reincarceration is for the original conviction. The leaning toward admissibility under the ten-year rule is counterbalanced by the requirement of a balancing test for probative value under 609(a).

◼▭◼

Quicknotes

FED. R. EVID. 609 Impeachment by evidence of conviction of crime committed by a witness may be permitted under certain circumstances, and if it involved dishonesty or false statement; the evidence will be admitted if its probative value outweighs its prejudicial effect to the accused.

LIMITING INSTRUCTION Directions given to a judge or jury prior to deliberation.

MOTION IN LIMINE Motion by one party brought prior to trial to exclude the potential introduction of prejudicial evidence.

PROBATIVE Tending to establish proof.

◼▭◼

CHAPTER 5

The Rape Shield Law

Quick Reference Rules of Law

People v. Abbot

State of New York (P) v. Convicted rapist (D)

N.Y. Sup. Ct. of Judicature, 19 Wend. (N.Y.) 192 (1838).

NATURE OF CASE: Appeal from conviction of rape.

FACT SUMMARY: [Facts not stated in casebook excerpt.]

🏛 RULE OF LAW
A woman's past sexual history is relevant to her credibility as an alleged victim of sexual assault because of the question of assent.

FACTS: [Facts not stated in casebook excerpt.]

ISSUE: Is a woman's past sexual history relevant to her credibility as an alleged victim of sexual assault because of the question of assent?

HOLDING AND DECISION: (Cowen, J.) Yes. A woman's past sexual history is relevant to her credibility as an alleged victim of sexual assault because of the question of assent. A virtuous virgin is more likely to be credible in her accusation of rape than a common prostitute who engages in sexual activity with men on a daily basis. The more varied a woman's sexual past, the greater question as to the validity of her assent or refusal to the sexual behavior at issue. "[W]ill you not more readily infer assent in the practiced Messalina, in loose attire, than in the reserved and virtuous Lucretia?" A rapist of a prostitute or concubine will be punished the same as the rapist of a virgin, but the evidence of utmost resistance must be stronger in the case of the prostitute or concubine. Reversed and remanded for retrial.

▶ *ANALYSIS*

Of course, this is not modern judicial thinking, but it, unfortunately, may be modern human thinking. The more a woman resists, the more "virtuous" the female victim, the more likely she did not assent to the sexual offense. The famous quote about Lucretia and Messalina involves two women of ancient Rome, one of whom was the virtuous officer's wife raped by a spurned admirer and the other the oft-described "conniving" and sexually adventurous woman. That quote has often been cited as justification for requiring additional evidence of struggle and resistance when a woman accuses a man of rape.

■■■■

Quicknotes

FED. R. EVID. 412 In sex offense cases, sets forth the rules governing the relevance of an alleged victim's past sexual behavior or alleged sexual predisposition, and when any exceptions may apply. It also sets out the procedure to determine admissibility. [Commonly known as the "Rape Shield" law.]

RAPE Unlawful sexual intercourse by means of fear or force and without consent.

■■■■

State v. Sibley

State (P) v. Convicted child rapist (D)

Mo. Sup. Ct., 131 Mo. 519, 132 Mo. 102, 33 S.W. 167 (1895).

NATURE OF CASE: Appeal from conviction for rape of a minor.

FACT SUMMARY: At defendant's trial for rape and the impregnation of his wife's minor daughter, witnesses testified to defendant's generally bad character for chastity and virtue. Defendant appealed, claiming that impeachment by proof of general reputation for unchastity applies only to females.

🏛 RULE OF LAW
Only female witnesses may be impeached by proof of general reputation for unchastity.

FACTS: Sibley (D) allegedly raped and impregnated his wife's minor daughter from a former marriage. Sibley (D) testified on his own behalf at his trial and denied the charges against him. Witnesses, however, testified that Sibley (D) had a generally bad reputation for chastity and virtue. Sibley (D) was convicted and he appealed, claiming the impeachment witnesses should not have been allowed to testify to his general reputation for chastity.

ISSUE: May only female witnesses be impeached by proof of general reputation for unchastity?

HOLDING AND DECISION: (Burgess, J.) Yes. Only female witnesses may be impeached by proof of general reputation for unchastity. Women's chastity or lack thereof directly bears on their truthfulness, while a man's reputation for truthfulness is unaffected completely by unchastity. Although more recent decisions of this court apply the impeachment rule to both sexes, this prior rule applying it only to female witnesses should control. "Many great and noble men" suffer from sexual weaknesses, but remain truthful, while women simply cannot make the same claim. Reversed and remanded.

DISSENT: (Gantt, J.) Impeachment should apply to both male and female. The majority relies upon an older Missouri case which cites a Massachusetts case, *Comm. v. Murphy*, 14 Mass. 387 (1817), which involved a female prostitute. The veracity of the male in that case should also have been questioned as he was the one choosing to engage the services of a prostitute.

▌ ANALYSIS

This is clearly not the status of judicial thought in modern times, but female victims must still cope with the after effects of generations of such case law. The character and past sexual history of female victims is very often the subject of much debate in sexual assault cases, while the male offenders' sexual background must fit within the confines of rules of evidence to be admissible. Statutory protections now exist to protect against the needless exposure of a sexual assault victim's sexual history, but the judicial system must be vigilant in guarding against "unchastity" equaling untruthfulness in women.

◼≡◼

Quicknotes

FED. R. EVID. 412 In sex offense cases, sets forth the rules governing the relevance of an alleged victim's past sexual behavior or alleged sexual predisposition, and when any exceptions may apply. It also sets out the procedure to determine admissibility. [Commonly known as the "Rape Shield" law.]

RAPE Unlawful sexual intercourse by means of fear or force and without consent.

REPUTATION EVIDENCE Evidence pertaining to an individual's general reputation in the community.

◼≡◼

State v. Smith

State (P) v. Convicted molester (D)

La. Sup. Ct., 743 So. 2d 199 (1999).

NATURE OF CASE: Appeal of conviction for attempted indecent behavior with a juvenile.

FACT SUMMARY: At defendant's trial for the attempted molestation of the minor victim, defendant sought to introduce evidence of the victim's prior false allegations of sexual abuse. The trial judge prohibited the evidence, which decision defendant appeals.

> ## 🏛 RULE OF LAW
> Prior false allegations of past sexual assault do not constitute past sexual behavior for purposes of the rape shield statute and are therefore admissible evidence.

FACTS: The 12-year-old victim accused Eual Howard Smith, Jr. (D) of attempting to molest her over a number of years. At trial, Smith (D) sought to introduce evidence through witness testimony that the victim previously made false allegations of molestation against her cousin. The trial judge conducted a hearing to determine if the evidence was admissible under La. Code of Evidence Art. 412 (similar to Fed. R. Evid. 412) which prohibits admission of evidence of most instances of the victim's sexual past. The trial judge heard the evidence and determined that the victim had not made prior false allegations, thus evidence of her past sexual misconduct was inadmissible under Rule 412. Smith (D) was convicted and the conviction was affirmed on appeal. This court granted certiorari to determine whether Rule 412 encompasses prior false allegations of sexual misconduct.

ISSUE: Do prior false allegations of sexual assault constitute past sexual behavior for purposes of the rape shield statute?

HOLDING AND DECISION: (Traylor, J.) No. Prior false allegations of sexual assault do not constitute past sexual behavior for purposes of the rape shield statute and are therefore admissible evidence. In this case, the victim had previously accused her cousin of molesting her and then promptly recanted. The victim and other witnesses testified to the allegations and then the cousin's brother testified to the recantation. A reasonable juror could find that the prior allegation was false. With that in mind, the question becomes whether a prior false allegation constitutes past sexual behavior protected from disclosure by Rule 412. It does not, and a Rule 412 hearing is unnecessary. The issue here was the credibility of the witness; therefore Smith (D) was prejudiced by the error in excluding the proffered evidence. Reversed and remanded.

DISSENT: (Victory, J.) The evidence should have been excluded under La. Code of Evidence 403.

▶ ANALYSIS

When the essence of a case is the credibility of the victim, a prior false allegation may certainly be probative. Consider, however, the prejudice to the prosecution in having to address a "she lied before so she must be lying now" argument. It comes suspiciously close to the old case law that required added proof of resistance when the complainant was "unchaste."

Quicknotes

ARTICLE 412 (La. C.E. Art.) Prevents the introduction of evidence of the victim's past sexual behavior, with limited exceptions.

CERTIORARI A discretionary writ issued by a superior court to an inferior court in order to review the lower court's decisions; the Supreme Court's writ ordering such review.

Olden v. Kentucky

Sexual crime convict (D) v. State (P)

488 U.S. 227 (1988).

NATURE OF CASE: Appeal of conviction for forcible sodomy.

FACT SUMMARY: Olden (D), accused of various sex crimes, was not permitted to cross-examine accusing witness Matthews regarding a relationship Olden (D) claimed Matthews was trying to protect by accusing him of sexual assault.

🏛 RULE OF LAW
The Confrontation Clause mandates that a defendant be permitted to cross-examine a witness on any relevant matter.

FACTS: Starla Matthews accused Olden (D) of rape. Olden (D) contended that Matthews had consented. Olden (D) attempted to elicit, on cross-examination, an admission from Matthews that she was involved in an extramarital relationship with one Russell. It was Olden's (D) contention that Matthews had invited him to have sex with her but, when Russell found out, she accused Olden (D) of rape. The trial court limited the cross-examination, holding that evidence that Matthews had a relationship with Russell would be prejudicial against Matthews. Olden (D) was convicted of forcible sodomy, and the Kentucky court of appeals affirmed. The Supreme Court granted review.

ISSUE: Does the Confrontation Clause mandate that a defendant be permitted to cross-examine a witness on any relevant matter?

HOLDING AND DECISION: (Per curiam) Yes. The Confrontation Clause mandates that a defendant be permitted to cross-examine a witness on any relevant matter. Cross-examination is an integral right under the Confrontation Clause. Any subject matter that tends to demonstrate an improper motive or bias by the witness is a proper subject of cross-examination. The only limit on this is that the court has discretion to limit repetitive or unduly harassing interrogation. Also, cross-examination on matters only marginally relevant is not a right. Here, however, the subject of the cross-examination was a possible motive for Matthews to lie, and this was central to the case against Olden (D). Cross-examination should have been permitted in this instance. Reversed and remanded.

▶ ANALYSIS

Many states have enacted "rape shield" laws, which prevent an alleged rape victim from being cross-examined on prior sexual conduct. It is not clear to what extent the present opinion cuts away at such laws. It appears that laws that per se prohibit such cross-examination would likely conflict with this decision.

Quicknotes

BIAS Predisposition; preconception; refers to the tendency of a judge to favor or disfavor a particular party.

CONFRONTATION CLAUSE A provision in the Sixth Amendment to the United States Constitution that an accused in a criminal action has the right to confront the witnesses against him, including the right to attend the trial and to cross-examine witnesses called on behalf of the prosecution.

CROSS-EXAMINATION The interrogation of a witness by an adverse party either to further inquire as to the subject matter of the direct examination or to call into question the witness's credibility.

SIXTH AMENDMENT Provides the right to a speedy and public trial by impartial jury, the right to be informed of the accusation, the right to confront witnesses, and the right to have the assistance of counsel in all criminal prosecutions.

Stephens v. Miller

Convicted attempted rapist (D) v. Unidentified party (P)

13 F.3d 998 (7th Cir.), *cert. denied*, 513 U.S. 808 (1994).

NATURE OF CASE: Appeal from denial of writ of habeas corpus.

FACT SUMMARY: Defendant's conviction for attempted rape was affirmed and the district court denied his writ of habeas corpus. Defendant appealed, contending the trial court erred in excluding his testimony about the victim's sexual preferences.

🏛 RULE OF LAW
A defendant's implicit right to testify in his own defense must yield to certain procedural and evidentiary rules.

FACTS: Lonnie Stephens (D) and Melissa Wilburn were at Wilburn's trailer with Wilburn's sister, brother-in-law, and nephew asleep in the other room. Wilburn claims that she awoke to find Stephens (D) in her trailer and that he attempted to sexually assault her. Stephens (D) claims that he and Wilburn engaged in consensual sex, that he said something that angered her, and she falsely accused him of rape in retaliation. At trial, Stephens (D) sought to introduce evidence that he angered Wilburn by saying that a mutual acquaintance had told him that Wilburn liked "doing it doggy fashion" and something about "switching partners." The trial judge excluded the evidence under the Indiana Rape Shield Statute (similar to Fed. R. Evid. 412). The jury convicted Stephens (D) of attempted rape, the appeals courts affirmed the convictions, and Stephens (D) was denied a writ of habeas corpus by the district court. He appealed, claiming the trial court erred in excluding the evidence because it was an unconstitutional denial of his right to testify fully in his own defense and explain his version of events, and that the testimony concerned the res gestae of the offense.

ISSUE: Must a defendant's implicit right to testify in his own defense yield to certain procedural and evidentiary rules?

HOLDING AND DECISION: (Bauer, J.) Yes. A defendant's implicit right to testify in his own defense must yield to certain procedural and evidentiary rules. Defendant's testimony would have done nothing to aid his defense, but serve only to humiliate the victim. Stephens (D) was otherwise allowed to provide his entire version of events and the exclusion was a minor imposition on Stephens's (D) right to testify. Stephens's (D) other argument about res gestae is nearly nonsensical because res gestae is not able to be defined for purposes of the Constitution and federal law. Affirmed.

DISSENT: (Cummings, J.) The defense was that Stephens (D) made such an offensive statement to Wilburn that she fabricated a rape charge in retaliation. It is arguable that application of the Rape Shield Statue to prevent the jury from hearing the content of that statement unconstitutionally denied Stephens (D) his right to present a complete defense. The rape shield rules are laudable and necessary, but Stephens (D) had to counter a detailed story from Wilburn with a story missing the essential details. The exception to the rape shield rule created by allowing Stephens's (D) testimony would be a narrow one and would not frustrate the purpose of the statute.

▶ ANALYSIS

The purpose of the rape shield statutes is to prevent unnecessary harassment and embarrassment of rape complainants. Criminal defendants have numerous evidentiary and procedural protections and must yield slightly to the occasional protection for the complainant. Consider, however, if the jury's knowledge of the exact nature of the statement would have resulted in a different verdict. The statement made could arguably anger the victim enough to cause her to falsely claim rape and the defendant may have been disadvantaged in not being able to fully explain his version. The trial courts must do careful balancing acts, but protection of the complainants should likely prevail over minor impositions on criminal defendants.

■■■

Quicknotes

FED. R. EVID. 412 In sex offense cases, sets forth the rules governing the relevance of an alleged victim's past sexual behavior or alleged sexual predisposition, and when any exceptions may apply. It also sets out the procedure to determine admissibility. [Commonly known as the "Rape Shield" law.]

HABEAS CORPUS A proceeding in which a defendant brings a writ to compel a judicial determination of whether he is lawfully being held in custody.

RAPE SHIELD LAW Law conferring a privilege on rape victims against harassing examination at trial regarding past sexual conduct.

RES GESTAE Any spontaneous statement spoken concurrently with an occurrence so that it carries a strong presumption of credibility.

■■■

United States v. Knox

Federal government (P) v. Convicted rapist (D)

1992 WL 97157 (U.S.A.F. Ct. Mil. Rev. 1992), *aff'd*, 41 M.J. 28 (Ct. Mil. App. 1994), *cert. denied*, 513 U.S. 1153 (1995).

NATURE OF CASE: Appeal from conviction for rape.

FACT SUMMARY: At defendant's trial for rape, he sought to introduce under Mil. R. Evid. 412 the victim's past sexual acts and reputation for being sexually promiscuous. The trial judge allowed some history, but not the individual sex acts. Defendant appealed his conviction for rape, contending all of the evidence was admissible to demonstrate his state of mind when he thought the victim was consenting.

RULE OF LAW
A rape victim's past sexual acts do not tend to prove or disprove the existence of present consent.

FACTS: Theresa and Knox (D) worked together at a military base. One evening, they were at a party with co-workers and Theresa had several beers. She and her boyfriend went to Knox's (D) room where she later awoke to find Knox (D) having sex with her. Theresa called the Rape Intervention Crisis Center and claimed that Knox (D) raped her. At Knox's (D) trial, he sought to introduce certain evidence under Mil. R. Evid. 412 to show his state of mind that night. Knox (D) wanted to show he believed Theresa consented. The evidence he sought to introduce included Theresa's reputation as a sexually promiscuous "bimbo" and several of her past individual sexual acts. The trial judge allowed some of the evidence, but denied admission of Theresa's past sexual acts or her reputation as known by Knox (D) because that evidence did not prove or disprove Theresa's consent. Knox (D) was convicted and he appealed, claiming all of the evidence was admissible under Rule 412 to show his frame of mind as to Theresa's consent.

ISSUE: Do a rape victim's past sexual acts tend to prove or disprove the existence of present consent?

HOLDING AND DECISION: (Hodgson, J.) No. A rape victim's past sexual acts do not tend to prove or disprove the existence of present consent. This case distilled down to one factual question—did Theresa consent? She claimed she was asleep and did not consent. Knox (D) claimed she was an awake, willing participant. Knox (D) sought to introduce evidence of Theresa's past "wild ways," but her reputation as he knew it did not tend to prove or disprove her consent. Similarly, her past individual sex acts do not tend to prove or disprove her willingness that night. Knox (D) tried to use Rule 412 to show Theresa as a loose woman "deserving" of rape, which is exactly what Rule 412 was enacted to prevent. Affirmed.

ANALYSIS

Compare this case with *People v. Abbot*, 19 Wend. (N.Y.) 192 (1838). That court would certainly have found evidence of Theresa's past promiscuity to be relevant to her present consent. This is fortunately no longer valid law or accepted social thought. Rape victims are now offered at least similar protections as criminal defendants in that their past behavior does not dictate present behavior and juries judge only present behavior.

Quicknotes

REPUTATION EVIDENCE Evidence pertaining to an individual's general reputation in the community.

STATE OF MIND A declarant's mental state; testimony regarding state of mind is ordinarily not considered hearsay because it is indicative of motivation and therefore has circumstantial guarantees of trustworthiness.

Note: There are no principal cases in Chapter 6 of the casebook.

CHAPTER

7

The Rule Against Hearsay

Quick Reference Rules of Law

Mahlandt v. Wild Canid Survival & Research Center, Inc.

Child (P) v. Animal center (D)

588 F.2d 626 (8th Cir. 1978).

NATURE OF CASE: Appeal from denial of damages for negligence.

FACT SUMMARY: The trial court hearing Daniel Mahlandt's (P) civil action against the Center (D) refused to let into evidence certain conclusionary statements against interest made by an employee of the Center (D).

🏛 RULE OF LAW
Fed. R. Evid. 801(d)(2)(D) makes statements made by agents within the scope of their employment admissible and there is no implied requirement that the declarant have personal knowledge of the facts underlying his statement.

FACTS: Nobody actually saw what happened, but young Daniel Mahlandt (P), who was just under four years old at the time, wound up in the enclosure where Mr. Poos (D), the Director of the Center (D), kept Sophie, a wolf belonging to the Center (D), but which he took around to schools and institutions where he showed films and gave programs regarding the nature of wolves. Sophie had been raised at the children's zoo and had there acted in a good-natured and stable manner while in contact with thousands of children. Sophie apparently bit Mahlandt (P) causing him serious injuries. There was some evidence indicating that the child might have crawled under the fence and thereby received his injuries. An offer was made to disprove this theory by introducing evidence that Poos (D) had left a note on the door of the Center's (D) president saying the wolf had bitten a child and that he had made a similar statement later that day when he met the president and was asked what happened. There was also an offer to introduce minutes of a meeting at the Center's (D) board that reflected a great deal of discussion about the legal aspects of the incident of Sophie biting the child. None of this was let into evidence, the judge reasoning that in each case those making the statements had no personal knowledge of the facts and the statements were thus hearsay. A judgment for the Center (D) followed.

ISSUE: Is it necessary to show that the agent had personal knowledge of the facts underlying his statement for a statement made by an agent within the scope of his employment to be admissible under Fed. R. Evid. 801(d)(2)(D)?

HOLDING AND DECISION: (Sickle, J.) No. Fed. R. Evid. 801(d)(2)(D) makes admissible statements made by agents within the scope of their employment. Rule 403 provides for the exclusion of relevant evidence if its probative value is substantially outweighed by the danger of unfair prejudice, etc. Rule 805 recites, in effect, that a statement containing hearsay within hearsay is admissible if each part of the statement falls within an exception to the hearsay rule. While each provides additional bases for excluding otherwise acceptable evidence, neither rule mandates for the introduction into Fed. R. Evid. 801(d)(2)(D) of an implied requirement that the declarant have personal knowledge of the facts underlying his statement. Thus, the two statements made by Poos (D) (one in the note he wrote and one he made verbally) were admissible against the Center (D). As to the minutes of the Center's (D) board meeting, there was no servant or agency relationship which justified admitting the evidence of these minutes as against Poos (D) (who was a nonattending, nonparticipating employee). The only remaining question is whether the trial court's rulings excluding these three items of evidence are at all justified under Rule 403. It is true that none of the statements involved were based on the personal knowledge of the declarant. However, it was recognized by the Advisory Committee on Proposed Rules that this does not necessarily mean they must be rejected as too unreliable to be admitted into evidence. In its discussion of 801(d)(2) exceptions to the hearsay rule, the Committee said: "The freedom which admissions have enjoyed from technical demands of searching for an assurance of trustworthiness in some against-interest circumstances, and from the restrictive influences of the opinion rule and the rule requiring first-hand knowledge, when taken with the apparently prevalent satisfaction with the results, calls for generous treatment of this avenue to admissibility." 28 U.S.C.A., Volume of Federal Rules of Evidence, Rule 801. So here, remembering that relevant evidence is usually prejudicial to the cause of the side against which it is presented, and that the prejudice which concerns us is unreasonable prejudice—and applying the spirit of Rule 801(d)(2)—Rule 403 does not warrant the exclusion of the evidence of Poos's (D) statements as against himself or the Center (D). But the limited admissibility of the corporate minutes, coupled with the repetitive nature of the evidence and the low probative value of the minutes-record, all justify supporting the judgment of the trial court, under Rule 403, not to admit them into evidence. Reversed and remanded for a new trial.

▶ ANALYSIS

One of the questions courts have struggled with in this area is whether or not in order to qualify as an admission the statement must have been made by the agent to an outsider (i.e., one other than his principal or another

Continued on next page.

agent). This often comes up when the opposing party in a suit against the principal wants to introduce into evidence a report written or given orally by an agent to the principal or another agent. Just as many courts have refused to let such evidence in as have let it in against the principal as an admission. The Federal Rules of Evidence have been interpreted as recognizing what Wigmore observed: that "communication to an outsider has not generally been thought to be an essential characteristic of an admission." See Wigmore on *Evidence*, § 1557.

■≡■

Quicknotes

FED. R. EVID. 403 Discretionary rule that allows a trial judge to exclude evidence if the danger of unfair prejudice to defendant outweighs its probative value.

FED. R. EVID. 801 The "hearsay rule," making out-of-court statements used to prove the truth of the matter asserted inadmissible at trial.

HEARSAY EXCEPTION Out-of-court statement made by a person other than the witness testifying at trial that is offered in order to prove the truth of the matter asserted, and is admissible at trial notwithstanding the fact that it is hearsay.

■≡■

Bourjaily v. United States

Conspirator (D) v. Federal government (P)

483 U.S. 171 (1987).

NATURE OF CASE: Appeal from conviction for conspiracy to distribute drugs.

FACT SUMMARY: Bourjaily (D) contended that the trial court erred in considering statements by an accomplice in determining whether a conspiracy existed as such a finding was a prerequisite to determining the admissibility of the statements.

> 🏛 **RULE OF LAW**
> A court may, in determining whether a conspiracy existed, consider the out-of-court statements which themselves are the subject of the inquiry into admissibility.

FACTS: Bourjaily (D) was charged with conspiracy to distribute cocaine. The Government (P) introduced out-of-court statements made by Lonardo, an accomplice, which arguably implicated Bourjaily (D) in the conspiracy. Under Fed. R. Evid. 801, out-of-court statements by a co-conspirator against a party, made during the course of the conspiracy, are not hearsay. The court made a preliminary evidentiary ruling based in part on Lonardo's out-of-court statements that a conspiracy existed and that Bourjaily (D) was a co-conspirator. This ruling was made solely as a preliminary step to determining whether the out-of-court statements fell under Rule 801, and were thus admissible. Bourjaily (D) was convicted and appealed, contending the court could not consider the statements themselves in determining whether a conspiracy existed where such determination was the threshold consideration in the statement's admissibility.

ISSUE: May a court, in making a preliminary determination of admissibility under Fed. R. Evid. 801, consider the subject statements?

HOLDING AND DECISION: (Rehnquist, C.J.) Yes. A court may, in making a preliminary determination of admissibility under Fed. R. Evid. 801, consider the subject statements to determine if a conspiracy exists. Although case authority exists to the contrary, the amendments to the Federal Rules have made it clear that the statements may be used. Once it is shown by a preponderance of the evidence that a conspiracy existed and that the defendant was involved, the statements are not hearsay. The statements themselves may be highly probative of the existence of a conspiracy and may be used. Affirmed.

▶ ANALYSIS

Rule 104 allows trial courts to consider hearsay evidence in making evidentiary determinations. Thus, the Court read

Rule 104 in conjunction with Rule 801 to arrive at its decision. It has been held, however, that if an agency relationship must be proved, the statements at issue cannot be considered.

Quicknotes

CONSPIRACY Concerted action by two or more persons to accomplish some unlawful purpose.

FED. R. EVID. 104 Permits a court to consider all nonprivileged matters, whether independently admissible or not, when determining preliminary issues of admissibility.

FED. R. EVID. 801 The "hearsay rule," making out-of-court statements used to prove the truth of the matter asserted inadmissible at trial.

United States v. Barrett

Federal government (P) v. Convicted thief (D)

539 F.2d 244 (1st Cir. 1976).

NATURE OF CASE: Appeal of theft conviction.

FACT SUMMARY: At defendant's trial for theft, the defense sought to admit admittedly hearsay testimony that defendant was not involved in the theft. The trial court excluded the testimony and defendant appealed.

🏛 RULE OF LAW
Hearsay evidence is admissible if it is a prior inconsistent statement, and that statement need not be plainly contradictory.

FACTS: Arthur "Bucky" Barrett (D) was charged in connection with the theft of stamps from a museum. At Barrett's (D) trial, an admitted thief, "Buzzy" Adams testified against Barrett (D) and said that Barrett (D) had admitted his involvement in the theft to him. The defense sought to admit the admittedly hearsay testimony of two witnesses who overheard Adams state that he knew that Barrett (D) was not involved in the theft. The trial judge excluded the evidence as hearsay falling within no exception. Barrett (D) was convicted and he appealed, contending the trial court erred in excluding the testimony of the two defense witnesses.

ISSUE: Is hearsay evidence admissible if it is a prior inconsistent statement even if that statement is not plainly contradictory?

HOLDING AND DECISION: (Campbell, J.) Yes. Hearsay evidence is admissible if it is a prior inconsistent statement, and that statement need not be plainly contradictory. Adams stated at trial that he knew that Barrett (D) was involved in the theft. The defense's potential witnesses, however, overheard Adams say earlier that he was sorry to hear that Barrett (D) had been arrested and that he knew that Barrett (D) was "not involved." Although the statement was vague, the jury could certainly have inferred that it was a contradictory statement to that he offered at trial. The trial court erred in excluding the testimony of the defense witnesses. Although the case against Barrett (D) was relatively strong, it is possible that the witnesses would have created a reasonable doubt in the jury's mind. Vacated and remanded.

▌ANALYSIS

Hearsay decisions are difficult calls for the most seasoned of judges. The courts usually choose to err on the side of excluding the information, but perhaps choosing to allow juries to hear more information would be the better decision. Here, the additional information could certainly have swayed the jury to a different verdict and the appeals court seems to encourage finding an exception to the hearsay rule.

■■■■

Quicknotes

FED. R. EVID. 613 Addresses the examination of a witness concerning prior statements or the extrinsic evidence of prior inconsistent statements.

FED. R. EVID. 801 The "hearsay rule," making out-of-court statements used to prove the truth of the matter asserted inadmissible at trial.

PRIOR INCONSISTENT STATEMENT A statement made before a witness's testimony that contradicts such testimony and which may be admitted in order to impeach the witness; the prior statements may not be admitted, however, to prove the truth of the matter asserted.

■■■■

United States v. Ince

Federal government (P) v. Firearms user (D)

21 F.3d 576 (4th Cir. 1994).

NATURE OF CASE: Appeal of evidentiary ruling after a conviction for assault.

FACT SUMMARY: The Government (P) introduced hearsay evidence to impeach a witness who it knew would refuse to testify about a conversation with the defendant.

> ## 🏛 RULE OF LAW
> A prior inconsistent statement may not be introduced to impeach one's own witness, thus circumventing the hearsay exclusion, where the original testimony was not damaging and the impeachment testimony is both prejudicial and lacking probative value as impeachment evidence.

FACTS: After a gun was fired at a concert on a military base, Ince (D) and his companions were stopped as they attempted to leave the base. Ince's (D) friend Neumann gave an unsworn statement to Military Policeman Stevens. She told Stevens that Ince (D) admitted to firing the gun, but he no longer had the weapon. Ince (D) was charged with assault with a dangerous weapon. Ince (D) was tried twice, with the first jury deadlocking. At both trials, the Government (P) called Neumann to testify. She said she could not recall the details of her conversation with Ince (D). The Government (P) attempted to refresh her recollection with the statement taken by Stevens. She still said she could not recall the conversation clearly. The prosecutor then called Stevens, over Ince's (D) objection, to testify as to what Neumann told him. The Government (P) was permitted to proceed when it was argued that the hearsay evidence was intended to impeach the credibility of Neumann, since she had claimed that she could not recall the conversation. Ince (D) was convicted after the second trial. Ince (D) appealed.

ISSUE: May a prior inconsistent statement be introduced to impeach one's own witness, thus circumventing the hearsay exclusion, if the impeachment testimony is prejudicial and of little probative value?

HOLDING AND DECISION: (Murnaghan, J.) No. A prior inconsistent statement may not be introduced to impeach one's own witness, thus circumventing the hearsay exclusion, where the original testimony was not damaging and the impeachment testimony is both prejudicial and lacking probative value as impeachment evidence. Impeachment by prior inconsistent statement was not intended as a vehicle to circumvent the hearsay rule. Where the witness has not damaged the case, an attack on credibility by impeachment is not necessary. Here,

Neumann merely refused to give testimony that the Government (P) hoped she would give. There was no reason to attack her credibility. By allowing Stevens to testify as to Ince's (D) supposed confession to Neumann, the jury was able to hear extremely prejudicial information. Reversed and remanded.

▌ ANALYSIS

One original justification for the rule that prohibited impeaching one's own witness was that a witness being attacked by both parties might just as well lie to end the confrontation. However, such concerns proved unpersuasive, and the rule has been abolished. Impeachment is now available to either party. But the tool may not be used where it is a ruse to introduce otherwise inadmissible evidence.

■≡■

Quicknotes

FED. R. EVID. 403 Discretionary rule that allows a trial judge to exclude evidence if the danger of unfair prejudice to defendant outweighs its probative value.

FED. R. EVID. 607 The credibility of a witness may be attacked by any party.

FED. R. EVID. 803 Rule setting forth certain exceptions to the hearsay rule, including present sense impressions, excited utterances, present state of mind, statements for medical diagnosis and past recollection recorded.

PAST RECORDED RECOLLECTIONS An exception to the hearsay rule for statements contained in a document as to which the witness no longer has recollection.

PRIOR INCONSISTENT STATEMENT A statement made before a witness's testimony that contradicts such testimony and which may be admitted in order to impeach the witness; the prior statements may not be admitted, however, to prove the truth of the matter asserted.

■≡■

Fletcher v. Weir

Prosecutor (P) v. Silent defendant (D)

455 U.S. 603 (1982).

NATURE OF CASE: Appeal from grant of writ of habeas corpus.

FACT SUMMARY: Weir (D) was convicted of manslaughter and filed a writ of habeas corpus, which was granted and affirmed by the court of appeals on the basis that Weir's (D) due process rights were violated when the prosecutor used Weir's (D) post-arrest silence to impeach.

🏛 RULE OF LAW
It is not a due process violation for a prosecutor to attempt to impeach a defendant on the stand using post-arrest silence absent affirmative government assurances, such as *Miranda* warnings.

FACTS: Weir (D) got involved in a fight with another man in a nightclub parking lot. Weir (D) stabbed the man and fled the scene. The victim later died from his injuries and Weir (D) was prosecuted for the man's death. At trial, Weir (D) claimed for the first time that his participation in the fight was in self-defense and the stabbing was accidental. On cross-examination, the prosecutor attempted to impeach Weir (D) on the stand by inquiring into Weir's (D) post-arrest silence as to the exculpatory explanation. A jury convicted Weir (D) of manslaughter and the Supreme Court of Kentucky affirmed. Weir (D) then filed a writ of habeas corpus in the U.S. District Court for the Western District of Kentucky, which granted the writ. The granted writ was affirmed by the Sixth Circuit Court of Appeals and the state appealed.

ISSUE: Is it a due process violation for a prosecutor to attempt to impeach a defendant on the stand using post-arrest silence absent affirmative government assurances, such as *Miranda* warnings?

HOLDING AND DECISION: (Per curiam) No. It is not a due process violation for a prosecutor to attempt to impeach a defendant on the stand using post-arrest silence absent affirmative government assurances, such as *Miranda* warnings. The Sixth Circuit gave an overly broad reading to this Court's holding in *Doyle v. Ohio*, 426 U.S. 610 (1976). *Doyle's* holding was that cross-examination on post-arrest silence violated due process because *Miranda* warnings implicitly encourage silence. Here, however, the record does not reflect that Weir (D) received *Miranda* warnings during the silence at issue. *Doyle* should not be expanded to include post-arrest, pre-*Miranda* warning silence. The Government (P) did not take affirmative action here to implicitly induce silence, so comment on that

silence for impeachment purposes does not violate due process. Reversed.

▌ ANALYSIS

A person under arrest is told that anything he says can be used against him and then the prosecution might seek to use the resulting silence against him as well. Even if *Miranda*-style warnings are not given, the act of taking a person into police custody is often enough to provoke silence. Using that silence against him puts the person in a "catch-22" situation. When the affirmative government action is missing, however, it seems natural that a person would protest or seek to absolve himself and a silence would be unnatural.

■=■

Quicknotes

DUE PROCESS RIGHTS The constitutional mandate requiring the courts to protect and enforce individuals' rights and liberties consistent with prevailing principles of fairness and justice, and prohibiting the federal and state governments from such activities that deprive its citizens of a life, liberty or property interest.

EXCULPATORY EVIDENCE A statement or other evidence that tends to excuse, justify, or absolve the defendant from alleged fault or guilt.

HABEAS CORPUS A proceeding in which a defendant brings a writ to compel a judicial determination of whether he is lawfully being held in custody.

MIRANDA WARNINGS Specified warnings that must be communicated to a person prior to a custodial interrogation; in the absence of the communication of such warnings, any communications made during the interrogation are inadmissible at trial.

■=■

Tome v. United States

Convicted sex offender (D) v. Federal government (P)

513 U.S. 150 (1995).

NATURE OF CASE: Appeal from conviction of felony sexual abuse of a child.

FACT SUMMARY: Tome (D), convicted of felony sexual abuse of a child, appealed, contending that the trial court abused its discretion by admitting out-of-court consistent statements made by his daughter to six prosecution witnesses who testified as to the nature of Tome's (D) sexual assaults on his daughter.

RULE OF LAW
Fed. R. Evid. 801(d)(1)(B) permits the introduction of a declarant's consistent out-of-court statements to rebut a charge of recent fabrication or improper influence or motive only when those statements were made before the charged recent fabrication or improper influence or motive.

FACTS: Tome (D) was charged by the Government (P) with felony sexual abuse of his daughter, A.T., who was four years old at the time of the alleged crime. Tome (D) and the child's mother were divorced in 1988, and Tome (D) was awarded physical custody of his daughter. In 1989, the mother of A.T. unsuccessfully petitioned the court for primary custody, but she was awarded custody for the summer of 1990. In August 1990, at the end of a court-approved summer-long visitation, the mother contacted authorities with allegations that Tome (D) had committed sexual abuse against A.T. Tome (D) argued that A.T.'s allegations were concocted so that the child would not be returned to Tome (D). At trial, A.T. (now six years old) testified first. Thereafter, cross-examination took place over two days. On the first day, A.T. answered all questions placed to her. Under cross-examination, however, A.T. was questioned regarding her conversations with the prosecutor but was reluctant to discuss them. The Government (P) then produced six witnesses who testified about seven statements made by A.T. describing Tome's (D) sexual assaults upon her. A.T.'s out-of-court statements, recounted by these witnesses, were offered under Fed. R. Evid. 801(d)(1)(B). The trial court admitted all of the statements over Tome's (D) objections, accepting the Government's (P) argument that they rebutted the implicit charges that A.T.'s testimony was motivated by a desire to live with her mother. Tome (D) was convicted and sentenced to twelve years' imprisonment. On appeal the Tenth Circuit Court of Appeals affirmed, and Tome (D) again appealed, contending that the district court judge had abused his discretion in admitting A.T.'s out-of-court statements.

ISSUE: Does Fed. R. Evid. 801(d)(1)(B) permit the introduction of a declarant's consistent out-of-court statements to rebut a charge of recent fabrication or improper influence or motive only when those statements were made before the charged recent fabrication or improper influence or motive?

HOLDING AND DECISION: (Kennedy, J.) Yes. Fed. R. Evid. 801(d)(1)(B) permits the introduction of a declarant's consistent out-of-court statements to rebut a charge of recent fabrication or improper influence or motive only when those statements were made before the charged recent fabrication or improper influence or motive. These conditions of admissibility were not established here. The prevailing common-law rule, before adoption of the Federal Rules of Evidence, was that a prior consistent statement introduced to rebut a charge of recent fabrication or improper influence or motive was admissible if the statement had been made before the alleged fabrication, influence, or motive came into being but inadmissible if made afterward. Rule 801 defines prior consistent statements as nonhearsay only if they are offered to rebut a charge of recent fabrication or improper influence or motive. Prior consistent statements may not be admitted to counter all forms of impeachment or to bolster the witness merely because she has been discredited. Here, the question is whether A.T.'s out-of-court statements rebutted the alleged link between her desire to be with her mother and her testimony, not whether they suggested that A.T.'s testimony was true. The Rule speaks of a party's rebutting an alleged motive, not bolstering the veracity of the story told. However, the requirement is that consistent statements must have been made before the alleged influence or motive to fabricate arose. The language of the Rule suggests that it was intended to carry over the common-law premotive rule. If the Rule were to permit introduction of prior statements as substantive evidence to rebut every implicit charge that a witness's in-court testimony results from recent fabrication, improper influence, or motive, the whole emphasis of the trial could shift to the out-of-court statements rather than the in-court ones. In response to a rather weak charge that A.T.'s testimony was a fabrication so that she could stay with her mother, the Government (P) was allowed to present a parade of witnesses who did no more than recount A.T.'s detailed out-of-court statements to them. Although those statements might have been probative on the question of whether the alleged conduct had occurred, they shed minimal light on whether A.T. had the charged motive to fabricate. Reversed and remanded.

CONCURRRENCE: (Scalia, J.) Advisory Committee Notes are drafted by experts, but they are not

Continued on next page.

authoritative on the meaning of the Federal Rules of Evidence. A promulgated Rule "says what it says" even if the Advisory Committee Notes seem to point to a different drafter's intent.

DISSENT: (Breyer, J.) No case law or commentary supports the absolute rule on the relevancy of postmotive statements, which has been adopted by the majority of courts. Trial courts may find it easier to apply an absolute rule, but a reasonable result may be more likely if trial courts can take a flexible approach. Here, the court of appeals appropriately used a flexible approach to consider A.T.'s prior consistent statements against a possible motive to lie.

▶ ANALYSIS

Justice Breyer, in his dissent, commented that prior consistent statements may rehabilitate a witness whose credibility has been questioned. In these circumstances, no improper influence or motive is alleged, and the prior statement does not need to precede it.

■═■

Quicknotes

COMMON LAW A body of law developed through the judicial decisions of the courts as opposed to the legislative process.

FED. R. EVID. 801 The "hearsay rule," making out-of-court statements used to prove the truth of the matter asserted inadmissible at trial.

PRIOR TESTIMONY EXCEPTION Exception to the hearsay rule for testimony given in a prior proceeding that may be offered in a later proceeding under certain circumstances.

RELEVANCE The admissibility of evidence based on whether it has any tendency to prove or disprove a matter at issue in the case.

■═■

Commonwealth v. Weichell

State (P) v. Convicted murderer (D)

Mass. Sup. Jud. Ct., 453 N.E.2d 1038, 390 Mass. 62 (1983), *cert. denied*, 465 U.S. 1032 (1984).

NATURE OF CASE: Appeal from first-degree murder conviction.

FACT SUMMARY: A composite sketch of the suspect was introduced at trial and emphasized in the prosecution's closing argument. The defendant contended that the sketch was prejudicial hearsay.

🏛 RULE OF LAW
Composite sketches are either admissible as statements of an out-of-court identification by a witness available for cross-examination or because the sketches are not a statement for hearsay purposes.

FACTS: Three witnesses heard shots fired in a parking lot and saw a man running from the scene. One of the witnesses, John Foley, saw the shooter under a street lamp for approximately one second when the shooter turned toward the threesome. The body of the victim was found in the parking lot. Foley later helped police prepare a composite sketch of the suspected shooter, which the Commonwealth (P) introduced at trial and emphasized in closing arguments as identification of Weichell (D). Weichell (D) was convicted of first-degree murder and appealed on the grounds that the composite was inadmissible hearsay.

ISSUE: Are composite sketches inadmissible hearsay?

HOLDING AND DECISION: (Lynch, J.) No. Composite sketches are either admissible as statements of an out-of-court identification by a witness available for cross-examination or because the sketches are not a statement for hearsay purposes. The Rules of Evidence allow for a prior statement of identification if the witness is available for cross-examination. Foley was available for cross-examination by the defendant and the composite prepared through his out-of-court statements is just as admissible as his out-of-court identification. Similarly, even if a composite sketch is classified as a statement, it is one of out-of-court identification and would still be admissible when the witness who helped develop the composite sketch is available for cross-examination. The court recently held that out-of-court identifications may be admissible as substantive evidence of guilt; therefore Weichell (D) was not prejudiced. Affirmed.

DISSENT: (Liacos, J.) Composite sketches have not been proven to be more reliable indicators of identification than in-court identifications. They should not be admitted as substantive evidence of guilt and the conviction should have been reversed.

▶ ANALYSIS

In *Weichell,* the court stated conclusively that a composite sketch is a "statement." That, however, is debatable and would certainly affect the admissibility of the sketch within the hearsay exceptions. Perhaps sketches should not be admissible as further evidence of identification because human nature is such that people would tend to dismiss dissimilar features in the sketch and focus on the features that look like the defendant sitting before them.

Quicknotes

HEARSAY EXCEPTION Out-of-court statement made by a person other than the witness testifying at trial that is offered in order to prove the truth of the matter asserted, and is admissible at trial notwithstanding the fact that it is hearsay.

United States v. Owens

Federal government (P) v. Convicted murderer (D)

484 U.S. 554 (1988).

NATURE OF CASE: Appeal of conviction for attempted murder.

FACT SUMMARY: Owens (D) was convicted of attempted murder after victim Foster, while unable to identify Owens (D) in court, testified that he had earlier identified him.

🏛 RULE OF LAW
A witness in a criminal trial may testify about an earlier identification even if he can no longer testify as to the basis for that identification.

FACTS: Foster, a prison guard, was severely beaten. While in the hospital, he identified Owens (D) as the attacker. He later lost independent recollection of the attack and could not explain the basis for his hospital identification. Over defense objection, Foster was allowed to testify regarding his hospital identification. Owens (D) was convicted and appealed. The Ninth Circuit reversed, holding that the Confrontation Clause barred such testimony. The Supreme Court granted review.

ISSUE: May a witness in a criminal trial testify about an earlier identification even if he can no longer testify as to the basis for that identification?

HOLDING AND DECISION: (Scalia, J.) Yes. A witness in a criminal trial may testify about an earlier identification even if he can no longer testify as to the basis for that identification. The Confrontation Clause of the Sixth Amendment has been read to require only the opportunity for effective cross-examination, not whatever sort of cross-examination the defense might wish. When a witness cannot recall the basis for an earlier identification, the opposing party already has a potent cross-examination tool, as a forgetful witness has inherent credibility problems. It has long been held that an expert may give an opinion even if he has forgotten the basis therefor, and this situation is no different. Here, Owens (D) had the opportunity to attack Foster on the basis of his forgetfulness, and that was all the Confrontation Clause required. Reversed and remanded.

DISSENT: (Brennan, J.) The right of confrontation ensures effective cross-examination. With respect to hearsay statements, a witness's mere presence in the courtroom is not sufficient to guarantee the opportunity for such examination.

▶ ANALYSIS

Owens (D) also contended that Foster's testimony violated the Federal Rules of Evidence. Specifically, Owens (D)

contended that Fed. R. Evid. 801(d)(1)(C)'s exclusion from hearsay of a prior identification required that the declarant be subject to cross-examination. Foster, stated Owens (D), was not so subject due to his memory loss. The Court disagreed for the same reasons noted in the discussion on the Confrontation Clause.

■■■■

Quicknotes

CONFRONTATION CLAUSE A provision in the Sixth Amendment to the United States Constitution that an accused in a criminal action has the right to confront the witnesses against him, including the right to attend the trial and to cross-examine witnesses called on behalf of the prosecution.

FED. R. EVID. 801 The "hearsay rule," making out-of-court statements used to prove the truth of the matter asserted inadmissible at trial.

FED. R. EVID. 802 Hearsay is not admissible except as provided by the Federal Rules of Evidence, the Supreme Court, or an Act of Congress.

FED. R. EVID. 804 Addresses the definition of an unavailable witness and outlines the exceptions to the hearsay rule.

■■■■

United States v. Duenas

Federal government (P) v. Drug dealer (D)

691 F.3d 1070 (9th Cir. 2012).

NATURE OF CASE: Appeal of the district court decision to permit the prior testimony of a now-deceased witness.

FACT SUMMARY: After arrest, Ray Duenas (D) invoked his *Miranda* rights to Drug Enforcement Administration (DEA) agents, but then provided incriminating statements to Officer Frankie Smith. At a pre-trial suppression hearing, Officer Smith testified and Duenas (D) argued the voluntariness of the statements after cross-examination. The district court denied the suppression motion. After Officer Smith's death, his suppression hearing testimony was admitted at trial as "former testimony."

🏛 RULE OF LAW
Former testimony cannot be introduced under Fed. R. Evid. 804(b)(1) without a showing of "similar motive."

FACTS: Ray Duenas (D) and his brother were drug dealers on the island of Guam who were arrested after the execution of a search warrant discovered both drugs and stolen items. Duenas (D) was interviewed by both DEA agents and Officer Frankie Smith. After invoking his *Miranda* rights while speaking with the DEA agents, Duenas (D) provided incriminating oral and written statements to Officer Smith. At a pre-trial suppression hearing, Duenas (D) cross-examined Officer Smith as to the voluntariness of the statements, arguing that they were procured in violation of his invocation of both his right to remain silent and a request for an attorney. The district court found Duenas's (D) statements to be voluntary and denied the motion to suppress. Subsequently Officer Smith died and the court allowed the Government (P) to introduce his suppression hearing testimony as an exception to the hearsay prohibition as "former testimony." After Duenas's (D) conviction, he appealed.

ISSUE: Can former testimony be introduced under Fed. R. Evid. 804(b)(1) without a showing of "similar motive"?

HOLDING AND DECISION: (Wardlaw, J.) No. Former testimony cannot be introduced under Fed. R. Evid. 804(b)(1) without a showing of "similar motive." "Former testimony" is not hearsay if a declarant is unavailable. "Former testimony" is testimony that: (A) was given as a witness at a trial, hearing, or lawful deposition, whether given during the current proceeding or a different one; and (B) is now offered against a party who had—or, in a civil case, whose predecessor in interest had—an opportunity and similar motive to develop it by direct, cross-, or

redirect examination. Smith was "unavailable" because he was deceased, and his former testimony was given during the pre-trial suppression hearing. Thus, the critical question is whether Duenas (D) had the "opportunity and similar motive" to develop Officer Smith's testimony by direct, cross-, or redirect examination at the suppression hearing as he would have had at trial. Because Duenas's (D) motive at the suppression hearing was solely to demonstrate that his statements were involuntary and obtained in violation of *Miranda*, and thus inadmissible, his motive for cross-examining Officer Smith at trial, to challenge the substance of the statements as opposed to the circumstances in which they were given, was substantially dissimilar. The record of the suppression hearing and written motion plainly shows that Duenas's (D) motive at that proceeding was to question Officer Smith about circumstances bearing on the voluntariness of the statement, and not to delve into the contents of the statement. Rather, Duenas's (D) "fundamental objective" at trial would have been to vigorously challenge Officer Smith on the details of the oral and written statements, to cast doubt on his credibility and on the reliability and completeness of his version of Duenas's (D) statement. Reversed.

▶ ANALYSIS

While "former testimony" is permitted as a hearsay exception when a declarant is unavailable, the key question is whether a party had an opportunity and similar motive in its examination. The "similar motive" determination focuses in on the "fundamental objective" of examination, not just the broad concept here of suppressing the defendant's statement. Because the focus of the examination of Officer Smith's testimony shifted from voluntariness to what would have been an attack on accuracy, the initial testimony did not fall into the hearsay exception.

■■■

Quicknotes

FORMER TESTIMONY EXCEPTION Exception to the hearsay rule for testimony given in a prior proceeding that may be offered in a later proceeding under certain circumstances.

HEARSAY EXCEPTION Out-of-court statement made by a person other than the witness testifying at trial that is offered in order to prove the truth of the matter asserted, and is admissible at trial notwithstanding the fact that it is hearsay.

Continued on next page.

***MIRANDA* WARNINGS** Specified warnings that must be communicated to a person prior to a custodial interrogation; in the absence of the communication of such warnings, any communications made during the interrogation are inadmissible at trial.

■■■

Lloyd v. American Export Lines, Inc.

Seaman (P) v. Shipping company (D)

580 F.2d 1179 (3d Cir.), *cert. denied*, 439 U.S. 969 (1978).

NATURE OF CASE: Counterclaim for damages for negligence and unseaworthiness.

FACT SUMMARY: In defending against a counterclaim brought by Alvarez (D), American Export Lines, Inc. (Export) (D) sought to introduce into evidence testimony that Lloyd (P) (who was unavailable) had given at a Coast Guard hearing regarding the fight between himself and Alvarez (D) aboard one of Export's (D) ships.

🏛 RULE OF LAW

The prior testimony of an unavailable witness is admissible under Fed. R. Evid. 804(b)(1) if the party against whom it is offered or a "predecessor in interest" had the "opportunity and similar motive to develop the testimony by direct, cross- or redirect examination."

FACTS: There was a fight between two crew members, Lloyd (P) and Alvarez (D), aboard one of American Export Lines, Inc.'s (Export's) (D) ships. Lloyd (P) sued Export (D), alleging negligence and unseaworthiness. Export (D) joined Alvarez (D) as a third-party defendant, and Alvarez (D) then counterclaimed against Export (D), alleging negligence and unseaworthiness (based on Export's (D) supposed failure to use reasonable precautions to safeguard him from one it knew to have dangerous propensities, i.e., Lloyd (P)). Lloyd's (P) case was dismissed when he repeatedly failed to show up for pretrial depositions and when his case was called for trial. Alvarez (D) proceeded with his counterclaim, testifying to his version of the fight that had occurred between himself and Lloyd (P). The trial court did not permit Export (D) to introduce into evidence Lloyd's (P) prior testimony at a Coast Guard hearing that had been held to determine whether his merchant mariner's document should have been suspended or revoked on the basis of charges of misconduct brought against him for the fight with Alvarez (D). That testimony contained Lloyd's (P) quite different account of the fight that had occurred. At that hearing, both Lloyd (P) and Alvarez (D) were represented by counsel and testified under oath. The jury found Export (D) negligent, and returned a verdict in favor of Alvarez (D). On appeal, Export (D) argued that the trial court had erred in ruling that this prior testimony was not admissible under Fed. R. Evid. 804(b)(1), which renders admissible the prior testimony of an unavailable witness if the party against whom it is offered or a "predecessor in interest" had the "opportunity and similar motive to develop the testimony by direct, cross- or redirect examination."

ISSUE: If a witness is unavailable, does Fed. R. Evid. 804(b)(1) make his prior testimony admissible if the party against whom it is offered or a "predecessor in interest" had the "opportunity and similar motive to develop the testimony by direct, cross- or redirect examination"?

HOLDING AND DECISION: (Aldisert, J.) Yes. Under Fed. R. Evid. 804(b)(1), the prior testimony of a witness who is "unavailable" is admissible if the party against whom it is offered or a "predecessor in interest" had the "opportunity and similar motive to develop the testimony by direct, cross or redirect examination." In this case, it is clear that the proponent of Lloyd's (P) statement was unable to procure his attendance by process or other reasonable means and that he must thus be considered to have been "unavailable." As to whether Export (D) can be considered a "predecessor in interest" of Lloyd (P), that is a more difficult question. Congress did not define that phrase, leaving it up to the courts to interpret it. As originally submitted by the Supreme Court, Rule 804(b)(1) would have allowed prior testimony of an unavailable witness to be received in evidence if the party against whom it was offered, or a person with "motive and interest similar," had an opportunity to examine the witness. The change in wording that occurred thereafter to that which is now set forth in Rule 804(b)(1) did not signal a return to the common-law approach to former testimony—which required privity or a common property interest between the parties. With that in mind, this court is satisfied there was a sufficient community of interest shared by the Coast Guard in its hearing and Alvarez (D) in the subsequent civil trial to satisfy Rule 804(b)(1). The Coast Guard investigating officer attempted to establish at the Coast Guard hearing what Alvarez (D) attempted to establish at the later trial: Lloyd's (P) intoxication, his role as the aggressor, and his prior hostility toward Alvarez (D). While the result sought in the two proceedings differed, the basic interest advanced by both was that of determining culpability and, if appropriate, exacting a penalty for the same condemned behavior thought to have occurred. Under the circumstances, this court is satisfied that there existed sufficient "opportunity and similar motive (for the Coast Guard investigating officer) to develop (Lloyd's) testimony" at the former hearing to justify its admission against Alvarez (D) at the later trial. It is this court's belief that Congress intended that when a party in a former suit had a like motive to cross-examine regarding the same matters as the present party would have and had an adequate opportunity to do so, the testimony thus procured in that former suit is admissible against the

Continued on next page.

present party because the previous party was, in the final analysis, a predecessor in interest to the present party. Reversed and remanded.

CONCURRENCE: (Stern, J.) While I agree with the result, I cannot agree with the analysis. I would hold that the prior testimony is admissible under the catch-all exception to the hearsay rule, 804(b)(5), and not under 804(b)(1). Under the majority's approach, it is sufficient that the Coast Guard investigator and Alvarez (D) shared a community of interest, which the majority seems to think means nothing more than similarity of interest or similarity of motive. But similar motive is a separate prerequisite to admissibility under 804(b)(1), and thus the majority's analysis which reads "predecessor in interest" to mean nothing more than person with "similar motive" eliminates the predecessor in interest requirement entirely. It seems clear that the phrase "predecessor in interest" is a term of art having a narrow, substantive law sense that historically requires it to be defined in terms of a privity relationship. No such relationship existed in this case. While the interests of Alvarez (D) and the Coast Guard may overlap, they do not coincide. The Coast Guard investigating officer was under no duty to advance every arguable issue against Lloyd (P) in vindication of Alvarez's (D) interests. He simply did not represent Alvarez (D).

▶ *ANALYSIS*

Just precisely when a witness is "unavailable" so that his prior testimony may be admissible is a problem that has plagued the courts. While some have held that a witness's loss of memory of the relevant matters does not render him "unavailable," the general consensus is that it does; so too does his refusal to testify.

■═■

Quicknotes

FED. R. EVID. 804 Addresses the definition of an unavailable witness and outlines the exceptions to the hearsay rule.

■═■

Williamson v. United States

Convicted drug dealer (D) v. Federal government (P)

512 U.S. 594 (1994).

NATURE OF CASE: Appeal from conviction of possession of cocaine with intent to distribute, conspiracy to possess cocaine with intent to distribute, and traveling interstate to promote the distribution of cocaine.

FACT SUMMARY: Williamson (D) contended that the district court erred in allowing the testimony of a DEA agent in court who related arguably self-inculpatory statements made out of court to him by Harris, one of Williamson's (D) employees, regarding the possession and transport of the cocaine.

🏛 RULE OF LAW
Fed. R. Evid. 804(b)(3) does not allow admission of non-self-exculpatory statements, even if they are made within a broader narrative that is generally self-inculpatory.

FACTS: Harris, an employee of Williamson (D), was stopped by the police while he was driving. The police, after searching the car, found 19 kilograms of cocaine in the car and arrested Harris. After his arrest, Harris was interviewed by telephone by Drug Enforcement Administration (DEA) Agent Walton. Harris told Walton that he had gotten the cocaine from a Cuban, that the cocaine belonged to Williamson (D), and that Harris was delivering it to a particular dumpster for pickup. Shortly thereafter, Walton interviewed Harris personally. Harris then told Walton he was transporting the cocaine to Atlanta for Williamson (D), Williamson (D) was traveling ahead of him in another car at the time of the arrest, and Williamson (D) had apparently seen the police searching Harris's car and had fled. Harris told Walton that he had initially lied about the source of the cocaine because he was afraid of Williamson (D). Harris implicated himself in his statements to Walton but did not want his story to be recorded and refused to sign a written transcript of the statement. Walton later testified that Harris was not promised any reward for cooperating. Williamson (D) was eventually charged and convicted of various drug-related offenses. When Harris was called to testify at Williamson's (D) trial, he refused to do so. The district court then ruled that, under Fed. R. Evid. 804(b)(3), Agent Walton could relate what Harris told him because Harris's statements were against his own interests. Williamson (D) was convicted, and the court of appeals affirmed. On appeal, Williamson (D) argued that both lower courts erred by allowing Walton to testify regarding Harris's out-of-court statements.

ISSUE: Does Fed. R. Evid. 804(b)(3) allow admission of non-self-inculpatory statements, even if they are made within a broader narrative that is generally self-inculpatory?

HOLDING AND DECISION: (O'Connor, J.) No. Fed. R. Evid. 804(b)(3) does not allow admission of non-self-inculpatory statements, even if they are made within a broader narrative that is generally self-inculpatory. The rationale behind the Rule is that a reasonable person would only make statements believed to be true when those statements are self-inculpatory. The admissibility of an entire statement, however, depends on the surrounding circumstances and not just on the fact that a few self-inculpatory facts were thrown into an otherwise exculpatory statement. A smart defendant will usually mix truth with lies, thus the self-inculpatory statements do not lend greater credibility to the collateral statements. In this case, Harris's confession was not fully self-inculpatory, and in fact, squarely implicated Williamson (D). The court of appeals must review Harris's statements to determine if each statement is in fact self-inculpatory and thus falls within the exception of Rule 804(b)(3). Vacated and remanded.

▌ ANALYSIS

As indicated by the Court in *Williamson*, Rule 804(b)(3) requires that self-inculpatory statements should be examined in terms of the reasonable person and that the declarant believes the statement to be against interest. In order to analyze whether the declarant truly believes his statement was against interest, the identity of the person to whom the statement was made should be considered. Although the situation wherein a declarant makes his statement to the authorities is the prime example of a statement against interest, if such a statement was made to a trusted friend (who was expected to keep the information secret), it has not necessarily been held that this eliminates the disserving nature of the statement.

■=■

Quicknotes

FED. R. EVID. 804(b)(3) A hearsay exception. Addresses a statement made contrary to the defendant's best interests; a reasonable person would not make the statement unless believing it to be true.

INCULPATORY Evidence tending to show a person's guilt in committing a criminal act.

■=■

Shepard v. United States

Convicted murderer (D) v. Federal government (P)

290 U.S. 96 (1933).

NATURE OF CASE: Appeal from conviction for murder.

FACT SUMMARY: Shepard (D) filed a writ of certiorari challenging the validity of his murder conviction, claiming that the court improperly admitted evidence of a dying declaration to his prejudice.

🏛 RULE OF LAW
In order for a statement to be considered a dying declaration, the declarant must have spoken without hope of recovery and in the shadow of impending death.

FACTS: Shepard (D) was convicted of murdering his wife by poisoning. Two days after Mrs. Shepard had become ill, while she was lying in bed, she had a conversation with Brown, a nurse. Mrs. Shepard asked Brown to bring her a particular bottle of liquor, told Brown that was what she was drinking right before she collapsed, asked Brown to test it for poison, and then stated, "Dr. Shepard (D) has poisoned me." The conversation was admitted after Brown testified that Mrs. Shepard said she was not going to get well, that she was going to die. At the time the conversation took place, all prospects for Mrs. Shepard's recovery were good. A fortnight after the conversation, Mrs. Shepard gave an indication that she was still hopeful of recovery. Shepard (D) was convicted, and the conviction was affirmed by the court of appeals. Shepard (D) then filed a writ of certiorari.

ISSUE: In order for a statement to be considered a dying declaration, must the declarant have spoken without hope of recovery and in the shadow of impending death?

HOLDING AND DECISION: (Cardozo, J.) Yes. In order for a statement to be considered a dying declaration, the declarant must have spoken without hope of recovery and in the shadow of impending death. Fear or even belief that illness will result in death will not suffice. There must be a "settled" hopeless expectation that death is near at hand, and what is said must have been spoken in the hush of its impending presence. Here, there was hope for recovery, and death was not imminent when the statement was made, and therefore it could not have been admitted as a dying declaration. It cannot be said that the admission of the declaration was mere unsubstantial error.

▌ *ANALYSIS*

There is no reason to believe that fear or even belief that one is going to die could not provide the guarantee of special reliability necessary to admit this type of hearsay evidence, since it is probably reasonable that persons so inclined would tell the truth. The strict application of the doctrine probably represents a basic lack of trust in "deathbed" statements generally.

Quicknotes

CERTIORARI A discretionary writ issued by a superior court to an inferior court in order to review the lower court's decisions; the Supreme Court's writ ordering such review.

DYING DECLARATION A statement spoken upon belief of impending death, usually not considered hearsay due to its circumstantial guarantees of trustworthiness.

United States v. Gray

Federal government (P) v. Convicted felon (D)

405 F.3d 227 (4th Cir.), *cert. denied*, 546 U.S. 912 (2005).

NATURE OF CASE: Appeal of conviction for mail and wire fraud.

FACT SUMMARY: Josephine Gray (D) allegedly killed two husbands and a boyfriend, and collected their life insurance. She was convicted for mail fraud and wire fraud related to the insurance proceeds. On appeal, she sought a new trial based on the district court's admission of testimony regarding several out-of-court statements made by her second husband, Robert Gray, during the three months before his murder.

> **RULE OF LAW**
> Under Fed. R. Evid. 804(b)(6), a defendant who wrongfully and intentionally renders a declarant unavailable as a witness in any court proceeding forfeits the right to exclude, on hearsay grounds, the declarant's statements at that proceeding and any subsequent proceeding.

FACTS: Josephine Gray (D) allegedly killed her first husband, Norman Stribbling, and collected his life insurance. She then allegedly killed her second husband, Robert Gray, with the help of her boyfriend, Clarence Goode, and collected his life insurance. Then, she allegedly killed Goode. She was convicted for mail fraud and wire fraud related to the insurance proceeds. On appeal, she sought a new trial based on the district court's admission of testimony regarding several out-of-court statements made by her second husband, Robert Gray, during the three months before his murder. Specifically, she sought to exclude a criminal complaint he filed alleging that Goode tossed a nine-millimeter handgun on the table to provoke an argument; a criminal complaint alleging that Gray (D) tried to stab Robert Gray and beat him with a club; statements made by Robert Gray to police claiming that Gray (D) and Goode assaulted him; and statements made by Robert Gray to family claiming that Goode pulled a gun on him outside a restaurant. The district court admitted the evidence under Fed. R. Evid. 804(b)(6).

ISSUE: Under Fed. R. Evid. 804(b)(6), does a defendant who wrongfully and intentionally renders a declarant unavailable as a witness in any court proceeding forfeit the right to exclude, on hearsay grounds, the declarant's statements at that proceeding and any subsequent proceeding?

HOLDING AND DECISION: (Shedd, J.) Yes. Under Fed. R. Evid. 804(b)(6), a defendant who wrongfully and intentionally renders a declarant unavailable as a witness in any court proceeding forfeits the right to exclude, on hearsay grounds, the declarant's statements at that proceeding and any

subsequent proceeding. The purpose of the forfeiture-by-wrongdoing exception is to prevent wrongdoers from profiting by their misconduct. The exception should be applied broadly. Gray (D) cannot be allowed to avoid the impact of statements made by her victim, whether or not she suspected the victim would be a witness at the trial in which the evidence was offered against her. Because the district court properly found by a preponderance of the evidence that Gray (D) engaged in some wrongdoing that was intended to procure Robert Gray's unavailability as a witness and that did, in fact, procure his unavailability, it did not abuse its discretion in admitting testimony concerning out-of-court statements made by Robert Gray. Affirmed.

▌ANALYSIS

The important thing to remember about this case is that the wrongdoing perpetrated by the defendant need not be done specifically with the intent to prevent the declarant from appearing as a witness in a particular trial. The test is whether the defendant should profit from her wrongdoing, not whether she committed the wrongdoing at a particular time, place, or with a particular intent related to a particular trial.

■■■

Quicknotes

DECLARANT Any person who is the source of offered testimony.

FED. R. EVID. 804 Addresses the definition of an unavailable witness and outlines the exceptions to the hearsay rule.

HEARSAY An out-of-court statement made by a person other than the witness testifying at trial that is offered in order to prove the truth of the matter asserted.

PREPONDERANCE OF THE EVIDENCE A standard of proof requiring the trier of fact to determine whether the fact sought to be established is more probable than not.

■■■

Mutual Life Insurance Co. v. Hillmon

Insurance company (D) v. Decedent's spouse (P)

145 U.S. 285 (1892).

NATURE OF CASE: Action to recover proceeds of insurance policy.

FACT SUMMARY: Mutual Life Insurance Co. (D) refused to pay off on a life insurance policy on Hillmon's life because of a conflict over the identity of the decedent.

> 🏛 **RULE OF LAW**
> Whenever a party's intention is, of itself, a distinct and material fact in a chain of circumstances, it may be proved by contemporaneous oral or written declarations of the party.

FACTS: Hillmon was missing. A body which could have been his or another's was buried at Crooked Creek. Hillmon's wife (P), the beneficiary of his life insurance, filed suit against three life insurance companies (D) to recover the policy proceeds. Mutual Life Insurance Co. (Mutual Life) (D) defended on the basis that it could not adequately be established that Hillmon was dead, since the body could not be positively identified. Some evidence was admitted which tended to show that Hillmon had gone to Crooked Creek at the same time the body was discovered. Mutual Life (D) contended that Walters was the actual decedent at Crooked Creek. It tried to introduce a letter written to Walters's fiancée that he intended to go to Crooked Creek at the time the body was discovered. It was alleged that this was within the business record exception to the hearsay rule. The letter was not admitted, and the jury found for Hillmon (P).

ISSUE: Where an actor's intentions are a material factor in a controversy, is evidence admissible to establish his intent?

HOLDING AND DECISION: (Gray, J.) Yes. Where a party's intention is, of itself, a distinct and material fact in a chain of circumstances, it may be proved by contemporaneous oral or written declarations of the party. Here, there is a controversy over the identity of the decedent. Mutual Life (D) contends that the decedent was Walters. While the letters were not within the business records exception as Mutual Life (D) argued, they are admissible as falling within the state of mind exception. The evidence of Walters's intention is admissible to create the inference that since he intended to go there at the time the letter was written, he did go there. It is not proof that he actually went there, only that it is more likely than not that he did. Since the issue was in controversy, it might have tended to influence the jury. Where the bodily or mental feelings of an actor are material to be proved, the usual expression of them is competent and admissible as an exception to the hearsay rules. After death, there is no other way of establishing such facts. Since the letters were probative as to Walters's current state of mind, it was error to exclude them. Judgment is reversed and the cause is remanded.

▶ ANALYSIS

Regarding this case, McCormick has said, "Despite the failure until recently to recognize the potential value of declarations of state of mind to prove subsequent conduct, it is now clear that out-of-court statements which tend to prove a plan, design or intention of the declarant are admissible, subject to the usual limitations as to remoteness in time and apparent sincerity common to all declarations of mental state, to prove that the plan, design, or intention of the declarant was carried out by declarant."

■▬■

Quicknotes

BUSINESS RECORDS EXCEPTION Exception to the hearsay rule for records made in the ordinary course of business.

DECLARANT Any person who is the source of offered testimony.

STATE-OF-MIND EXCEPTION An exception to the hearsay rule for the admission of an out-of-court declaration to prove the declarant's present reason for action despite the declarant's unavailability.

■▬■

Shepard v. United States

Convicted murderer (D) v. Federal government (P)

290 U.S. 96 (1933).

NATURE OF CASE: Appeal from conviction for murder.

FACT SUMMARY: Trial court had permitted the introduction of testimony that Mrs. Shepard, the victim, had stated shortly before her death, "Dr. Shepard has poisoned me."

🏛 RULE OF LAW
Declarations of present memory, looking backwards to a prior occurrence, are inadmissible to prove, or tend to prove, the existence of the occurrence.

FACTS: Dr. Shepard (D) was charged with the poison-killing of his wife. At his trial, the court permitted the prosecution to introduce testimony of a nurse who attended Mrs. Shepard shortly before her death. The nurse testified that Mrs. Shepard asked her to fetch a bottle of whisky from the defendant's room. The nurse said the wife had drunk from this bottle before collapsing, requested a test, insisting that the smell and taste were strange, and added, "Dr. Shepard has poisoned me." Dr. Shepard (D) was convicted, and the conviction was affirmed by the court of appeals.

ISSUE: Are declarations of present memory, looking backwards to a prior occurrence, inadmissible to prove, or tend to prove, the existence of the occurrence?

HOLDING AND DECISION: (Cardozo, J.) Yes. Declarations of present memory, looking backwards to a prior occurrence, are inadmissible to prove, or tend to prove, the existence of the occurrence. Since the testimony had been offered and received as proof of a dying declaration, the Government (P) may not now argue an appeal that the declarations were offered to show a persistency of a will to live. Because of the stated purpose of the testimony, Dr. Shepard (D) was put off his guard. It would now be unfair for the Government (P) to shift its ground. The purpose for which normally hearsay evidence is sought to be admitted must be made clear at the time it is introduced. The Government (P) did not use the declarations by Mrs. Shepard to prove her present thoughts and feelings, or even her thoughts and feelings in times past. Rather, they were offered as proof of an act committed by someone else as evidence that she was dying of poison by her husband. The jury is incapable of distinguishing in its mind between these declarations as mere indications of a state of mind and as pointing the finger of guilt at Dr. Shepard (D). The ruling in *Mutual Life Ins. Co. v. Hillmon,* 145 U.S. 285 (1892), represents the high-water line beyond which courts may not go; in that case, the testimony looked forward to prove an occurrence. Here, it looks backward to a past act, and, more importantly, to an act by someone not the speaker. Reversed and remanded.

▶ *ANALYSIS*

The rule enunciated here has been heavily criticized but has, nonetheless, survived in the case law. One exception has been in probate cases where the testator's declarations, made after the disputed occurrence, are admitted to prove that he has made or revoked a will. The reason for this is that the testator is unavailable. Extending this rationale, the Model Code of Evidence would admit all hearsay declarations including statements of memory, when the declarant is unavailable to testify.

■■■

Quicknotes

DYING DECLARATION A statement spoken upon belief of impending death, usually not considered hearsay due to its circumstantial guarantees of trustworthiness.

■■■

United States v. Iron Shell

Federal government (P) v. Sex offender (D)

633 F.2d 77 (8th Cir. 1980), *cert. denied*, 450 U.S. 1001 (1981).

NATURE OF CASE: Appeal from rape conviction.

FACT SUMMARY: Iron Shell (D) objected to the admission at his trial of statements made to an examining physician by the nine-year-old girl he allegedly tried to rape.

🏛 **RULE OF LAW**
Under Fed. R. Evid. 803(4), an exception to the hearsay rule is created that permits admission of statements made for purposes of medical diagnosis or treatment.

FACTS: Lucy, the nine-year-old Indian girl the jury found Iron Shell (D) had assaulted with intent to commit rape, had made certain statements to the doctor who examined her on the night of the assault. He elicited various statements from her concerning the cause of her injuries. At trial, the doctor was permitted to testify that she had told him she was dragged into the bushes, then her clothes were removed, that the man had tried to force something into her vagina that hurt, and that she had tried to scream but was unable to because he put his hand over her mouth and neck. Lucy was unable to detail what happened to her after she was assaulted but did manage to respond to a series of leading questions on direct and thus tell some of her story. Defense counsel did not explore any of the substantive issues on cross-examination, nor did he examine Lucy concerning her statements to the doctor. On appeal, Iron Shell (D) argued that these statements were not ones falling within the hearsay exception for statements made for purposes of medical diagnosis or treatment.

ISSUE: Are statements made for purposes of medical diagnosis or treatment admissible?

HOLDING AND DECISION: (Stephenson, J.) Yes. Federal Rule 803(4) significantly liberalized prior practice concerning admissibility of statements made for purposes of medical diagnosis or treatments (i.e., those reasonably pertinent to diagnosis or treatment). To ascertain if this exception to the hearsay rule applied, it must be determined if the statement communicated a fact of the type reasonably relied upon by experts in a particular field in forming opinions. Actually, a two-part test is appropriate in these cases: first, is the declarant's motive consistent with the purpose of the rule; and second, is it reasonable for the physicians to rely on the information in diagnosis or treatment. Both parts of the test seem satisfied by the circumstances of this case. Thus, admission of the statements Lucy made to the examining doctor was proper. Affirmed.

▶ **ANALYSIS**

While a number of states have adopted the federal rule, others have maintained a more orthodox and restrictive stance. The federal rule dropped the distinction between the doctor who was consulted for the purpose of treatment and one consulted only in order to testify as a witness. Many states have not.

■═■

Quicknotes

FED. R. EVID. 803 Rule setting forth certain exceptions to the hearsay rule, including present sense impressions, excited utterances, present state of mind, statements for medical diagnosis and past recollections recorded.

■═■

Johnson v. State

Convicted murderer (D) v. State (P)

Tex. Crim. App. Ct., 967 S.W.2d 410 (1998).

NATURE OF CASE: Appeal from capital murder conviction and death sentence.

FACT SUMMARY: A witness at defendant's murder trial had no recollection of the events noted in his prior sworn statement to the police nor did he guarantee the accuracy or truthfulness of the assertions in that statement. Defendant contends that the statement was inadmissible hearsay and should not have been read into evidence.

> ## 🏛 RULE OF LAW
> The past recollection recorded hearsay exception requires a present showing that the past recording was accurate or that the factual assertions therein contained were true.

FACTS: Arnold Johnson (Johnson) (D) was allegedly involved in the murder of Frank Johnson, Jr. The State (P) contended that Johnson (D) was driving a car in which the victim, the shooter, and Reginald Taylor were riding. Taylor provided a written statement to the police just after the murder, implicating Johnson (D) and making several factual assertions about the murder. At Johnson's (D) trial for capital murder, the state called Taylor as an eyewitness, but Taylor was not cooperative on the stand. The State (P) attempted to refresh Taylor's memory with the written statement, but he testified that he did not remember the events of that date nor did he make assurances that the statement was correct when he wrote it. Taylor was not familiar with its contents at the time of trial. Over objection, the trial judge allowed the statement to be read into evidence as a past recorded recollection exception to the hearsay rule. Johnson (D) was convicted of capital murder and sentenced to death. He appealed, contending that the exception should not have applied because the reliability of Taylor's statement was not established.

ISSUE: Does a past recollection recorded hearsay exception require a present showing that the past recording was accurate or that the factual assertions contained therein were true?

HOLDING AND DECISION: (Mansfield, J.) Yes. The past recollection recorded hearsay exception requires a present showing that the past recording was accurate or that the factual assertions therein contained were true. At the very least, the witness should testify that he would not have signed the statement had he not believed it to be accurate and truthful at the time he made it. Taylor testified that he did not remember giving the statement, anything in the statement, or the events of that day. Although Taylor's statement contained boilerplate language asserting the truthfulness of the statement, the past recorded recollection cannot be self-proving. The State (P) did not demonstrate the reliability of Taylor's statement and it was inadmissible hearsay. Reversed and remanded.

▶ ANALYSIS

Although it must have been frustrating to the prosecution to have their witness fall apart on the stand, the rationale behind the rule of his case is an important one. Past recorded recollections cannot be self-proving. Attorneys, sheriffs, and anyone involved in the drafting of legal documents routinely put self-affirming language on documents. Relying on those documents alone could lead to abuses of the system where witnesses may or may not have accurately recorded facts and details in the first place.

■═■

Quicknotes

HEARSAY EXCEPTION Out-of-court statement made by a person other than the witness testifying at trial that is offered in order to prove the truth of the matter asserted, and is admissible at trial notwithstanding the fact that it is hearsay.

PAST RECORDED RECOLLECTIONS An exception to the hearsay rule for statements contained in a document as to which the witness no longer has recollection.

■═■

Palmer v. Hoffman

Railroad trustee (D) v. Injured claimant (P)

318 U.S. 109 (1943).

NATURE OF CASE: Action for personal injuries arising out of a railroad accident.

FACT SUMMARY: The engineer of a train involved in an accident, who died before trial, made a statement to the railroad company regarding the accident. This statement was not allowed into evidence.

RULE OF LAW

A record is considered to be "in the regular course of business" if made systematically or as a matter of routine to reflect events or transactions of the business.

FACTS: Hoffman (P) was injured in an accident with a railroad train and brought suit against Palmer (D), a trustee of the railroad. Shortly after the accident, the engineer of the train made a statement to the superintendent of the railroad and to a representative of the public utilities commission. It was the custom of the railroad to record such statements whenever there was an accident. The engineer died before the trial, and Palmer (D) attempted to introduce the statement into evidence. A statute allowed business records to be admitted if made in the course of regular business, but the court would not allow it into evidence.

ISSUE: Is a record considered to be "in the regular course of business" if made systematically or as a matter of routine to reflect events or transactions of the business?

HOLDING AND DECISION: (Douglas, J.) Yes. To be considered made "in the regular course of business" a record must be made in relation to the inherent nature of the business and in the methods systematically employed for the conduct of the business as a business. The keeping of accident reports, while customary, is not essential to the efficient operation of a railroad. If the mere custom of making a record of non-essential activity could bring that record within the meaning of "regular course" of business, then any company could bring any type of record into court. The primary purpose of the record in this case was not for the efficient management of a railroad, but for litigation. Therefore, the record was not within the regular course of business and was properly excluded. Affirmed.

▶ ANALYSIS

This is the leading case recognized for records that are kept in the regular course of business. Many scholars have criticized the decision as being contrary to the statute, and therefore lower courts have dealt with the case in varying ways. Current analysis of this case does not create a blanket rule of exclusion for "self serving" accident reports or other such records kept by businesses. Instead, it gives trial courts the discretion to exclude evidence which falls under the business records exception to the hearsay rule. The motive and the opportunity to falsify are the primary factors in using this case to exclude records.

Quicknotes

BUSINESS RECORDS EXCEPTION Exception to the hearsay rule for records made in the ordinary course of business.

United States v. Vigneau

Federal government (P) v. Convicted money launderer (D)

187 F.3d 70 (1st Cir. 1999), *cert. denied*, 528 U.S. 1172 (2000).

NATURE OF CASE: Appeal from conviction for money laundering and illegal drug distribution.

FACT SUMMARY: Vigneau (D) claimed that Western Union's "To Send Money" forms that contained his name, address, and telephone number were inadmissible hearsay and not admissible under the business records exception.

🏛 RULE OF LAW
The business records exception to the hearsay rule does not embrace statements contained within a business record that are made by one who is an outsider to the business where the statements are offered for their truth.

FACTS: Vigneau (D) was convicted on twenty-one counts of money laundering in connection with a drug distribution scheme. At trial, the court allowed the Government (P) to introduce, without redaction and for all purposes, Western Union's "To Send Money" forms, under the theory that the forms fell under the business records exception to the hearsay rule. These forms are handed by the sender of money to a Western Union agent after the sender completes the left side of the form by writing (1) the sender's name, address and telephone number; (2) the amount of the transfer; and (3) the intended recipient's name and location. The Western Union clerk then fills in the right side of the form with the clerk's signature, date, amount of the transfer and fee, and a computer-generated control number. At the time Vigneau (D) allegedly filled out these forms, independent proof of the sender's identity was not required. The Government (P) had either the original forms completed by the sender or computer records of such forms. Vigneau (D) argued that his name, address and telephone number on the "To Send Money" forms were inadmissible hearsay to identify him as the sender.

ISSUE: Does the business records exception to the hearsay rule embrace statements contained within a business record that are made by one who is an outsider to the business where the statements are offered for their truth?

HOLDING AND DECISION: (Boudin, J.) No. The business records exception to the hearsay rule does not embrace statements contained within a business record that are made by one who is an outsider to the business where the statements are offered for their truth. The forms literally comply with the business records exception because each form (or the computerized information representing the form) is a business record. The problem, however, is that the business records exception does not

apply where the statements contained in the record were made by a stranger to the business. That is because when the stranger fills out the forms, there are no safeguards of business regularity or business checks to assure the truth of the statement to the business. Fed. R. Evid. 803(6), which codifies the business records exception, provides in part that a business record is inadmissible if found to lack trustworthiness. That reference to "trustworthiness," however, does not comprise an independent hearsay exception. Sometimes, the statement by the "outsider" may be admissible not for its truth but for some other purpose. The weakness in the Government's (P) position here is that the forms were admitted for all purposes. Clearly, the forms were relevant to the Government's (P) case because they showed money transfers that supported the description of drug and money laundering activities. Thus, the forms could have been submitted in redacted form, omitting the information identifying Vigneau (D) as the sender. But because the forms were not redacted, they should not have been admitted for their truth. Here, the error is not harmless. Vacated and remanded as to the money laundering charges.

▶ ANALYSIS

As the court in this case notes, if there had been independent evidence that the writer of the forms was Vigneau (D), the statements in those forms—his name, address, and telephone number—would constitute party-opponent admissions and would technically not be hearsay under Fed. R. Evid. 801(d)(2). Without such independent evidence, however, the prosecution could not use the forms themselves as bootstrap-proof that Vigneau (D) was the one who made the admission.

■=■

Quicknotes

BUSINESS RECORDS EXCEPTION Exception to the hearsay rule for records made in the ordinary course of business.

FED. R. EVID. 801 The "hearsay rule," making out-of-court statements used to prove the truth of the matter asserted inadmissible at trial.

FED. R. EVID. 803 Rule setting forth certain exceptions to the hearsay rule, including present sense impressions, excited utterances, present state of mind, statements for medical diagnosis and past recollection recorded.

■=■

Beech Aircraft Corp. v. Rainey

Aircraft manufacturer (D) v. Decedent's survivors (P)

488 U.S. 153 (1988).

NATURE OF CASE: Appeal of reversal of denial of damages for wrongful death.

FACT SUMMARY: In Rainey's (P) wrongful death action, the trial court admitted portions of a government investigative report which contained the investigator's conclusions.

🏛 RULE OF LAW
Governmental reports that contain the report makers' conclusions are admissible as a hearsay exception.

FACTS: A Navy aircraft accident involving an airplane made by Beech Aircraft Corp. (D) resulted in the deaths of the two pilots aboard. A governmental investigative report was prepared by appropriate authorities. The report contained both factual findings and analysis/conclusions. The report's basic conclusion was that the exact cause was unascertainable, but was most likely pilot error. In a wrongful death suit brought by Rainey (P) and the other decedent's survivors, the district court admitted both the report's factual findings and conclusions under the "public records and reports" hearsay exception embodied in Fed. R. Evid. 803(8). A jury returned a defense verdict. The Eleventh Circuit reversed, holding that only factual findings, as opposed to conclusions, were admissible under Fed. R. Evid. 803(8). The Supreme Court granted review.

ISSUE: Are governmental reports that contain the report makers' conclusions admissible as a hearsay exception?

HOLDING AND DECISION: (Brennan, J.) Yes. Governmental reports that contain the report makers' conclusions are admissible as a hearsay exception. Fed. R. Evid. 803(8) creates a hearsay exception for reports containing "factual findings." It is clear that "factual findings" should be read to mean raw data only, as opposed to conclusions based on such data. Further, the rule does not limit admissibility only to "factual findings," but rather makes admissible "reports . . . setting forth . . . factual findings." Thus, the Rule on its face makes no distinction between fact and opinion. Also, in any given situation, the difference between what is fact and what is conclusion may be difficult to distinguish. Finally, the legislative history behind Fed. R. Evid. 803(8) gives no indication that Congress intended to create a fact/conclusion dichotomy. In light of this, the fact/conclusion distinction made by the Eleventh Circuit here was analytically incorrect. Reversed.

▶ ANALYSIS

Prior to this case, there had been a conflict among the circuits on this issue. The Fifth Circuit, in *Smith v. Ithaca Corp.*, 612 F.2d 215 (1980), had embraced the narrow view of Rule 803(8) adopted by the Eleventh Circuit in this case. Every other circuit which had decided the issue had come to the opposite conclusion.

Quicknotes

FED. R. EVID. 803 Rule setting forth certain exceptions to the hearsay rule, including present sense impressions, excited utterances, present state of mind, statements for medical diagnosis and past recollection recorded.

PUBLIC RECORDS EXCEPTION Exception to the hearsay rule for the introduction of public records and reports made within the scope of a public employee's official duties, made close to the time of the event and with other indicia of trustworthiness.

Dallas County v. Commercial Union Assurance Co.

County (P) v. Insurance company (D)

286 F.2d 388 (5th Cir. 1961).

NATURE OF CASE: Action to collect under insurance policy.

FACT SUMMARY: Commercial Union Assurance Co. (D) offered into evidence a 1901 newspaper article.

🏛 RULE OF LAW
In matters of local interest, when the fact in question is of such a public nature it would be generally known throughout the community, and when the questioned fact occurred so long ago that the testimony of an eyewitness would probably be less trustworthy than a contemporary newspaper account, a federal court may relax the hearsay exclusionary rules to the extent of admitting the newspaper article in evidence.

FACTS: In 1957, in Dallas County, the clock tower of the courthouse collapsed. In order to collect under an insurance policy which covered loss caused by lightning, Dallas County ("the County") (P) reported the presence of charcoal and charred timbers found in the tower debris. To refute this at trial, Commercial Union Assurance Co. (D) ("the insurer") (D), claiming that the charred remains were present in the building prior to its collapse, offered into evidence a local 1901 newspaper article, unsigned, which reported a fire in the courthouse. The County (P) objected to the introduction of the article on the ground of hearsay.

ISSUE: May a federal court ever admit into evidence a newspaper article?

HOLDING AND DECISION: (Wisdom, J.) Yes. A federal court is permitted to follow any rule that favors the reception of evidence. Although nearly all newspaper articles constitute hearsay, a federal court may recognize its own exceptions. First, it is due to necessity that the article should be admitted. Witnesses to the 1901 fire would now either be dead or possess a faulty memory. Secondly, the article itself carries sufficient indicia of trustworthiness. A small town newspaper reporter in 1901 would not report a local fire unless there had, in fact, been one. The reporter would simply lack any motive to falsify. The article is admissible into evidence. Affirmed.

▌ ANALYSIS

Newspaper articles, printed books, or publications are usually not admissible into evidence. This is because, absent some special indication of reliability, as in the instant case, there is no opportunity to cross-examine their authors, and the statements within were not made under oath.

Quicknotes

ANCIENT DOCUMENT EXCEPTION EVIDENCE RULE Permits the admission of a document if it meets the ancient writing requirements.

FED. R. EVID. 901 Requires the authentication or identification of evidence as a condition precedent to admissibility.

Confrontation and Compulsory Process

Quick Reference Rules of Law

Mattox v. United States

Convicted murderer (D) v. Federal government (P)

156 U.S. 237 (1895).

NATURE OF CASE: Appeal from murder conviction.

FACT SUMMARY: Two witnesses at defendant's first trial for murder died prior to defendant's retrial. Defendant contended that their absence violated his confrontation rights when their transcribed testimony from the first trial was read into evidence at his second trial.

> 🏛 **RULE OF LAW**
> The law declares that the rights of the public shall not be wholly sacrificed in order that an incidental benefit may be preserved to the accused.

FACTS: Mattox (D) was tried and convicted for the murder of John Mullen, but this Court reversed that conviction and remanded for a new trial. Prior to the second trial, two key witnesses for the prosecution died. A reporter had transcribed the testimony of the deceased from the first trial and testified as to the transcription's accuracy at the second trial. The transcribed testimony was read into evidence and was the strongest evidence against Mattox (D), who was once again convicted of murder. He again appealed, claiming his constitutional right to confront his accusers had been violated.

ISSUE: Is there an exception to the defendant's constitutional right to confrontation?

HOLDING AND DECISION: (Brown, J.) Yes. The law declares that the rights of the public shall not be wholly sacrificed in order that an incidental benefit may be preserved to the accused. The constitutional protections enjoyed by defendants were never meant to allow a defendant to escape justice completely. If following the constitutional provisions to the technical letter puts the public safety in jeopardy, then an exception is warranted and necessary. The witnesses originally made their statements under oath and the defendant had ample opportunity at that time for cross-examination. Their untimely deaths do not provide him with a way to avoid justice. Affirmed.

▶ ANALYSIS

The holding in this case is similar to the rule preventing a defendant from benefiting from harassment or removal of a witness against him. Although the defendant in this case did nothing to affirmatively prevent the testimony of the witnesses, he should not benefit from the untimely death of the witnesses.

Quicknotes

CONFRONTATION CLAUSE A provision in the Sixth Amendment to the United States Constitution that an accused in a criminal action has the right to confront the witnesses against him, including the right to attend the trial and to cross-examine witnesses called on behalf of the prosecution.

CROSS-EXAMINATION The interrogation of a witness by an adverse party either to further inquire as to the subject matter of the direct examination or to call into question the witness's credibility.

Crawford v. Washington

Criminal defendant (D) v. State (P)

541 U.S. 36 (2004).

NATURE OF CASE: Appeal from a criminal conviction.

FACT SUMMARY: When the prosecution played the tape-recorded statement of a witness against him at trial, which did not afford the opportunity for cross-examination, Crawford (D) argued he was denied the Sixth Amendment's guarantee of confrontation.

🏛 RULE OF LAW
Where testimonial statements are at issue, the only indicium of reliability sufficient to satisfy constitutional demands is the one the Constitution actually prescribes: confrontation.

FACTS: Michael Crawford (D) stabbed a man who allegedly tried to rape his wife, Sylvia. At his trial, the prosecution played for the jury Sylvia's tape-recorded statement to the police describing the stabbing, even though Crawford (D) had no opportunity for cross-examination. The jury found Crawford (D) guilty. The Washington court of appeals reversed, but the Washington Supreme Court upheld the conviction after determining that Sylvia's statement was reliable. Crawford (D) appealed to the U.S. Supreme Court, contending that the State of Washington's (P) procedure of playing the tape violated the Sixth Amendment's guarantee that in all criminal prosecutions the accused shall enjoy the right to confront the witnesses against him.

ISSUE: Where testimonial statements are at issue, is confrontation the only indicium of reliability sufficient to satisfy constitutional demands?

HOLDING AND DECISION: (Scalia, J.) Yes. Where testimonial statements are at issue, the only indicium of reliability sufficient to satisfy constitutional demands is confrontation. Here, the state admitted Sylvia's testimonial statement against Crawford (D) despite the fact that he had no opportunity to cross-examine her. That alone is sufficient to make out a violation of the Sixth Amendment. This Court will not mine the record in search of indicia of reliability. Although where nontestimonial hearsay is at issue, it is wholly consistent with the Framers' design to afford the states flexibility in their development of hearsay law. Where testimonial evidence is at issue, the Sixth Amendment demands what the common law required: unavailability and a prior opportunity for cross-examination. Whatever else the term "testimonial" covers, it applies at a minimum to prior testimony at a preliminary hearing, before a grand jury, or at a former trial, and to police interrogations. These are the modern practices with

closest kinship to the abuses at which the Confrontation Clause was directed. The Constitution prescribes the procedure for determining the reliability of testimony in criminal trials, and this Court, no less than the state courts, lacks authority to replace it with one of our own devising. By replacing categorical constitutional guarantees with open-ended balancing tests, we would do violence to the Framers' design. Reversed and remanded.

CONCURRENCE: (Rehnquist, C.J.) The Court's adoption of a new interpretation of the Confrontation Clause is not backed by sufficiently persuasive reasoning to overrule long-established precedent. The decision of the Court here casts a mantle of uncertainty over future criminal trials in both federal and state courts and is by no means necessary to decide the instant case. The Court's distinction between testimonial and nontestimonial statements is no better rooted in history than the Court's current doctrine.

▶ ANALYSIS

In *Crawford*, the Supreme Court makes clear that where testimonial statements are involved in criminal cases, the framers did not intend to leave the Sixth Amendment's protection to the vagaries of the rules of evidence, much less to amorphous notions of "reliability." Legal authorities and scholars do not acknowledge any general reliability exception to the common-law confrontation rule. In this regard, the *Crawford* decision notes that admitting statements simply because they are deemed reliable by a judge is fundamentally at odds with the right of confrontation. While the Sixth Amendment's ultimate goal is to ensure reliability of evidence, it is a procedural rather than a substantive guarantee. It commands, not that evidence be reliable, but that reliability be assessed in a particular manner: by cross-examination.

■▬■

Quicknotes

CONFRONTATION CLAUSE A provision in the Sixth Amendment to the United States Constitution that an accused in a criminal action has the right to confront the witnesses against him, including the right to attend the trial and to cross-examine witnesses called on behalf of the prosecution.

CROSS-EXAMINATION The interrogation of a witness by an adverse party either to further inquire as to the

Continued on next page.

subject matter of the direct examination or to call into question the witness's credibility.

HEARSAY An out-of-court statement made by a person other than the witness testifying at trial that is offered in order to prove the truth of the matter asserted.

SIXTH AMENDMENT Provides the right to a speedy and public trial by impartial jury, the right to be informed of the accusation, the right to confront witnesses, and the right to have the assistance of counsel in all criminal prosecutions.

Michigan v. Bryant

State (P) v. Murderer (D)

131 S. Ct. 1143 (2011).

NATURE OF CASE: Appeal from state court decision reversing a murder conviction.

FACT SUMMARY: A shooting victim made statements to the police implicating the defendant Bryant (D) as the shooter. The victim later died and his statements to the police were introduced at trial.

🏛 RULE OF LAW
Where the primary purpose of an interrogation of a witness is to allow police to respond to an ongoing emergency, statements made by a witness will not qualify as testimonial statements and the Confrontation Clause will not bar their admission at trial.

FACTS: When the police found Anthony Covington, he was alive but fatally wounded. After asking him a series of questions about "what had happened, who has shot him, and where the shooting occurred," Covington identified Richard Bryant (D) as the shooter and where it had occurred. Covington later died at the hospital. At trial, the State (P) was allowed to introduce Covington's statements identifying Bryant (D) as the shooter. Upon conviction, Bryant (D) appealed. The state supreme court reversed, holding Covington's statements were testimonial. The State (P) then appealed.

ISSUE: Where the primary purpose of an interrogation of a witness is to allow police to respond to an ongoing emergency, do statements made by a witness qualify as testimonial statements and will the Confrontation Clause bar their admission at trial?

HOLDING AND DECISION: (Sotomayor, J.) No. Where the primary purpose of an interrogation of a witness is to allow police to respond to an ongoing emergency, statements made by a witness will not qualify as testimonial statements and the Confrontation Clause will not bar their admission at trial. Out-of-court statements can evade the basic objective of the Confrontation Clause, which is to prevent the accused from being deprived of the opportunity to cross-examine the declarant about statements taken for use at trial. When the primary purpose of an interrogation is to respond to an "ongoing emergency," its purpose is not to create a record for trial and thus is not within the scope of the Clause. In making the "primary purpose" determination, standard rules of hearsay, designed to identify some statements as reliable, will be relevant. Where no such primary purpose exists, the admissibility of a statement is the concern of state and federal rules of evidence, not the Confrontation Clause.

To determine whether the "primary purpose" of an interrogation is "to enable police assistance to meet an ongoing emergency," which would render the resulting statements nontestimonial, requires an objective evaluation of the circumstances in which the encounter occurs and the statements and actions of the parties. The circumstances in which an encounter occurs—at, or near the scene of the crime, versus at the police station, during an emergency or afterwards—are clearly matters of objective fact. The statements and actions of the parties must also be objectively evaluated. The relevant inquiry is not the subjective or actual purpose of the individuals involved in a particular encounter, but rather the purpose that reasonable participants would have had.

An emergency focuses the participants on something other than proving past events potentially relevant to later criminal prosecution. Rather, it focuses them on ending a threatening situation. Implicit in the idea that because the prospect of fabrication in statements given for the primary purpose of resolving that emergency is presumably significantly diminished, the Confrontation Clause does not require such statements to be subject to cross examination. As *Davis v. Washington*, 547 U.S. 813 (2006), made clear, whether an ongoing emergency exists is simply one factor that informs the ultimate inquiry regarding the "primary purpose" of an interrogation. Another factor is the importance of informality in an encounter between a victim and police. Formality suggests the absence of an emergency and therefore an increased likelihood that the purpose of the interrogation is to establish or prove past events potentially relevant to later criminal prosecution. Informality does not necessarily indicate the presence of an emergency or the lack of testimonial intent. The questioning in this case occurred in an exposed, public area, prior to the arrival of emergency medical services, and in a disorganized fashion. All of those facts make this case distinguishable from the formal station-house interrogation.

Statements made to assist the police in addressing an ongoing emergency presumably lack the testimonial purpose that would subject them to the requirement of confrontation. As the context of this case brings into sharp relief, the existence and duration of an emergency depend on the type and scope of danger posed to the victim, the police, and the public. Nothing Covington said to the police indicated that the cause of the shooting was a purely private dispute or that the threat from the shooter had ended. The potential scope of the dispute and therefore emergency in this case thus encompasses a threat potentially to the police and the public. The questions asked were the exact type of questions necessary to allow

Continued on next page.

the police to assess the situation, the threat to their own safety, and possible danger to the potential victim and to the public. In other words, they solicited the information necessary to enable them to meet an ongoing emergency. Likewise, the informality suggests that the interrogators' primary purpose was simply to address what they perceived to be an ongoing emergency, and the circumstances lacked any formality that would have alerted Covington to or focused him on the possible future prosecutorial use of his statements.

Because the circumstances of the encounter, as well as the statements and action of Covington and the police, objectively indicate that the "primary purpose" of the interrogation was to enable police assistance to meet an ongoing emergency, Covington's identification and description of the Bryant (D) as the shooter and the location of the shooting were not testimonial hearsay and the Confrontation Clause did not bar their admission at trial. Vacated and remanded.

CONCURRENCE: (Thomas, J.). Covington's questioning by the police lacked sufficient "formality" for them to be considered testimonial. The majority's analysis relies on what the police knew when they arrived at the scene, the specific questions they asked, the particular information Covington conveyed, the weapon involved, and Covington's medical condition which illustrates the uncertainty in the test created. Rather, the Court should consider the extent to which the interrogation resembles those historical practices that Confrontation Clause addressed (formal interrogations). Here, the police questioning was not a formalized dialogue and did not result in formalized testimonial materials . . . nor is there any indication that the statements were offered at trial in order to evade confrontation. Covington's statements were not testimonial because they occurred in an informal setting. The statements did not therefore "bear testimony" against Bryant (D).

DISSENT: (Scalia, J.) The declarant's intent is what counts. For an out-of-court statement to qualify as testimonial, the declarant must intend the statement to be a solemn declaration rather than an unconsidered or off-hand remark; and he must make the statement with the understanding that it may be used against the accused. A declarant-focused inquiry is also the only inquiry that would work in every fact pattern implicating the Confrontation Clause. From Covington's perspective, his statements had little value except to ensure the arrest and eventual prosecution of Bryant (D). The majority's decision is not only a gross distortion of the facts, it is a gross distortion of the law—a revisionist narrative in which reliability continues to guide our Confrontation Clause jurisprudence.

DISSENT: (Ginsburg, J.) Covington's statements are testimonial. The cloak protecting the accused against admission of out-of-court testimonial statements was removed for dying declarations. This historic exemption applied to statements made by a person about to die and aware that death was imminent. Were the issue properly tendered in this case (which was abandoned by the prosecutor), the question should be whether an exception for dying declarations survives the Confrontation Clause.

ANALYSIS

Testimonial statements made by an unavailable declarant implicate the Sixth Amendment's Confrontation Clause, which generally prohibits their introduction. The significance of this case is that assessing the admissibility of such statements requires an inquiry into whether the "primary purpose" of the interrogation was part of (1) an ongoing emergency, and (2) where informality in the encounter existed to a lack of focus that statements would be later used in a criminal prosecution. Justice Scalia's withering dissent alleges the majority's total distortion of the facts, an unbridled expansion of what constitutes an "emergency situation," and a confusing focus on what would be the appropriate test of the reliability of the victim's statement. The easy question (and probably winnable) posed by Justice Ginsburg, as to whether Covington's statement would have fallen within the dying declaration hearsay exception, went unanswered because it was never argued by the State (P).

Quicknotes

CONFRONTATION CLAUSE A provision in the Sixth Amendment to the United States Constitution that an accused in a criminal action has the right to confront the witnesses against him, including the right to attend the trial and to cross-examine witnesses called on behalf of the prosecution.

DYING DECLARATION A statement spoken upon belief of impending death, usually not considered hearsay due to its circumstantial guarantees of trustworthiness.

Bullcoming v. New Mexico

Drunk Driver (P) v. Government (D)

131 S. Ct. 2705 (2011).

NATURE OF CASE: Appeal of the state court decision to permit the surrogate testimony of a forensic analyst who was otherwise not involved in the forensic examination of the introduced evidence.

FACT SUMMARY: Petitioner Donald Bullcoming (P) was arrested on charges of driving while intoxicated and a blood alcohol test proved he was drunk. At trial, instead of calling the forensic analyst who produced the test results, another analyst was called to testify. The state court found the introduction of this "testimonial" evidence did not violate the Confrontation Clause and the state's highest court upheld the conviction.

🏛 RULE OF LAW

The Confrontation Clause does not permit the prosecution to introduce a forensic laboratory report containing a testimonial certification, made in order to prove a fact at a criminal trial, through the in-court testimony of an analyst who did not sign the certification or personally perform or observe the performance of the test reported in the certification.

FACTS: Petitioner Donald Bullcoming (P) was arrested on charges of driving while intoxicated. The principal evidence against Bullcoming (P) was a forensic laboratory report certifying that his blood alcohol concentration was well above the threshold for aggravated driving while intoxicated (DWI). At trial, the State (D) did not call the analyst who signed the certification. Instead, the State (D) called another analyst who was familiar with the laboratory's testing procedures, but who neither participated in nor observed the test on Bullcoming's (P) blood sample. The trial court admitted this surrogate testimony and Bullcoming (P) was convicted, and later appealed.

ISSUE: Does the Confrontation Clause permit the prosecution to introduce a forensic laboratory report containing a testimonial certification, made in order to prove a fact at a criminal trial, through the in-court testimony of an analyst who did not sign the certification or personally perform or observe the performance of the test reported in the certification?

HOLDING AND DECISION: (Ginsburg, J.) No, the Confrontation Clause does not permit the prosecution to introduce a forensic laboratory report containing a testimonial certification, made in order to prove a fact at a criminal trial, through the in-court testimony of an analyst who did not sign the certification or personally perform or observe the performance of the test reported in the certification. Surrogate testimony of that order does not meet the constitutional requirement. The accused's right is to be confronted with the analyst who made the certification, unless that analyst is unavailable at trial, and the accused had an opportunity, pretrial, to cross-examine that particular scientist.

In *Melendez-Diaz v. Massachusetts*, 129 S. Ct. 2527 (2009), this Court held that a forensic laboratory report stating that a suspect substance was cocaine ranked as testimonial for purposes of the Sixth Amendment's Confrontation Clause. The report had been created specifically to serve as evidence in a criminal proceeding. Absent stipulation, the Court ruled, the prosecution may not introduce such a report without offering a live witness competent to testify to the truth of the statements made in the report.

In light of *Melendez-Diaz*, the state supreme court here also acknowledged that the blood-alcohol report introduced at Bullcoming's (P) trial qualified as testimonial evidence. Like the affidavits in *Melendez-Diaz*, the court observed, the report was "functionally identical to live, in-court testimony, doing precisely what a witness does on direct examination. The state supreme court held surrogate testimony adequate to satisfy the Confrontation Clause in this case because the analyst "simply transcribed the resul[t] generated by the gas chromatograph machine," presenting no interpretation and exercising no independent judgment. Bullcoming's (P) "true 'accuser,'" the court said, was the machine, while the testing analyst role was that of "mere scrivener."

The analyst's certification, however, reported more than a machine-generated number. The analyst certified that he received Bullcoming's (P) blood sample intact with the seal unbroken, that he checked to make sure that the forensic report number and the sample number "correspond[ed]," and that he performed on Bullcoming's (P) sample a particular test, adhering to a precise protocol. He further represented, by leaving the "[r]emarks" section of the report blank, that no "circumstance or condition . . . affect[ed] the integrity of the sample or . . . the validity of the analysis." These representations, relating to past events and human actions not revealed in raw, machine-produced data, are meat for cross-examination.

In all material respects, the laboratory report in this case resembles those in *Melendez-Diaz*. Here, as in *Melendez-Diaz*, a law enforcement officer provided seized evidence to a state laboratory required by law to assist in police investigations. Like the analysis in *Melendez-Diaz*, the analyst tested evidence and prepared a certificate concerning the result of his analysis. All of this is considered testimonial subject to cross examination. Reversed and remanded.

Continued on next page.

CONCURRENCE: (Sotomayor, J.) To determine if a statement is testimonial, it must be decided whether it has "a primary purpose of creating an out-of-court substitute for trial testimony." *Michigan v. Bryant*, 131 S. Ct. 1142 (2011). When the "primary purpose" of a statement is "not to create a record for trial," "the admissibility of [the] statement is the concern of state and federal rules of evidence, not the Confrontation Clause." As applied to a scientific report, *Melendez-Diaz* explained that pursuant to Fed. R. Evid. 803, "[d]ocuments kept in the regular course of business may ordinarily be admitted at trial despite their hearsay status," except "if the regularly conducted business activity is the production of evidence for use at trial." In that circumstance, the hearsay rules bar admission of even business records. Relatedly, in the Confrontation Clause context, business and public records "are generally admissible absent confrontation . . . because— having been created for the administration of an entity's affairs and not for the purpose of establishing or proving some fact at trial—they are not testimonial." Because the purpose of the certificates of analysis was use at trial, they were not properly admissible as business or public records under the hearsay rules, nor were they admissible under the Confrontation Clause. The hearsay rule's recognition of the certificates' evidentiary purpose thus confirmed the decision that the certificates were testimonial under the primary purpose analysis required by the Confrontation Clause.

DISSENT: (Kennedy, J.) The majority takes the new and serious misstep of extending that holding to instances like this one. Here a knowledgeable representative of the laboratory was present to testify and to explain the lab's processes and the details of the report; but because he was not the analyst who filled out part of the form and transcribed onto it the test result from a machine printout, the Court finds a confrontation violation. Before today, the Court had not held that the Confrontation Clause bars admission of scientific findings when an employee of the testing laboratory authenticates the findings, testifies to the laboratory's methods and practices, and is cross-examined at trial. Far from replacing live testimony with "systematic" and "extrajudicial" examinations, *Davis v. Washington*, 547 U.S. 813 (2006), these procedures are fully consistent with the Confrontation Clause and with well-established principles for ensuring that criminal trials are conducted in full accord with requirements of fairness and reliability and with the confrontation guarantee.

Requiring the State (D) to call the technician who filled out a form and recorded the results of a test is a hollow formality. The defense remains free to challenge any and all forensic evidence. It may call and examine the technician who performed a test. And it may call other expert witnesses to explain that tests are not always reliable or that the technician might have made a mistake. The jury can then decide whether to credit the test, as it did here. The states, furthermore, can assess the progress of scientific testing and enact or adopt statutes and rules to ensure that only reliable evidence is admitted. Rejecting these commonsense arguments and the concept that reliability is a legitimate concern, the Court today takes a different course. It once more assumes for itself a central role in mandating detailed evidentiary rules.

▶ *ANALYSIS*

Here, the Supreme Court reaffirmed the general rule that every criminal defendant enjoys the right to confront witnesses who offer evidence against them, as guaranteed by the Sixth Amendment's Confrontation Clause. There are, however, certain exceptions, including certain "testimonial" statements made by unavailable witnesses where the defendant had a prior opportunity to cross-examine. However seemingly trivial or burdensome it would seem to be to have a forensic analyst testify about a blood test result generated by a piece of equipment, the Court declined to permit a surrogate technician to offer testimony when they neither participated in nor observed the test results. In what was seen as expanding the requirement of who is needed to testify about lab test results, Justice Kennedy believed that this was better dealt with through the state and federal evidence rules.

■=■

Quicknotes

CONFRONTATION CLAUSE A provision in the Sixth Amendment to the United States Constitution that an accused in a criminal action has the right to confront the witnesses against him, including the right to attend the trial and to cross-examine witnesses called on behalf of the prosecution.

■=■

Bruton v. United States

Convicted robber (D) v. Federal government (P)

391 U.S. 123 (1968).

NATURE OF CASE: Appeal from conviction for robbery.

FACT SUMMARY: The Government (P) contended that Bruton's (D) robbery conviction based upon the confession of a co-conspirator was valid.

🏛 RULE OF LAW
The conviction of a defendant at a joint trial must be set aside despite a jury instruction that a co-defendant's confession incriminating the defendant must be disregarded in determining his guilt or innocence.

FACTS: Evans was arrested and charged with armed postal robbery. In the course of his confinement, he orally confessed to the postal authorities that both he and Bruton (D) committed the robbery. A joint trial was held wherein Evans's confession was admitted into evidence. The court instructed the jury that while the confession was substantive evidence against Evans, it could not be used to determine the guilt of Bruton (D). Both individuals were convicted, and Evans's conviction was overturned when it was determined that his confession should not be used against him. However, Bruton's (D) conviction was affirmed, based upon the trial judge's limiting instruction. Bruton (D) appealed, contending the use of the confession in a joint trial constituted reversible error as to his conviction.

ISSUE: Must the conviction of a defendant at a joint trial be set aside despite a trial court's limiting instruction that the confession of a co-defendant cannot be used as substantive evidence?

HOLDING AND DECISION: (Brennan, J.) Yes. The conviction of a defendant at a joint trial must be set aside despite a jury instruction that a co-defendant's confession incriminating the defendant must be disregarded in determining his guilt or innocence. The use of such a confession presents a substantial risk that the jury, despite the instructions to the contrary, will look to the incriminating extrajudicial statements in determining a defendant's guilt. As a result, the use in the case of the confession deprived Bruton (D) of his right of cross-examination under the confrontation clause of the Sixth Amendment. Although there are many circumstances wherein the reliance upon the jury's following the court's order to disregard certain pieces of evidence and to use it only for particular purposes will be harmless, some pieces of evidence are so prejudicial as to require their exclusion. The risk of misuse is simply too high where such use potentially robs the co-defendant of his constitutional rights. Further, the confession of a co-defendant is so lacking in reliability with regard to the nonconfessing defendant that the hearsay rule must be strictly applied. Reversed.

DISSENT: (White, J.) The practical result of the Court's opinion in this case is to severely limit the ability of prosecutors to hold joint trials for defendants. The great value in using an uncoerced admission against one defendant when that would render the codefendant's conviction questionable will surely dissuade prosecutors from joint trials. This will greatly increase the judicial workload and the benefits of joint trials will be lost.

▶ ANALYSIS

There is no question that the use of a co-defendant's admission against another defendant is clearly hearsay. It is an out-of-court statement offered for its truth. It also contains several elements of unreliability including the fact that it is made under a stressful condition and usually made in an attempt to exalt the declarant at the expense of the co-defendant. As a result of this unreliability, the court is unwilling to allow it into evidence at all in a joint trial. Even though, as the dissent points out, there are great benefits to using an uncoerced confession against the declarant, many commentators have indicated that this benefit is clearly outweighed by the risk of the nondeclarant defendant's loss of his constitutional rights.

■■■

Quicknotes

CONFRONTATION CLAUSE A provision in the Sixth Amendment to the United States Constitution that an accused in a criminal action has the right to confront the witnesses against him, including the right to attend the trial and to cross-examine witnesses called on behalf of the prosecution.

CROSS-EXAMINATION The interrogation of a witness by an adverse party either to further inquire as to the subject matter of the direct examination or to call into question the witness's credibility.

EXTRAJUDICIAL Outside of court; taking place outside of formal proceedings.

REVERSIBLE ERROR A substantial error that might reasonably have prejudiced the party complaining.

SIXTH AMENDMENT Provides the right to a speedy trial by impartial jury, the right to be informed of the accusation, to confront witnesses and to have the assistance of counsel in all criminal prosecutions.

■■■

Cruz v. New York

Convicted murderer (D) v. State (P)

481 U.S. 186 (1987).

NATURE OF CASE: Appeal from felony murder conviction.

FACT SUMMARY: Defendant and his brother murdered a gas station attendant, and the brother's videotaped confession implicated defendant. Defendant confessed only to a friend. The videotaped confession was introduced at their joint trial, and defendant contends that this constituted a deprivation of his Sixth Amendment confrontation rights.

RULE OF LAW
A defendant's Sixth Amendment confrontation rights are denied when his nontestifying codefendant's incriminating confession is introduced at the joint trial, even when that confession is corroborated by the defendant's own.

FACTS: Eulogio Cruz (D) and his brother, Benjamin, robbed a gas station. During the robbery, the gas station attendant shot Cruz (D) in the arm, and Benjamin killed the attendant. In a later conversation with a friend, Cruz (D) confessed to what happened. The police questioned Benjamin in an unrelated murder, and Benjamin spontaneously confessed to the murder of the gas station attendant. His detailed confession implicating Cruz (D) was videotaped and he and Cruz (D) were indicted for felony murder. At their joint trial, Benjamin's confession was admitted as evidence, although the judge warned the jury to use the confession only against Benjamin. The friend to whom Cruz (D) confessed testified to that confession at trial, but the videotaped confession was the only direct evidence linking Cruz (D) to the murder. The jury convicted both brothers. Cruz (D) appealed, but the court of appeals affirmed on the grounds the codefendant's confession did not have to be excluded because Cruz's (D) confession to his friend corroborated Benjamin's. Cruz (D) appealed to the U.S. Supreme Court, which granted certiorari.

ISSUE: Are a defendant's Sixth Amendment confrontation rights denied when his nontestifying codefendant's incriminating confession is introduced at the joint trial, even when that confession is corroborated by the defendant's own confession admitted against him?

HOLDING AND DECISION: (Scalia, J.) Yes. A defendant's Sixth Amendment confrontation rights are denied when his nontestifying codefendant's incriminating confession is introduced at the joint trial even when that confession is corroborated by the defendant's own confession admitted against him. *Bruton v. United States*, 391 U.S.

123 (1968), held that a codefendant's incriminating confession may not be introduced at a joint trial because it violates the defendant's confrontation rights. That case did not address a situation where the defendant's confession corroborated that of the codefendant's and his own confession was introduced against him. This Court attempted to resolve that question in *Parker v. Randolph*, 442 U.S. 62 (1979), but the Court remained evenly divided and left the question for another day. Today, this Court follows the reasoning of Justice Blackmun in *Parker*. The introduction of the codefendant's confession is always a violation of the Confrontation Clause even though the defendant's "interlocking" confession renders that violation harmless. In this case, the "interlocking" confession of Cruz (D) was not necessarily devastating to his defense because it depended entirely upon the credibility of the testifying friend. The videotaped confession implicating Cruz (D) and seemingly corroborating Cruz's (D) confession to his friend, however, was devastating to Cruz's (D) defense. It is common sense that a jury is more likely to lend credence to a codefendant's confession implicating the defendant when the defendant seems to corroborate that version of events, even in the face of jury instructions to disregard the codefendant's confession as to defendant. Here, the introduction of Benjamin's confession violated Cruz's (D) Sixth Amendment confrontation rights. Whether or not the admission of Cruz's (D) confession was harmless may be considered on appeal. Reversed and remanded.

DISSENT: (White, J.) The majority finds the traditional presumption that juries follow the instructions from the judge to be "illogical." To the contrary, most juries understand that presumptively unreliable evidence is not to be used against a defendant. Also, not every interlocking confession will be devastating to the defense. Where an interlocking codefendant's confession exists, it may be introduced against the defendant without violation of the defendant's confrontation rights.

ANALYSIS

The dissenting judge points out the majority's lack of faith in the intelligence of the average jury. The majority, however, may simply be pointing out a fact—juries are comprised of human beings who tend to believe a story is true when more than one person tells nearly the same tale. It would be difficult for a person to discount a defendant's confession when it is nearly identical to the

Continued on next page.

confession of a codefendant incriminating the defendant. The holding in this case is a logical way to avoid potential confusion caused by human nature.

—■≡■—

Quicknotes

CERTIORARI A discretionary writ issued by a superior court to an inferior court in order to review the lower court's decisions; the Supreme Court's writ ordering such review.

CONFRONTATION CLAUSE A provision in the Sixth Amendment to the United States Constitution that an accused in a criminal action has the right to confront the witnesses against him, including the right to attend the trial and to cross-examine witnesses called on behalf of the prosecution.

FELONY MURDER The unlawful killing of another human being while in the commission of, or attempted commission of, specified felonies.

SIXTH AMENDMENT Provides the right to a speedy and public trial by impartial jury, the right to be informed of the accusation, the right to confront witnesses, and the right to have the assistance of counsel in all criminal prosecutions.

—■≡■—

Gray v. Maryland

Convicted murderer (D) v. State (P)

523 U.S. 185 (1998).

NATURE OF CASE: Appeal from a murder conviction.

FACT SUMMARY: The trial judge permitted the State (P) to introduce Bell's (D) confession against Bell (D) and Gray (D) at their joint trial for murder.

🏛 RULE OF LAW
In a joint trial, a confession which contains the use of blanks, the word "delete," symbols or other indication of redaction, is so prejudicial that limiting instructions are not effective.

FACTS: Stacy Williams died in 1993 after a severe beating. Anthony Bell (D) gave a confession to the Baltimore City police, admitting that he, Kevin Gray (D) and Jacquin "Tank" Vanlandingham participated in the beating resulting in Williams's death. A Maryland grand jury indicted Bell (D) and Gray (D) for murder, and the State of Maryland (P) tried them jointly. The trial judge denied Gray's (D) motion for a separate trial, and admitted a redacted version of Bell's (D) confession into evidence. The police detective who read the confession into evidence read the word "deleted" or "deletion" whenever Gray's (D) name appeared. The State (P) also introduced into evidence a written version of the confession with Gray's (D) name omitted, leaving in its place a blank white space separated by commas.

ISSUE: In a joint trial, is a confession which contains the use of blanks, the word "delete," symbols or other indication of redaction, so prejudicial that limiting instructions are not effective?

HOLDING AND DECISION: (Breyer, J.) Yes. According to *Bruton v. United States*, 391 U.S. 123 (1968), certain "powerfully incriminating extrajudicial statements of a codefendant" which name the defendant are so prejudicial that limiting instructions are not effective. In this case, the trial court admitted a confession accusing the defendant, but with the defendant's name omitted and replaced with the word "deletion." A jury will often react similarly to an unredacted confession and one redacted in such a way that a name is simply replaced with an obvious blank space or a word such as "deleted." Further, the obvious deletion draws the juror's attention to the removed name and the jury may be directly accusatory of the deleted name. The judgment of the court of appeals is vacated.

DISSENT: (Scalia, J.) The majority erroneously concludes that "deleted" amounts to a description which clearly identifies the defendant. To present a redacted confession without such marks of redaction would threaten the integrity of the justice system.

▶ ANALYSIS

The majority in *Gray* supported their decision by looking to the policy behind excluding confessions that incriminated "by connection" from *Bruton v. United States'* protective rule, noting that including the use of blanks, the word "delete," symbols or other indication of redaction in *Bruton's* protective rule runs no risk of provoking mistrials or prosecutor hesitancy to pursue confession or joint trials.

■■■

Quicknotes

EXTRAJUDICIAL Outside of court; taking place outside of formal proceedings.

REDACT To edit or revise a document.

■■■

Chambers v. Mississippi

Convicted murderer (D) v. State (P)

410 U.S. 284 (1973).

NATURE OF CASE: Appeal from conviction for murder.

FACT SUMMARY: Chambers (D) was convicted of murder after not being allowed to show that a witness whom he called to testify confessed to the killing to three of his friends on the ground that such confessions were hearsay.

🏛 RULE OF LAW
Where constitutional rights directly affecting the ascertainment of guilt are implicated, the hearsay rule may not be applied mechanically so to defeat the ends of justice.

FACTS: Chambers (D) was tried and convicted of murdering a policeman during a confrontation between a few policemen and several townspeople when the former were attempting to arrest one of the latter. McDonald, a town resident, after talking to Rev. Stokes, agreed to see Chambers's (D) lawyers and confess to the killing. He did so, was jailed, but was later released upon repudiating his confession, which he claimed was prompted by a promise of a share in a tort recovery which Chambers (D) would get from the town. At trial, Chambers (D) tried to show that McDonald committed the crime. Hardin testified that he saw McDonald, his long-time friend, shoot the officer. Additionally, Chambers (D) sought to show that McDonald not only confessed to his lawyers, but that he confessed to three of his friends. Chambers (D) called McDonald to testify when the State (P) failed to do so. McDonald again repudiated his confession. The court denied Chambers's (D) motion that McDonald be declared an adverse witness. It also prevented three of McDonald's friends from testifying that he confessed to them on the ground that such a confession was hearsay. Under Mississippi law, a person who presents a witness vouches for his credibility, and the hearsay exception for declarations against interest applies only when that interest is pecuniary, while here it was not. Chambers (D) appealed his conviction on due process grounds.

ISSUE: Where constitutional rights directly affecting the ascertainment of guilt are implicated, may the hearsay rule be applied mechanically so to defeat the ends of justice?

HOLDING AND DECISION: (Powell, J.) No. Where constitutional rights directly affecting the ascertainment of guilt are implicated, the hearsay rule may not be applied mechanically to defeat the ends of justice. Chambers (D) was not allowed to subject McDonald's repudiation and alibi to cross-examination. Cross-examination is fundamen-

tal to assuring the accuracy of the truth-determining process. The voucher rule, which does not allow a party to impeach his own witness, bears little usefulness to the criminal process. Here, it not only precluded cross-examination, it restricted the scope of direct examination. The right to confront and cross-examine has never depended on who put the witness on the stand. As for declarations against interest, most states will not admit them even when they are against a penal interest. But here, several circumstances assured the declaration's reliability: (1) Each of McDonald's confessions was spontaneous and made shortly after the killing; (2) each one was corroborated by some other evidence; (3) each was unquestionably against interest; and (4) McDonald was present in the courtroom to explain under oath his declaration. The testimony was absolutely critical to Chambers's (D) defense. Reversed and remanded.

▶ ANALYSIS

The Court specifically noted that by this case it was not creating any new principles in constitutional law. Rather, the trial rules in question were not "in accord with traditional and fundamental standards of due process." Further, the decision was not intended to diminish each state's ability to create its own trial rules. It would appear arguable, however, that the Court believes hearsay statements should be admitted when trustworthy. The Court does not require the states to go that far so long as their rules do not offend notions of due process.

■=■

Quicknotes

CROSS-EXAMINATION The interrogation of a witness by an adverse party either to further inquire as to the subject matter of the direct examination or to call into question the witness's credibility.

DECLARATION AGAINST INTEREST Exception to the hearsay rule for statements made by a declarant that are against his interest at the time of their utterance.

DUE PROCESS The constitutional mandate requiring the courts to protect and enforce individuals' rights and liberties consistent with prevailing principles of fairness and justice and prohibiting the federal and state governments from such activities that deprive its citizens of life, liberty, or property interest.

HEARSAY An out-of-court statement made by a person other than the witness testifying at trial that is offered in order to prove the truth of the matter asserted.

■=■

Lay Opinions and Expert Testimony

Quick Reference Rules of Law

United States v. Ganier

Federal government (P) v. Criminal defendant (D)

468 F.3d 920 (6th Cir. 2006).

NATURE OF CASE: Appeal of district court's exclusion of evidence.

FACT SUMMARY: The district court granted a motion by Albert Ganier (D) to exclude the proposed testimony of a Government (P) computer specialist, on grounds that it was expert testimony for which the Government (P) was required under federal criminal procedure rules to provide a written summary. The Government (P) appealed.

RULE OF LAW

The results of forensic tests run on computers and related testimony constitutes "scientific, technical, or other specialized knowledge" within the scope of Fed. R. Evid. 702 if making sense of the results requires interpretation by a forensic computer specialist.

FACTS: Albert Ganier (D) was under investigation for improprieties and favoritism in connection with contracts awarded to Ganier's (D) company by the state of Tennessee, and the solicitation of Tennessee and Texas officials for additional contracts. After subpoenas were issued, Ganier (D) began deleting documents and e-mail from company and personal computers. In accordance with the Federal Rules of Criminal Procedure, Ganier (D) filed a summary of expected expert testimony indicating that the files in question were transferred to the recycle bin rather than deleted, and that duplicates and other drafts remained on the computers and could easily be found using "search" functions on the computers. The Government's (P) forensic computer specialist, Wallace Drueck of the Internal Revenue Service, used forensic software to search the computers, and found evidence indicating that some documents may have been deliberately deleted by Ganier (D) to avoid conviction. The Government (P) planned to have Drueck interpret the reports at trial. The district court granted a motion by Ganier (D) to exclude the proposed testimony and the report, on grounds that it was expert testimony for which the Government (P) was required under federal criminal procedure rules to provide a written summary. The Government (P) appealed.

ISSUE: Do the results of forensic tests run on computers and related testimony constitute "scientific, technical, or other specialized knowledge" within the scope of Fed. R. Evid. 702 if making sense of the results requires interpretation by a forensic computer specialist?

HOLDING AND DECISION: (Moore, J.) Yes. The results of forensic tests run on computers and related testimony constitute "scientific, technical, or other specialized knowledge" within the scope of Fed. R. Evid. 702 if making sense of the results requires interpretation by a forensic computer specialist. The forensic tests Drueck ran are like specialized medical tests run by physicians, and Drueck needed to interpret the reports that were generated in order to make sense of them. Thus, he had to apply specialized knowledge. The district court did not err by concluding that Drueck's proposed testimony could be offered only under Fed. R. Evid. 702, and therefore was subject to criminal procedure rules mandating a written summary of the testimony, but the Government (P) did not fail to provide the summary in bad faith, and remedies less severe than exclusion might have been given by the district court. The decision is therefore vacated and remanded.

▶ ANALYSIS

Note that the advisory committee's note to the 2000 amendment to Fed. R. Evid. 701 implies that while a lay witness may not offer opinion testimony based on "specialized knowledge," the witness may do so based on his or her "particularized knowledge" gained by "his or her position in [a] business." Arguably, the "particularized knowledge" on which lay opinion may be based could also constitute "specialized knowledge."

Quicknotes

BAD FAITH Conduct that is intentionally misleading or deceptive.

EXPERT TESTIMONY Testimonial evidence about a complex area of subject matter relevant to trial, presented by a person competent to inform the trier of fact due to specialized knowledge or training.

SUBPOENA A command issued by court to compel a witness to appear at trial.

United States v. Johnson

Federal government (P) v. Convicted drug offender (D)

575 F.2d 1347 (5th Cir. 1978), *cert. denied*, 440 U.S. 907 (1979).

NATURE OF CASE: Appeal from drug conviction.

FACT SUMMARY: At trial for drug offenses, the Government (P) offered testimony from a witness claiming he could identify the origin of the marijuana at issue from past experience. Defendant claims it was error to admit the testimony as expert testimony.

> 🏛 **RULE OF LAW**
> Fed. R. Evid. 702 allows for expert testimony derived from experience as well as formal training or education.

FACTS: The Government (P) needed to prove that the marijuana at issue came from outside the United States' customs territory. Johnson (D) argued that the origin of the marijuana was impossible to prove without objective indicia. A witness for the Government (P), de Pianelli, testified as an expert the marijuana came from Colombia. De Pianelli's expertise came from admitted significant use of marijuana and previous experience identifying marijuana through the physical appearance of the plant. Johnson (D) appealed the admission of de Pianelli's testimony, contending he should not have been qualified as an expert under Fed. R. Evid. 702 and the jury should not have been allowed to consider his testimony.

ISSUE: Can expert testimony under Fed. R. Evid. 702 derive from experience as well as formal training or education?

HOLDING AND DECISION: (Clark, J.) Yes. Fed. R. Evid. 702 allows for expert testimony derived from experience as well as formal training or education. The defense cross-examined de Pianelli during voir dire and the judge was satisfied that de Pianelli's experience qualified him as an expert. Formal training or education is not required in addition to experience under Fed. R. Evid. 702 and de Pianelli demonstrated ample experience with the identification of marijuana. Aiding the jury in identifying the source of the marijuana was vital, as the average juror likely has little experience in identifying illegal narcotics. The trial court did not err in allowing de Pianelli to testify as an expert witness. The defense also took the opportunity to put its own expert witness on the stand to testify that determining the origins of a marijuana plant through examination of physical characteristics is impossible. The defense expert did, however, concede that plants grown in different climates could produce identifiable differences. Given the ambiguity of the defense expert's testimony, the jury certainly could choose to favor the prosecution's expert testimony. Affirmed.

▶ *ANALYSIS*

An expert witness does not become an expert through mere passing familiarity with a topic. The experience, training, or education must be such that the average juror will be aided by the testimony. If training and education are not the qualifying characteristics, the experience should be extensive and thorough in that narrow field. De Pianelli admitted to such extensive experience using and identifying marijuana that he qualified as an expert. Most jurors are not going to be familiar enough with illegal narcotics or botany in general to be able to have made determinations as to the origin of the plants on their own.

■■■

Quicknotes

EXPERT TESTIMONY Testimonial evidence about a complex area of subject matter relevant to trial, presented by a person competent to inform the trier of fact due to specialized knowledge or training.

FED. R. EVID. 702 Permits a witness qualified as an expert to testify in the form of an opinion.

VOIR DIRE Examination of potential jurors on a case.

■■■

Jinro America, Inc. v. Secure Investments, Inc.

Korean corporation (P) v. International business partner (D)

266 F.3d 993 (9th Cir. 2001).

NATURE OF CASE: Appeal from summary judgment.

FACT SUMMARY: Plaintiff and defendant ostensibly entered into a business arrangement, but defendant rescinded and claimed that the entire arrangement was fraudulent. At trial, defendant presented expert testimony from a private investigator who testified concerning corrupt Korean business practices in general. The plaintiff appealed, contending that the investigator was not a qualified expert.

> ### 🏛 RULE OF LAW
> Substantial, practical expertise, formal training, or education in the particular relevant field is necessary to qualify a witness as an expert under Fed. R. Evid. 702.

FACTS: Jinro America, Inc. (Jinro) (P) and Secure Investments, Inc. (D) entered into an international arrangement involving frozen chicken. The deal fell apart and Jinro (P) sued on several grounds to recover millions of dollars. Secure Investments (D) claimed that the entire deal was a fraud and presented expert testimony from David Herbert Pelham to support that claim. Pelham was a private investigator living in Korea, married to a Korean woman, who enjoyed studying Korean business practices as a hobby. His testimony consisted of indictments against the Korean corporate culture in general and relied heavily on newspaper articles and anecdotal evidence. None of Pelham's testimony related to Jinro (P) specifically. The jury agreed with Secure Investments (D) and the trial court sua sponte entered summary judgment against Jinro (P). Jinro (P) appealed, claiming that Pelham should not have been qualified as an expert.

ISSUE: What qualifications are necessary to classify an expert witness under Fed. R. Evid. 702?

HOLDING AND DECISION: (Fisher, J.) Substantial, practical expertise, formal training, or education in the particular relevant field is necessary to qualify a witness as an expert under Fed. R. Evid. 702. Pelham offered general impressions of Korean business practices derived from reading newspaper articles and indulging in his hobby of studying Korean corporate culture. He had no formal training as an attorney, financial expert, or anthropologist. His position as a private investigator did not provide him much more than exposure to corrupt practices in a business focused on unearthing corrupt behavior. His qualifications were "glaringly inadequate" and he should not have been permitted to testify as an expert on Korean corporate culture. Reversed and remanded.

CONCURRENCE AND DISSENT: (Wallace, J.) Pelham's testimony was irrelevant and prejudicial because it painted a guilt-by-association portrait of Jinro (P) as a Korean corporation. Pelham, however, was certainly qualified to testify as an expert. It is not a requirement of Fed. R. Evid. 702 an expert witness be an attorney or have additional formal education. Pelham had significant interaction with Korean businesses, had served in the military in Korea, lived in Korea for a number of years, and was intimately familiar with Korean business practices through his profession as a provider of security and information services for international companies doing business with Korean companies. Although Pelham's interest was characterized as a hobby, he still qualified as an expert. The irrelevancy of his testimony to this case does not render him unqualified to testify as an expert witness.

▶ ANALYSIS

The dissenting judge took the same information that the majority had concerning Pelham's qualifications and argued that Pelham's extensive experience qualified him as an expert. It is a fine line for judges to travel in determining how much experience is necessary in a particular area to allow a witness to testify as an expert and how much experience just qualifies as a "hobby." It seems that personal experience must be relatively extensive if formal education or training is lacking.

Quicknotes

EXPERT TESTIMONY Testimonial evidence about a complex area of subject matter relevant to trial, presented by a person competent to inform the trier of fact due to specialized knowledge or training.

FED. R. EVID. 702 Permits a witness qualified as an expert to testify in the form of an opinion.

SUA SPONTE An action taken by the court by its own motion and without the suggestion of one of the parties.

Hygh v. Jacobs

Victim (P) v. Police officer (D)

961 F.2d 359 (2d Cir. 1992).

NATURE OF CASE: Appeal from judgment for constitutional violations.

FACT SUMMARY: Plaintiff sued defendant and was awarded judgment for violations of his constitutional civil rights in a 42 U.S.C. § 1983 claim. Defendant appealed the award, contending the plaintiff's expert testimony impermissibly invaded the province of the jury.

> 🏛️ **RULE OF LAW**
> An expert witness may not express a legal conclusion directly related to the ultimate issue of the case.

FACTS: William Jacobs (D), a police officer, was called to a residence to address William Hygh's (P) threatening presence. Hygh (P) and Jacobs (D) got into an altercation, and Jacobs (D) hit Hygh (P) in the cheek. The injury to Hygh's (P) cheek was extensive, required plastic surgery, and resulted in permanent nerve damage. Hygh (P) sued Jacobs (D) under 42 U.S. § 1983 for violation of his civil rights. At trial, the testimony revealed that Jacobs (D) hit Hygh (P) with his flashlight. Hygh (P) offered the expert testimony of Terry C. Cox, a law enforcement expert. Cox testified that Jacobs's (D) actions in using the flashlight against Hygh (P) involved "deadly physical force," were "totally improper," and not "warranted under the circumstances." Judgment was awarded to Hygh (P), and Jacobs (D) appealed on the ground Cox's conclusory statements invaded the province of the jury.

ISSUE: May an expert witness express a legal conclusion directly related to the ultimate issue of the case?

HOLDING AND DECISION: (Mahoney. J.) No. An expert witness may not express a legal conclusion directly related to the ultimate issue of the case. Cox's testimony blatantly told the jury how to decide on the question of whether Jacobs's (D) actions were appropriate under the circumstances. Cox also invaded the judge's province when he offered a definition of "deadly physical force" that differed somewhat from the state statutory definition. The expert witness is supposed to offer the jury a guide to the truth in explaining matters outside the knowledge base of the average juror. The expert is not supposed to supplant the jury's function by informing the jury of the "correct" conclusion, nor is the expert supposed to instruct the jury on statutory definitions. Fed. R. Evid. 704 does not permit all expert opinions although it abolished the common-law "ultimate issue" rule that expert opinion testimony may not address an ultimate issue

more appropriately left to the trier of fact. Cox certainly crossed the line in delivering conclusory testimony concerning Jacobs's (D) behavior. In this case, however, the jury heard Cox's testimony within the larger framework of an explanation of proper police procedures during arrests and the jury could easily have come to the same conclusions expressed by Cox. Additionally, the judge's jury instructions were extensive. Therefore, although Cox's testimony impermissibly crossed the line into the jury's province, the error was harmless. Affirmed.

▶ **ANALYSIS**

Expert opinions are intended to guide the jury to find the truth when the issues involved are beyond the knowledge of the average juror. The expert is not supposed to act as judge and inform the jury of the "right" verdict. Fed. R. Evid. 704 allows opinion testimony, but that opinion still cannot invade the provinces of the judge and the jury.

Quicknotes

EXPERT TESTIMONY Testimonial evidence about a complex area of subject matter relevant to trial, presented by a person competent to inform the trier of fact due to specialized knowledge or training.

HARMLESS ERROR An error taking place during trial that does not require the reviewing court to overturn or modify the trial court's judgment in that it did not affect the appellant's substantial rights or the disposition of the action.

ULTIMATE FACT A fact upon which a judicial determination is made and which is inferred from the evidence presented at trial.

State v. Batangan

State (P) v. Convicted sex offender (D)

Haw. Sup. Ct., 799 P.2d 48, 71 Haw. 552 (1990).

NATURE OF CASE: Appeal from conviction for sexual abuse.

FACT SUMMARY: The prosecution's expert witness in defendant's trial for the sexual abuse of his minor daughter implied that the daughter was truthful and credible. Defendant appealed, claiming the expert testimony should have been inadmissible under Hawaii Rule of Evidence 702 as invading the jury's province.

🏛 RULE OF LAW
An expert witness may not render legal conclusions or conclusory opinions that invade the jury's province.

FACTS: Felomino Batangan (D) was indicted for second degree rape and first degree sexual abuse when his minor daughter accused him of sexually abusing her on several occasions. She later recanted that accusation, but testified to the abuse at trial. Batangan (D) was acquitted of the rape charge, but the judge declared a mistrial on the sexual abuse charge due to a hung jury. At the second trial on the sexual abuse charge, the prosecution (P) offered expert testimony from Dr. John Bond as a clinical psychologist with a subspecialty in sexually abused children. Dr. Bond testified to his examination of the daughter, his experience with the behavior of sexually abused children in general, and then he implied that the daughter's testimony was credible and should be believed. The jury convicted Batangan (D) of first-degree sexual abuse, and Batangan (D) appealed. He contended that Dr. Bond's testimony was inadmissible under Hawaii Rule of Evidence 702 because it provided a conclusory opinion to the jury that Batangan (D) was guilty.

ISSUE: May an expert witness render legal conclusions or conclusory opinions that invade the jury's province?

HOLDING AND DECISION: (Wakatsuki, J.) No. An expert witness may not render legal conclusions or conclusory opinions that invade the jury's province. Dr. Bond did not explicitly state that the daughter was telling the truth, but his implications were enough that the jury did not have to make the connection between his expert testimony concerning child sexual abuse victims in general and the behavior of the daughter. The jury is supposed to, and is quite capable of, making that connection. When the expert witness makes the connection for the jury in the form of a conclusory or legal opinion, then the testimony is inadmissible under Hawaii Rule of Evidence 702. Rule 704 permits opinion testimony regarding the ultimate issue, but it does not permit the expert to inform the jury of

the "correct" conclusion. Dr. Bond's testimony here was inappropriate and prejudicial to Batangan (D). Reversed and remanded.

▶ ANALYSIS

The judicial system puts much faith in the ability of jurors to listen to expert testimony on a topic outside of their average knowledge and then to compare that general testimony to the specific case at hand. Jurors are also supposed to discern the truthfulness and overall credibility of each witness. Some scholars argue that jurors are simply not up to this task, and that expert opinions relating to the ultimate issue are necessary to help jurors in assessing expert information and credibility of witnesses. Of course, the question remains whether the experts are any better at assessing credibility than the jurors.

■=■

Quicknotes

EXPERT WITNESS A witness providing testimony at trial who is specially qualified regarding the particular subject matter involved.

■=■

State v. Guilbert

State (P) v. Possible shooter (D)

Conn. Sup. Ct., 306 Conn. 218 (2012).

NATURE OF CASE: Appeal from state court decision reversing a double murder conviction.

FACT SUMMARY: At the double murder trial of Brady Guilbert (D), the court precluded his introduction of expert testimony concerning the fallibility of eyewitness identification testimony.

🏛 RULE OF LAW
Expert testimony concerning the fallibility of eyewitness testimony is permitted.

FACTS: Brady Guilbert (D) was tried for the murder of two individuals. The defense raised the issue of the reliability of the eyewitness identifications, and sought to present expert testimony as to the fallibility of this type of testimony. The State (P) objected, and after an evidentiary hearing, the trial court found the proffered defense expert testimony to be unnecessary as it was generally within the common knowledge of jurors. The testimony of eyewitness and other corroborating evidence was introduced at trial. Guilbert (D) then appealed his conviction.

ISSUE: Is expert testimony concerning the fallibility of eyewitness testimony permitted?

HOLDING AND DECISION: (Palmer, J.) Yes, expert testimony concerning the fallibility of eyewitness testimony is permitted. It is well settled that the true test of admissibility of expert testimony is whether the witnesses offered as experts have any peculiar knowledge or experience, not common to the world, which renders their opinions founded on such knowledge or experience any aid to the court or the jury in determining the questions at issue. In now overruling prior decisions, there is widespread judicial recognition that eyewitness identifications are potentially unreliable in a variety of ways unknown to the average juror. This broad-based judicial recognition tracks a near perfect scientific consensus. The scientific evidence is both reliable and useful. Consensus exists among the experts within the research community that many vagaries exist of memory encoding, storage and retrieval, the malleability of memory, the contaminating effects of extrinsic information, the influence of police interview techniques and identification procedures, and the many other factors that bear on the reliability of eyewitness identification. Although these findings are widely accepted by scientists, they are largely unfamiliar to the average person. As a result of this strong scientific consensus, federal and state courts around the country have recognized that the methods traditionally employed for alerting juries to the fallibility of eyewitness identifica-

tion—cross-examination, closing argument and generalized jury instructions on the subject—frequently are not adequate to inform them of the factors affecting the reliability of such identifications. Expert testimony on the reliability of eyewitness identification does not invade the province of the jury to determine what weight or effect it wishes to give to eyewitness testimony.

However, corroborative evidence of the defendant's guilt may render harmless the trial judge's error in excluding an expert's proposed testimony. Here, the corroborative evidence against Guilbert (D) (five different eyewitnesses, four of which were familiar with him) was substantial. This convincing evidence of Guilbert's (D) guilt ensured that the trial court's erroneous exclusion of the expert's testimony on the reliability of an eyewitness' identification did not substantially affect the verdict. Affirmed.

CONCURRENCE: (Zarella, J.) Trial courts should be allowed to consider substantial corroborating evidence when determining whether to admit expert testimony because, in cases in which the record contains such evidence, the importance of expert testimony is correspondingly diminished and would be an unnecessary distraction to the jury. Such expert testimony would be not only time consuming and costly, but potentially confusing rather than helpful to the jury.

▶ ANALYSIS

In overturning well established state law, the court held that expert testimony concerning the fallibility of eyewitness testimony can be introduced. The failure of the trial court in this case was harmless, given the overwhelming corroborating testimony of other witnesses.

■≡■

Quicknotes

EXPERT TESTIMONY Testimonial evidence about a complex area of subject matter relevant to trial, presented by a person competent to inform the trier of fact due to specialized knowledge or training.

■≡■

Frye v. United States

Convicted murderer (D) v. Federal government (P)

293 F. 1013 (D.C. Cir. 1923).

NATURE OF CASE: Appeal from second-degree murder conviction.

FACT SUMMARY: At defendant's murder trial, he sought to introduce expert testimony regarding a deception test that was not yet widely accepted in the scientific community. The trial judge denied defendant's motion to include expert testimony and defendant appealed on that ground.

🏛 RULE OF LAW
Scientific expert testimony must attain standing and scientific recognition in the applicable field in order to become accepted as admissible testimony.

FACTS: Frye (D) was indicted for second-degree murder. At trial, he sought to introduce expert testimony regarding a systolic blood pressure deception test given to the defendant. The test involved measuring a subject's blood pressure as the subject attempts to deceive the examiner. The theory is that the blood pressure will increase when the subject is lying and remain steady when the subject is telling the truth. The Government (P) objected to the admission of this evidence and the trial court sustained the objection. Frye (D) was convicted of second-degree murder and he appealed on the ground that the expert testimony should have been admitted.

ISSUE: Must scientific expert testimony attain standing and scientific recognition in the applicable field in order to be accepted as admissible testimony?

HOLDING AND DECISION: (Van Orsdel, J.) Yes. Scientific expert testimony must attain standing and scientific recognition in the applicable field in order to be accepted as admissible testimony. It is difficult to ascertain when a scientific test moves from experimental to demonstrable, but acceptance within the appropriate scientific community is a reliable indicator. The systolic blood pressure deception test has not yet attained such acceptance. Affirmed.

▶ ANALYSIS

Frye presented the court with a novel theory and remained the standard for scientific admissibility until the U.S. Supreme Court decided *Daubert v. Merrell Dow Pharmaceuticals, Inc.*, 509 U.S. 579 (1993). The test of general acceptance within the appropriate community had enough flexibility to allow attorneys latitude to make arguments, but also provided judges with a rule to follow.

■━■

Quicknotes

ADMISSIBILITY OF EVIDENCE Refers to whether particular evidence may be received by the court to aid the jury in determining the resolution of a controversy.

EXPERT TESTIMONY Testimonial evidence about a complex area of subject matter relevant to trial, presented by a person competent to inform the trier of fact due to specialized knowledge or training.

■━■

Daubert v. Merrell Dow Pharmaceuticals, Inc.

Prescription drug user (P) v. Drug company (D)

509 U.S. 579 (1993).

NATURE OF CASE: Review of summary judgment dismissing product liability action.

FACT SUMMARY: Daubert's (P) proffered expert witnesses were excluded because the opinions they intended to introduce were not based on methods generally accepted in the scientific community.

🏛 RULE OF LAW
An expert opinion does not need to be generally accepted in the scientific community to be admissible.

FACTS: Daubert (P) and Schuller (P) filed a lawsuit against Merrell Dow Pharmaceuticals, Inc. (Merrell) (D), alleging that they suffered in utero injuries due to maternal ingestion of the drug Bendectin. Merrell (D) moved for summary judgment, introducing expert opinions to the effect that there was no causal link between Bendectin and birth defects. Daubert (P) and Schuller (P) countered with a series of declarations from eight medical experts, contending that such a link existed. The district court held that the plaintiff's experts had used methodologies not generally accepted in the scientific community. Specifically, they had based their opinions on in vitro and animal studies, as well as chemical structure analysis. Merrell's (D) motion for summary judgment was granted, dismissing the action. The Ninth Circuit affirmed, and the Supreme Court granted review.

ISSUE: Does an expert opinion need to be generally accepted in the scientific community to be admissible?

HOLDING AND DECISION: (Blackmun, J.) No. An expert opinion does not need to be generally accepted in the scientific community to be admissible. The admissibility of expert opinions is governed by Fed. R. Evid. 702. The Rule provides that "If scientific or other specialized knowledge will assist the trier of fact to understand the evidence or to determine a fact in issue," an expert may testify thereto. Nothing in this Rule provides that general scientific acceptance is a condition to admissibility. This being so the broad relevance requirement of Fed. R. Evid. 104 takes precedence, which also provides no such requirement. Consequently, no such requirement should be inferred. However, this does not mean that there are no limits on admissibility of expert testimony. The Rule requires "knowledge," so guesses or speculations are inadmissible. A necessary corollary to this is that the expert must base his opinion on sound principles and valid deductions. In this analysis, such factors as peer review, publication, and even general acceptance may be relevant.

No one issue will be determinative, however. Here, the courts below held general acceptance to be determinative, and this was erroneous. Reversed and remanded.

CONCURRENCE AND DISSENT: (Rehnquist, C.J.) Everything in the present opinion going beyond the main holding that general acceptance is not required is dicta and should not have been included.

▶ ANALYSIS

The "general acceptance" rule was first enunciated in *Frye v. U.S.*, 293 F. 1013 (1923). For seventy years after *Frye*, the general acceptance requirement was adopted by most courts, although the rule was a matter of great controversy. The present opinion appears to have settled this issue.

Quicknotes

CAUSATION The aggregate effect of preceding events that brings about a tortious result; the causal connection between the actions of a tortfeasor and the injury that follows.

DICTUM Statement by a judge in a legal opinion that is not necessary for the resolution of the action.

EXPERT WITNESS A witness providing testimony at trial who is specially qualified regarding the particular subject matter involved.

FED. R. EVID. 104 Permits a court to consider all non-privileged matters, whether independently admissible or not, when determining preliminary issues of admissibility.

FED. R. EVID. 702 Permits a witness qualified as an expert to testify in the form of an opinion.

FED. R. EVID. 703 Rule governing the admissibility of expert testimony.

SUMMARY JUDGMENT Judgment rendered by a court in response to a motion made by one of the parties, claiming that the lack of a question of material fact in respect to an issue warrants disposition of the issue without consideration by the jury.

Daubert v. Merrell Dow Pharmaceuticals, Inc.

Prescription drug user (P) v. Drug company (D)

43 F.3d 1311 (9th Cir.), *cert. denied*, 516 U.S. 869 (1995).

NATURE OF CASE: Action seeking damages for liability for birth defects on remand from the Supreme Court.

FACT SUMMARY: Two minors (P) brought suit against Merrell Dow Pharmaceuticals, Inc. (D), claiming they suffered limb-reduction birth defects because their mothers took the drug Bendectin, prescribed for morning sickness.

⚖ RULE OF LAW
Under Fed. R. Evid. 702, scientific evidence is admissible if it rests on a reliable scientific foundation and is relevant to the task at hand.

FACTS: Bendectin, a drug manufactured by Merrell Dow Pharmaceuticals, Inc. (Merrell Dow) (D), was prescribed for morning sickness to about seventeen and a half million pregnant women between 1957 and 1982. Daubert (P) and another minor (P) brought suit against Merrell Dow (D) claiming they suffered limb-reduction birth defects because their mothers took Bendectin during their pregnancies. At trial, the district court granted Merrell Dow's (D) motion for summary judgment, and the court of appeals affirmed. The primary reason that summary judgment was granted was that the standard used to evaluate scientific evidence was whether the evidence was generally accepted as reliable within the scientific community. The courts concluded that the expert opinions offered by Daubert (P) at trial were counter to the substantial consensus in the scientific community, and not one scientist stated affirmatively that Bendectin causes limb birth defects. On appeal, the Supreme Court determined that the standard used by the district and appellate courts was incorrect, and remanded the case with instructions for applying the appropriate test.

ISSUE: Under Fed. R. Evid. 702, is scientific evidence admissible if it rests on a reliable scientific foundation and is relevant to the task at hand?

HOLDING AND DECISION: (Kozinski, J.) Yes. Under Fed. R. Evid. 702, scientific evidence is admissible if it rests on a reliable scientific foundation and is relevant to the task at hand. Establishing that an expert's testimony grows out of prelitigation research or that the research has been subjected to peer review are two principal ways the proponent of such testimony can satisfy the first part of the test under Rule 702. However, none of Daubert's (P) experts claim to have studied the effect of Bendectin on limb-reduction defects before being hired to testify in this or related cases, and none of the experts has had his work

on Bendectin published in a scientific journal or solicited formal review from his colleagues. Daubert's (P) experts have provided only their qualifications, their conclusions, and their assurances. The second part of the test under Rule 702 requires that the proffered evidence be helpful and pertinent to the question at issue. The issue here is one of causation since Daubert (P) has alleged that Bendectin caused the limb-reduction birth defects. Under California tort law, a plaintiff must show by statistical proof that a mother's ingestion of Bendectin more than doubled the likelihood of birth defects. None of Daubert's (P) epidemiological experts claimed that the children of mothers who took Bendectin were more than twice as likely to develop limb-reduction defects as those whose mothers did not. The strongest statement any of Daubert's (P) experts could assert was that Bendectin could possibly have caused the defects. The district court's grant of summary judgment is affirmed.

▶ ANALYSIS

Although the changed standard for expert scientific testimony did not have an effect on the outcome of this case, it is a significant one. The new *Daubert* standard will permit more new and controversial scientific testimony into evidence provided that it is well substantiated and relevant, even if it is not yet generally accepted. Some critique the new standard for this very reason, arguing that it is more appropriate for the scientific community to determine the relevance of such testimony than a non-scientifically trained judge.

■▬■

Quicknotes

CAUSATION The aggregate effect of preceding events that brings about a tortious result; the causal connection between the actions of a tortfeasor and the injury that follows.

FED. R. EVID. 702 Permits a witness qualified as an expert to testify in the form of an opinion.

REMAND To send back for additional scrutiny or deliberation.

SUMMARY JUDGMENT Judgment rendered by a court in response to a motion made by one of the parties, claiming that the lack of a question of material fact in respect to an issue warrants disposition of the issue without consideration by the jury.

■▬■

United States v. Semrau

Federal government (P) v. Doctor (D)

693 F.3d 510 (6th Cir. 2012).

NATURE OF CASE: Appeal from a conviction for health care fraud.

FACT SUMMARY: Dr. Semrau's (D) defense during a criminal health care fraud trial brought by the Government (P) intended to introduce expert testimony based on results for a new type of lie detector test showing his general truthfulness. The district court precluded his introduction of the test based on Fed. R. Evid. 403.

🏛 RULE OF LAW
Lie detection test results are not considered admissible evidence.

FACTS: Dr. Lorne Semrau (D) was tried for various health care fraud and money laundering counts. The defense requested the admissibility of expert testimony of Dr. Steven Laken based on the results of a lie detection/truth verification using "fMRI" (an MRI that examines a subject's blood oxygen levels in the brain). Laken's analysis of Semrau (D) was challenged by the Government (P) based on its failure to be admissible under Fed. R. Evid. 403. Specifically, the magistrate's decision held that Laken's test could not satisfy the test for admissibility of scientific evidence. The magistrate's decision was upheld by the federal district court, and Semrau (D) subsequently appealed his conviction.

ISSUE: Are lie detection test results considered admissible evidence?

HOLDING AND DECISION: (Stranch, J.) No. Lie detection test results are not considered admissible evidence. The magistrate judge's decision, which was adopted by the district court, excluded Dr. Laken's testimony under Fed. R. Evid. 403. Rule 403 permits a court to exclude relevant evidence if its probative value is subsequently outweighed by a danger of confusing the issues or misleading the jury. A district court has very broad discretion in making this determination. The magistrate judge recommended excluding the fMRI evidence under Rule 403 for three reasons. First, the test was unilaterally obtained without the Government's (P) knowledge, so the Government (P) had no supervision of the testing and Dr. Semrau (D) risked nothing because the results would never have been released had he failed. Second, the use of lie detector test results solely to bolster a witness's credibility is highly prejudicial, especially where credibility issues are central to the verdict. Finally, a jury would not be assisted by hearing that Dr. Semrau's (D) answers were truthful "overall" without learning which specific questions he answered truthfully or deceptively.

Dr. Semrau's reliance on *U.S. v. Bonds*, 12 F.3d 540 (1993), where DNA evidence was admissible, is wrong. Unlike other expert witnesses who testify about factual matters outside the jurors' knowledge, such as the analysis of DNA found at a crime scene, a polygraph expert can supply the jury only with another opinion, in addition to its own, about whether the witness was telling the truth. Where an accurate lie detector developed, the jury's unique role in determining witness credibility would be called into question. The district court did not abuse its discretion in excluding the fMRI evidence pursuant to Rule 403 in light of (1) the questions surrounding the reliability of the fMRI detection tests in general and as performed on Dr. Semrau (D), (2) the failure to give the prosecution an opportunity to participate in the testing, and (3) the test result's inability to corroborate Dr. Semrau's (D) answers as to the particular offenses for which he was charged. Affirmed.

▶ ANALYSIS

In upholding the magistrate and district court decisions, lie detection tests were again held to violate the admissibility requirements of Rule 403. Such evidence, while relevant, offered little in the way of reliability, but was more likely to cause confusion or mislead the trier of fact. Had Dr. Semrau's (D) test results been verifiable, the need for a jury would have been unlikely.

Quicknotes

ADMISSIBILITY OF EVIDENCE Refers to whether particular evidence may be received by the court to aid the jury in determining the resolution of a controversy.

EXPERT TESTIMONY Testimonial evidence about a complex area of subject matter relevant to trial, presented by a person competent to inform the trier of fact due to specialized knowledge or training.

PROBATIVE Tending to establish proof.

Kumho Tire Company v. Carmichael

Tire manufacturer (D) v. Customer (P)

526 U.S. 137 (1999).

NATURE OF CASE: Review of order declaring evidence inadmissible and judgment for defendant.

FACT SUMMARY: Carmichael (P) claimed that his expert witness testimony was improperly excluded at trial and successfully appealed the trial court's application of the *Daubert* factors to determine the admissibility of technical evidence.

> ⚖ **RULE OF LAW**
> A trial court must examine the reliability of expert testimony for not only "scientific" knowledge but "technical" or other "specialized" knowledge as well and may flexibly apply one or more of *Daubert*'s specific factors to determine the admissibility of a technical expert's testimony based on its relevancy and reliability.

FACTS: The right rear tire on Carmichael's (P) minivan blew out and caused an accident in which one passenger died and others were severely injured. Carmichael (P) alleged that the tire was defective and sued the manufacturer, Kumho Tire Company (Kumho) (D). Carmichael (P) rested his case in significant part upon deposition testimony provided by an expert in tire failure analysis, who intended to testify in support of his conclusion. Kumho's (D) motion to exclude that testimony was granted on the ground that the tire expert's methodology failed Rule 702's reliability requirement. The specific factors discussed in *Daubert v. Merrell Dow Pharmaceuticals, Inc.*, 509 U.S. 579 (1993), to determine whether scientific expert testimony is both relevant and reliable, were applied by the court. These factors include testing, peer review, error rules, and the "acceptability" in the relevant scientific community. The court agreed with Kumho (D) it should act as a *Daubert*-type gatekeeper, even though one might consider the testimony technical, rather than scientific. Carmichael's (P) motion for reconsideration was then granted, but the court later affirmed its earlier order and granted Kumho's (D) motion for summary judgment. The Eleventh Circuit reversed, concluding that the testimony fell outside the scope of *Daubert*, whose holding was expressly limited to the application of scientific principles, and not to skill or experience-based observation. Kumho (D) appealed, and the Supreme Court granted certiorari.

ISSUE: Must a trial court examine the reliability of expert testimony for not only "scientific" knowledge, but "technical" or other "specialized" knowledge as well, and could the court flexibly apply one or more of *Daubert*'s specific factors to determine the admissibility of a technical expert's testimony based on its relevancy and reliability?

HOLDING AND DECISION: (Breyer, J.) Yes. A trial court must examine the reliability of expert testimony for not only "scientific" knowledge but "technical" or other "specialized" knowledge as well and may flexibly apply one or more of *Daubert*'s specific factors to determine the admissibility of a technical expert's testimony based on its relevancy and reliability. A trial judge has a special obligation to ensure that any and all scientific testimony is not only relevant, but reliable. *Daubert* applies to technical or other specialized, non-specific knowledge where expert testimony is being proffered. Thus, some of *Daubert*'s questions can help to evaluate the reliability even of experience-based testimony. Whether *Daubert*'s specific factors are, or are not, reasonable measures of reliability in a particular case, is a matter the law grants the trial judge broad latitude to determine. The trial judge in this case determined the testimony fell outside the area where experts might reasonably differ, and where the jury must decide among the conflicting views of different experts, even though the evidence is shaky. The doubts that triggered the trial court's initial inquiry here were reasonable, as was the court's ultimate conclusion. Fed. R. Evid. 702 grants the district judge the discretionary authority, reviewable for its abuse, to determine reliability in light of the particular facts and circumstances of the particular case. The district court did not abuse its discretionary authority in this case. Reversed.

▶ ANALYSIS

Justice Stevens concurred with the first two parts of the Court's decision here, but dissented from the disposition of the case. He wrote that the question of the exclusion of the expert testimony should be decided by the court of appeals since it involved a study of the record. *Daubert* itself made clear that its list of factors was meant to be helpful, not definitive.

■=■

Quicknotes

CERTIORARI A discretionary writ issued by a superior court to an inferior court in order to review the lower court's decisions; the Supreme Court's writ ordering such review.

DEPOSITION A pretrial discovery procedure whereby oral

Continued on next page.

or written questions are asked by one party of the opposing party or of a witness for the opposing party under oath in preparation for litigation.

EXPERT TESTIMONY Testimonial evidence about a complex area of subject matter relevant to trial, presented by a person competent to inform the trier of fact due to specialized knowledge or training.

EXPERT WITNESS A witness providing testimony at trial who is specially qualified regarding the particular subject matter involved.

FED. R. EVID. 702 Permits a witness qualified as an expert to testify in the form of an opinion.

SUMMARY JUDGMENT Judgment rendered by a court in response to a motion made by one of the parties, claiming that the lack of a question of material fact in respect to an issue warrants disposition of the issue without consideration by the jury.

■=■

State v. Kinney

State (P) v. Convicted kidnapper and rapist (D)

Vt. Sup. Ct., 171 Vt. 239, 762 A.2d 833 (2000).

NATURE OF CASE: Appeal from conviction for kidnapping, aggravated sexual assault, and lewd and lascivious behavior.

FACT SUMMARY: Kinney (D) was convicted of kidnapping, aggravated sexual assault, and lewd and lascivious behavior. Kinney (D) contended that it was error for the trial court to admit testimony by Tyler, an expert on rape trauma syndrome and the characteristics and conduct of rape victims.

🏛 **RULES OF LAW**
(1) Expert evidence of rape trauma syndrome and the associated typical behavior of adult rape victims are admissible.
(2) Expert evidence of the rate of false reporting of rape accusations is inadmissible.

FACTS: Kinney (D) was convicted of kidnapping, aggravated sexual assault, and lewd and lascivious behavior. At trial, the State (P) called Tyler, an expert on rape trauma syndrome and the characteristics and conduct of rape victims. Tyler testified that rape trauma syndrome is a set of behaviors and symptoms experienced by victims of severe trauma. These symptoms generally include nightmares, anxiety, and fear, and, for rape victims, they may include guilt, shame, sexual dysfunction, and difficulty in interpersonal relationships. Tyler also testified about the responses of rape victims to their attacker, and about the typical patterns of reporting of rapes by the victims. Tyler also testified about the rate of false reporting of rape, indicating that at least 98 percent of the rapes reported actually occur. Kinney (D) contended that the trial court should have excluded Tyler's testimony. The Vermont Supreme Court granted review.

ISSUES:
(1) Are expert evidence of rape trauma syndrome and the associated typical behavior of adult rape victims admissible?
(2) Is expert evidence of the rate of false reporting of rape accusations admissible?

HOLDING AND DECISION: (Dooley, J.)
(1) Yes. Expert evidence of rape trauma syndrome and the associated typical behavior of adult rape victims are admissible. Most of Tyler's evidence, other than her testimony about the rate of false reporting, is admissible. This evidence is of the type this court has found admissible with respect to child sexual abuse, where evidence regarding post-traumatic stress disorder (PTSD) suffered by child victims of sexual abuse was

held admissible to assist the jury, given the unique psychological effects involved. The admission of such evidence was allowed under a flexible standard of admissibility that is consistent with *Daubert*, 509 U.S. 579 (1993), and that places emphasis on whether the evidence will "assist the trier of facts to understand the evidence." Here, Tyler's evidence regarding adult rape victims is admissible under that same standard. It will assist the jury to understand and evaluate the evidence, and to respond to defense claims that the victim's behavior after the alleged rape is inconsistent with the claim the rape occurred. Moreover, the evidence used here is professionally recognized and sufficiently reliable to be admitted, and is the type of evidence that minimizes the risk of improper usage or excessive prejudice. Tyler never interviewed the victim and offered no opinion whether the victim suffered from rape trauma syndrome or exhibited any of the behavior of a rape victim. Thus, there was little risk that Tyler would be seen by the jury as a truth detector.
(2) No. Expert evidence of the rate of false reporting of rape accusations is inadmissible. The jury could infer from Tyler's testimony that scientific studies have shown that almost no woman falsely claims to have been raped. This testimony was not relevant as to whether the alleged rape victim here made a false claim, and the prejudicial effect of the testimony outweighs its probative value because the jury could convict Kinney (D) on the basis of the testimony. The testimony was tantamount to an expert opinion that the victim was telling the truth and, therefore, it invaded the province of the jury. Although the testimony regarding the incidence of false reporting of rape accusations was inadmissible, (Kinney (D) failed to preserve this issue for appeal), the failure to exclude it did not cause a miscarriage of justice in this case. Affirmed.

▶ **ANALYSIS**

"Syndrome" means a group of symptoms or signs typical of an underlying cause or disease. Some commentators have pointed out that evidence of psychological "syndromes" is not based on the most dependable science. In part, this is because the "cause" of the syndrome may be constructed partly from the symptoms themselves, and because there are ethical restrictions on experimental research into behavioral syndromes making most of the data used the product of inherently less reliable methodology. Other factors that may reduce reliability is the fact that researchers

Continued on next page.

and therapists may be one and the same, being both the supplier of initial data, and then being the ones who analyze the data, which may lead to their not being as objective as possible. For all these reasons, it is very important that courts check the available research to see if the empirical record supports experts' testimony.

■══■

Quicknotes

EXPERT WITNESS A witness providing testimony at trial who is specially qualified regarding the particular subject matter involved.

■══■

Authentication, Identification, and the Best Evidence Rule

Quick Reference Rules of Law

United States v. Stelmokas

Federal government (P) v. Nazi war criminal (D)

100 F.3d 302 (3d Cir. 1996), *cert. denied*, 520 U.S. 1241 (1997).

NATURE OF CASE: Appeal from revocation of United States citizenship.

FACT SUMMARY: At the trial to revoke Stelmokas's (D) citizenship, the Government (P) introduced ancient documents against defendant. Stelmokas appealed the revocation of his citizenship, contending that the documents could not be authenticated and should have been inadmissible as hearsay.

🏛 RULE OF LAW

Ancient documents are admissible as exceptions to the hearsay rule provided they are in authentic condition, in a place where they likely would be located if authentic, and have been in existence for 20 years or more at the time offered.

FACTS: Jonas Stelmokas (D), born in Russia and residing in Lithuania, petitioned the U.S. in 1949 to be classified as a displaced person under the Displaced Persons Act of 1948. Being so classified would allow him to immigrate to the United States. Stelmokas (D) misrepresented facts about his past to the interviewing officer, was deemed eligible for displaced person status, and was so certified in July 1949. In 1995, the U.S. Government (P) brought a complaint against Stelmokas (D) claiming he was a voluntary member of the Lithuanian Schutzmannschaft, an armed unit aiding the Germans during WWII in the murder and persecution of Jews and Lithuanian civilians. The Government (P) introduced archived records that clearly demonstrated Stelmokas's (D) enlistment, involvement, and assignments. The documents were retrieved from the Lithuanian capital and other German sources. Two expert witnesses testified to the authenticity of the documents. Stelmokas's (D) citizenship was revoked, and he appealed on the basis that the documents introduced against him were not authenticated and did not fall within the hearsay exceptions.

ISSUE: Are ancient documents admissible as exceptions to the hearsay rule provided they are in authentic condition, in a place where they likely would be located if authentic, and have been in existence for 20 years or more at the time offered?

HOLDING AND DECISION: (Greenberg, J.) Yes. Ancient documents are admissible as exceptions to the hearsay rule provided they are in authentic condition, in a place where they likely would be located if authentic, and have been in existence for 20 years or more at the time offered. Fed. R. Evid. 901(b) provides these methods for authentication, and the methods were certainly met in this

case. One of the experts testifying to the documents' condition was for all practical purposes unimpeachable because of the extent of his experience and knowledge concerning these documents. Their authentic condition was not in the least suspicious. Stelmokas (D) next argued that the documents were not found in a likely location given that they were German records, but the records concerned Lithuanian units and the Lithuanian capital is the logical place for the archives. Finally, Stelmokas's (D) other argument that the Government's (P) chain of custody cannot be established fails because Fed. R. Evid. 901(a) does not require a perfect chain of custody for authentication purposes. The documents were properly admitted as exceptions to the hearsay rule, and there was no error below. Affirmed.

▎ ANALYSIS

Proving chain of custody is easier with unique items that have more recently been seized and tracked, such as a particular gun. Using chain of custody for authentication is even more important when dealing with a common item such as a packet of narcotics. Ancient documents pose a much more complex problem than either of these things because of the requirement of authentication, usually done by experts, negating any suspicion as to the authenticity of the documents. Chain of custody is less useful in such a case because the inquiry must still be made as to the likelihood of authenticity due to appearance, location, and age.

Quicknotes

ADMISSIBILITY OF EVIDENCE Refers to whether particular evidence may be received by the court to aid the jury in determining the resolution of a controversy.

AUTHENTICATION (OF DOCUMENTARY EVIDENCE) The validity of documentary evidence that must be established prior to its admission into evidence, usually by showing that a document is that it purports to be.

CHAIN OF CUSTODY One who offers evidence must account for custody of the item from the time it is taken into custody until it is offered as evidence.

FED. R. EVID. 901 Requires the authentication or identification of evidence as a condition precedent to admissibility.

Continued on next page.

HEARSAY EXCEPTION Out-of-court statement made by a person other than the witness testifying at trial that is offered in order to prove the truth of the matter asserted, and is admissible at trial notwithstanding the fact that it is hearsay.

■═■

State v. Small

Government (P) v. Convicted murder (D)

Ohio Ct. App., 2007 Ohio 6771 (2007).

NATURE OF CASE: Appeal of murder conviction.

FACT SUMMARY: Dean D. Small (D) was identified as a participant in a phone call in which he incriminated himself through his accent, the content of the conversation, and the use of a nickname that his wife testified he used. The trial court admitted testimony about the call.

🏛 RULE OF LAW
Statements made during a telephone conversation in which the defendant was not specifically identified as one of the parties to the conversation are admissible under the party opponent admission exception to the hearsay rule if the state can authenticate that the person speaking on the telephone was the defendant.

FACTS: Dean D. Small (D) was charged with the aggravated murder of Robel Medhin. Tesfalem Ellos, a friend of Medhin, testified that Medhin believed his life was in danger because of a debt. On the night of the murder, Medhin used Ellos's phone and told the person who answered that he did not have the money. After Medhin's death, Ellos retrieved the phone number Medhin called, and called it. The person who answered had a Jamaican accent and said his name was Dominique. Ellos and Dominique discussed arrangements under which Ellos would repay Medhin's debt. Small's (D) wife also testified at trial that Dominique was a name that Small (D) used. The trial court admitted testimony from Ellos about the call.

ISSUE: Are statements made during a telephone conversation in which the defendant was not specifically identified as one of the parties to the conversation admissible under the party opponent admission exception to the hearsay rule if the state can authenticate that the person speaking on the telephone was the defendant?

HOLDING AND DECISION: (Bryant, J.) Yes. Statements made during a telephone conversation in which the defendant was not specifically identified as one of the parties to the conversation are admissible under the party opponent admission exception to the hearsay rule if the state can authenticate that the person speaking on the telephone was the defendant. Here, the State (P) needed to authenticate that the person to whom Ellos spoke on the phone was Small (D), that is, that Small (D) is "Dominique." One method for authenticating a telephone conversation is through the distinctive characteristics that indicate that the caller could only be Small (D). To effec-

tively authenticate the call using this method, contents of the conversation, characteristics of the speech, or circumstances of the call must make it improbable that the caller could be anyone other than the person identified. The conversation between Ellos and Dominique contains enough evidence to identify Dominique as Small (D). Dominique's Jamaican accent, his claim that Medhin owed him money, and the testimony of Small's (D) wife that Small (D) was known as Dominique, had a Jamaican accent, and was owed money by Medhin, make it highly improbable that the person answering the phone was not Small (D). In addition, Ellos initiated the call, and did not know Small (D) or his wife, and the chance that an imposter also would have a Jamaican accent and would respond to an unexpected phone call in a manner that tends to incriminate Small (D) is slim. Therefore, the evidence authenticates Small (D) as "Dominique," and the statements made by Small (D) to Ellos during the phone call constitute party opponent admissions, and are admissible. Affirmed.

▶ ANALYSIS

Two other methods for authenticating a telephone conversation—evidence that the call was made to a number assigned by the telephone company to the person identified, or voice identification, where the caller knows the defendant's voice—are acceptable for purposes of Fed. R. Evid. 801(d)(2)(A), and are probably less vulnerable to cross-examination. Note that both direct and circumstantial evidence can be used to authenticate under any method.

━━■

Quicknotes

HEARSAY EXCEPTION Out-of-court statement made by a person other than the witness testifying at trial that is offered in order to prove the truth of the matter asserted, and is admissible at trial notwithstanding the fact that it is hearsay.

━━■

Simms v. Dixon

Driver (D) v. Driver (P)

D.C. Ct. App. 291 A.2d 184 (1972).

NATURE OF CASE: Appeal from judgment for defendant.

FACT SUMMARY: Simms (D) and Dixon (P) were involved in a motor vehicle collision and the trial revolved around the issue of who hit whom and where the vehicles were struck. Simms (D) sought to introduce photographs of her vehicle post-accident, which the trial judge denied. She appealed on the basis that the photographs should have been admitted.

🏛 RULE OF LAW
The essential test for the admissibility of photographs is whether the photographs accurately depict what is shown.

FACTS: Cheryl Simms (D) and Herbert Dixon (P) were involved in a motor vehicle collision. At trial, the two had conflicting stories of who hit whom and where the vehicles were struck. Simms (D) had six photographs of her vehicle post-accident, which she sought to admit into evidence. The trial judge denied their admission absent the presence of the photographer to testify to how the photographs were taken. The photographer could not be located and the trial court again held that Simms's (D) testimony was an insufficient foundation to permit the admission of the photographs. Simms (D) appealed the judgment, arguing that the photographs should have been admitted.

ISSUE: Is the essential test for the admissibility of photographs whether the photographs accurately depict what is shown?

HOLDING AND DECISION: (Fickling, J.) The essential test for the admissibility of photographs is whether the photographs accurately depict what is shown. A photographer's testimony would only be required to establish dimension and perspective, not whether the facts shown in the photograph are accurately depicted. Someone familiar with the facts may lay the foundation for the admissibility of the photographs. In this case, Simms's (D) testimony would be sufficient. Reversed and remanded for a new trial.

▶ ANALYSIS

Requiring the photographer's testimony is a cautious decision on the part of the court, but an unnecessary one. The photographer may not necessarily be able to testify as to the accuracy of the facts depicted by the photograph while someone more intimately familiar with the subject matter can.

Quicknotes

ADMISSIBILITY OF EVIDENCE Refers to whether particular evidence may be received by the court to aid the jury in determining the resolution of a controversy.

FOUNDATION The validity of proffered evidence that must be established prior to admission at trial, usually by demonstrating its authenticity or that it is what it purports to be.

Wagner v. State

Convicted cocaine dealer (D) v. State (P)

Fla. Dist. Ct. App., 707 So. 2d 827 (1998).

NATURE OF CASE: Appeal from drug conviction.

FACT SUMMARY: During defendant's trial for cocaine dealing, the prosecution introduced a videotape purportedly showing the transaction at issue. Upon conviction, defendant appealed claiming the videotape was not properly authenticated and was thus not admissible against him.

🏛 RULE OF LAW
Relevant, reliable photographic evidence is admissible upon a consideration of five enumerated factors.

FACTS: A police officer arranged for a confidential informant to purchase cocaine from Wagner (D) while the transaction was being videotaped. The police officer placed the recording equipment in a county car, verified that it worked, recorded the date and time, and then the confidential informant drove that car to the meeting with Wagner (D). The police officer followed the informant's car, but did not witness the transaction personally. As soon as the transaction was complete, the officer and the informant met at a prearranged site and the officer kept the videotape in his exclusive custody and control until trial. At trial, the videotape was introduced as evidence against Wagner (D) and the officer testified as to the installation and operation of the recording equipment. No evidence was introduced to suggest that the tape was altered or edited. The informant was not available to testify, but another witness identified Wagner (D) from the videotape. The jury convicted Wagner (D) of selling cocaine within 1000 feet of a school and Wagner (D) appealed, claiming the videotape was not properly authenticated and was thus not admissible as evidence against him.

ISSUE: Is relevant, reliable photographic evidence admissible upon a consideration of five enumerated factors rather than strictly under the "pictorial testimony" theory?

HOLDING AND DECISION: (Lawrence, J.) Yes. Relevant, reliable photographic evidence is admissible upon a consideration of five enumerated factors. Traditionally, the "pictorial testimony" theory provided the testimony of a witness who could verify that the subject matter of the photograph or videotape was an accurate representation. Here, the informant was unavailable so this method of authentication was not possible. Since it is not always possible to have a person who can vouch for the accuracy of the photograph, "silent witness" authentication is permissible. This allows the photograph or videotape to "speak for itself" as a "silent witness" so long as a witness can verify the installation and operation of the equipment producing the photographic evidence. The police officer in this case gave detailed and extensive testimony as to the installation and operation of the recording equipment, which is sufficient authentication for the videotape. The trial judge, once determining the relevancy and reliability of the photographic evidence, should also consider five evidentiary factors related to the photographic evidence: (1) time and date of the photograph or videotape, (2) possible editing or tampering, (3) operation, accuracy, and reliability of the equipment, (4) installation, security, and testing of the equipment, and (5) identification of the relevant participants depicted. Once these factors are considered and supported, the photographic evidence should be admitted. Affirmed.

▶ ANALYSIS

Having a live witness to identify the people in the photographic evidence, the accuracy of the background depicted, and to authenticate every detail in the evidence is always preferable. That is simply not always possible, as in the *Wagner* case where the informant ran away possibly because of pending, unrelated charges. This decision may provide police more leeway in using recording devices or images from security cameras without having to find a willing witness to authenticate every portion of the image.

■=■

Quicknotes

ADMISSIBILITY OF EVIDENCE Refers to whether particular evidence may be received by the court to aid the jury in determining the resolution of a controversy.

AUTHENTICATION The demonstration that a document or writing is the writing it purports to be so that it may be rendered admissible at trial.

PICTORIAL TESTIMONY Evidence offered as testimony through photographs of events or people.

SILENT WITNESS THEORY Permits admission of photographic evidence where the photographs have not been altered and a witness testifies the photos accurately depict what was observed.

■=■

Seiler v. Lucasfilm

Designer (P) v. Movie company (D)

808 F.2d 1316 (9th Cir. 1986), *cert. denied*, 484 U.S. 826 (1987).

NATURE OF CASE: Appeal from a denial of damages for copyright infringement.

FACT SUMMARY: Seiler (P) contended that pictures of his creations were not covered by the Best Evidence Rule.

🏛 RULE OF LAW
Pictures and nonverbal facsimiles are writings and are covered by the Best Evidence Rule.

FACTS: Seiler (P) sued Lucasfilm (D), contending characters he created in 1976 and copyrighted in 1981 were used by Lucasfilm (D) in the 1980 film, "The Empire Strikes Back." Seiler (P) was precluded from showing copies of his work to the jury on the basis of the Best Evidence Rule. He could produce no original evidence that the characters existed prior to 1980. He appealed from entry of summary judgment, contending his work was artwork and not subject to the Best Evidence Rule.

ISSUE: Are pictures and other nonverbal facsimile writings subject to the Best Evidence Rule?

HOLDING AND DECISION: (Farris, J.) Yes. Pictures and other nonverbal facsimiles are writings covered by the Best Evidence Rule. In this case, the key issue is the similarity between the two characters. Facsimiles created after the Lucasfilm (D) characters were created are of dubious probative value. Because they are subject to the Best Evidence Rule, it must be shown that the originals were lost or destroyed by no fault of Seiler (P). Because this was not done, the facsimiles cannot be used. Affirmed.

▶ ANALYSIS

Writings are often defined extremely broadly under most jurisdictions' evidence codes. The term includes traditional verbal communications as well as motion pictures, audio recordings, and videotape. Any type of recording method may be classified as a writing and be made subject to the Best Evidence Rule.

Quicknotes

BEST EVIDENCE RULE An evidentiary rule requiring that an original document be introduced if possible; secondary evidence is admissible only after proof that the original was lost or destroyed through no fault of the proponent of the evidence.

SUMMARY JUDGMENT Judgment rendered by a court in response to a motion made by one of the parties, claiming that the lack of a question of material fact in respect to an issue warrants disposition of the issue without consideration by the jury.

United States v. Jackson

Federal government (P) v. Accused pedophile (D)

488 F. Supp. 2d 866 (D. Neb. 2007).

NATURE OF CASE: In limine motion to exclude evidence.

FACT SUMMARY: [Defendant's first name omitted from casebook excerpt.] In a trial against an accused sex offender, the Government (P) sought to introduce an electronic document containing the cut-and-pasted online chat conversation between Jackson (D) and an underage girl.

🏛 **RULE OF LAW**

A document containing a cut-and-pasted online chat conversation does not constitute the best evidence of the conversation.

FACTS: [Defendant's first name omitted from casebook excerpt.] A local sheriff's office and the Federal Bureau of Investigation worked together on the investigation of Jackson's (D) possible involvement in inappropriate conduct with underage girls. Agent David Margritz, known in Internet chat rooms as "k8tee4fun," identified himself to Jackson (D) as a fourteen-year-old girl. They set up a meeting, but Jackson (D) did not stop and returned home. Officers then searched his home and seized his computers. The first U.S. Attorney assigned to the case, on November 3, 2002, did not work on it before his retirement on October 1, 2004. On September 28, 2004, Assistant U.S. Attorney Michael Norris was assigned to the case, and on February 24, 2005, a grand jury indicted Jackson for using a computer to knowingly attempt to "persuade, induce, and entice a minor to engage in sexual activity." None of the conversations were saved, because Margritz wiped his computer clean during a routine upgrade. The Government (P) therefore tried to introduce a document containing the conversation as it was cut-and-pasted by Margritz, and which Margritz annotated. Jackson (D) sought to prevent the Government (P) from introducing the document. A computer forensics expert testified that a bit-stream image of the hard drive, which is a forensic copy of the hard drive, is the best way to confirm the chat and the only way to see it exactly as it appeared during the conversations. He also said that Margritz's method was the least effective way to capture the chat, and that information about the chat log was missing from his document that would have appeared in a bit-stream image.

ISSUE: Does a document containing a cut-and-pasted online chat conversation constitute the best evidence of the conversation?

HOLDING AND DECISION: (Bataillon, J.) No. A document containing a cut-and-pasted online chat conversation does not constitute the best evidence of the conversation. None of the methods for capturing the chats, as described credibly by the forensics expert, were utilized, and the cut-and-pasted document is not an accurate original or duplicate because it does not accurately reflect the entire conversations between Jackson (D) and Margritz. In addition, Margritz changed the document by adding his editorial comments. Therefore, the document is inadmissible. Defendant's motion in limine granted.

▶ **ANALYSIS**

Though not part of the court's reasoning with respect to the Best Evidence Rule, the court also found that the Government's (P) two-year delay in prosecuting Jackson (D) was "extremely reckless" and may have amounted to bad faith, and that if the charges had been promptly filed, reliable evidence would have been available. The total amount of time that lapsed before the trial—four years—was a contributing factor to the loss of the evidence.

■■■

Quicknotes

BAD FAITH Conduct that is intentionally misleading or deceptive.

BEST EVIDENCE RULE An evidentiary rule requiring that an original document be introduced if possible; secondary evidence is admissible only after proof that the original was lost or destroyed through no fault of the proponent of the evidence.

EXPERT TESTIMONY Testimonial evidence about a complex area of subject matter relevant to trial, presented by a person competent to inform the trier of fact due to specialized knowledge or training.

RECKLESSNESS Conduct that is conscious and that creates a substantial and unjustifiable risk of harm to others.

■■■

Privileges: General Principles

Quick Reference Rules of Law

Jaffee v. Redmond

Executor of estate (P) v. Police officer (D)

518 U.S. 1 (1996).

NATURE OF CASE: Appeal from reversal of an award of damages in a wrongful death action.

FACT SUMMARY: Redmond (D), a police officer, underwent counseling sessions after shooting a man and sought to keep those sessions confidential in the subsequent federal civil action brought by the man's estate (P).

🏛 RULE OF LAW
Confidential communications between a psychotherapist and her patients in the course of diagnosis and treatment are protected from compelled disclosure under Rule 501 of the Federal Rules of Evidence.

FACTS: Redmond (D), a police officer, shot and killed Allen while on duty. Jaffee (P), the executor of Allen's estate, filed a wrongful death action against Redmond (D). Following the shooting, Redmond (D) had participated in fifty counseling sessions with Beyer, a clinical social worker. Jaffee (P) sought access to Beyer's notes for use at trial. Redmond (D) asserted that the counseling sessions were confidential and privileged. The district court disagreed, but Redmond (D) and Beyer refused to comply with the discovery order to disclose the notes. At the end of the trial, the court informed the jury that the refusal to turn over the notes was not justified and that the jury should presume the contents were unfavorable to Redmond (D). The jury awarded $545,000 in damages to Jaffee (P), but Redmond (D) appealed and prevailed. Jaffee (P) appealed the reversal of the award.

ISSUE: Are confidential communications between a psychotherapist and her patients protected from compelled disclosure?

HOLDING AND DECISION: (Stevens, J.) Yes. Confidential communications between a psychotherapist and her patients in the course of diagnosis and treatment are protected from compelled disclosure under Rule 501 of the Federal Rules of Evidence. Rule 501 of the Federal Rules of Evidence authorizes federal courts to define new privileges by interpreting common-law principles in the light of reason and experience. Thus, it was recognized that the recognition of privileges would change over time. The recognition of a privilege based on a confidential relationship should be determined on a case-by-case basis, taking into account the public good that would result from allowing the privilege. Of course, privileges should still be rare because they are an exception to the general rule favoring access to all probative evidence. The psychotherapist-patient privilege is rooted in the imperative need for confidence and trust. Successful treatment for mental illnesses depends on complete openness between the psychotherapist and the patient. The mental health of the public depends in part on the confidentiality between patients and psychotherapists. In contrast, the evidentiary benefit from denying the privilege would be modest. Patients would be chilled from expression in situations where litigation was imminent. The privilege should be extended to all licensed social workers who perform mental health treatment. Accordingly, the communications between Redmond (D) and Beyer were privileged and the trial court should not have directed the jury to make a negative inference from the refusal to divulge the contents of Beyer's notes. Affirmed.

DISSENT: (Scalia, J.) While the majority goes to great lengths to show the benefit that will result from this privilege, they give short shrift to the loss of probative evidence that will cause injustice in many cases. Furthermore, the majority does not make it clear why the privilege should extend to social workers when the privilege has usually been limited to those who actually practice medicine.

⬥ ANALYSIS

Prior to this decision, the court of appeals had split on this issue. Most states recognize this privilege, although most of these states extend the privilege through statute rather than common-law principles. Justice Scalia also pointed out in dissent that it was not realistic to suggest that people would fail to seek therapy because the therapist might have to turn over notes by court order.

■══■

Quicknotes

FED. R. EVID. 501 Provides that privilege principles shall be based on common law.

PSYCHOTHERAPIST-PATIENT PRIVILEGE The right of a patient to refuse to reveal confidential information given during the course of a relationship with a physician entered into for the purpose of treatment.

■══■

In re Grand Jury Subpoena, Judith Miller

Reporter (D) v. Federal government (P)

397 F.3d 964 (D.C. Cir.), *cert. denied*, 545 U.S. 1150 (2005), *reissued* 438 F.3d 1141 (2006).

NATURE OF CASE: Appeal from orders of the district court finding civil contempt of court.

FACT SUMMARY: Judith Miller (D) and other reporters refused to divulge the names of their sources for information included in published stories about certain covert government operations. The lower court held them in civil contempt for refusing to comply with the grand jury subpoenas.

🏛 RULE OF LAW
The identities of news reporters' sources are not protected under the First Amendment of the U.S. Constitution or common law.

FACTS: Judith Miller (D) was a Pulitzer Prize-winning journalist for the New York Times. She had written a series of articles on Osama bin Laden, the subject of which caused her to become involved in a grand jury investigation calling for her to disclose the names of her sources for the series. The investigation stemmed from President Bush's Jan. 28, 2003, statement that the British government had learned that Saddam Hussein sought significant quantities of uranium from Africa. In a July 6, 2003, *New York Times* op-ed piece, former Ambassador Joseph Wilson wrote that he had been sent to Niger in 2002 by the Central Intelligence Agency (CIA) to investigate whether Iraq had sought to purchase uranium from Niger and found that there was no credible evidence that it had. Then, on July 14, 2003, columnist Robert Novak wrote in a column in the *Chicago Sun-Times* that "two senior administration officials" told him Wilson's selection for the Niger trip was at the suggestion of Wilson's wife, Valerie Plame, whom Novak identified as a CIA operative on weapons of mass destruction. A grand jury issued a subpoena to Miller (D), among other reporters, concerning Wilson, Wilson's trip, Plame, and the CIA, in order to find out the identities of the administration officials who acted as sources and divulged what appeared to be sensitive and top secret information, in violation of federal law. Miller (D) and another reporter refused to divulge the names of their sources. The lower court held them in civil contempt for refusing to comply with the grand jury subpoenas.

ISSUE: Are the identities of news reporters' sources protected under the First Amendment of the U.S. Constitution or common law?

HOLDING AND DECISION: (Sentelle, J.) No. The identities of news reporters' sources are not protected under the First Amendment of the U.S. Constitution or common law. The Supreme Court considered and rejected

the same claim of First Amendment privilege on similar facts in *Branzburg v. Hayes*, 408 U.S. 665 (1972). There is no First Amendment privilege protecting journalists from providing evidence to a grand jury. While the three members of the panel of the court differ about whether there is a common-law privilege, all agree if there is a common-law privilege, it is not absolute and may be overcome in appropriate circumstances. Affirmed.

CONCURRENCE: (Sentelle, J.) Reporters refusing to testify before grand juries as to their "confidential sources" enjoy no common law privilege beyond the protection against harassing grand juries conducting groundless investigations that is available to all other citizens. The language used by the Supreme Court in *Branzburg* applied not only to the First Amendment privilege issue, but the common-law privilege issue as well. In addition, Federal Rule of Evidence 501 does not by itself work a change in the law that empowers departure from the Supreme Court's clear precedent in *Branzburg*. Even if Rule 501 did authorize courts to create a common-law privilege, the policy issues associated with defining the scope of the privilege are more appropriately considered by the legislature.

CONCURRENCE: (Henderson, J.) Nothing more needs to be decided than that the interests represented by the grand jury investigation outweigh the reporters' privilege, if one exists, to protect the identity of their sources.

CONCURRENCE: (Tatel, J.) Federal Rule of Evidence 501 delegates to courts congressional authority with respect to common-law privilege, and courts are obliged under the Rule to look at the necessity and desirability of a reporter privilege from a common-law perspective. Reason and experience mandate a qualified privilege for reporters' confidential sources, just as a common-law psychotherapist privilege was recognized in *Jaffe v. Redmond*, 518 U.S. 1 (1996). The public harm that would come from undermining all source relationships would be huge, as is reflected in the fact that the majority of states, along with the Justice Department, recognize a qualified immunity for reporters' sources. Other courts can draw the contours of the privilege as the need arises. But the modern consensus favors recognizing a common-law privilege. When set against the public interest in compelling disclosure in this case, however, the privilege must give way. The question in this case is whether Miller's (D) sources released information more harmful than newsworthy, and if so, the public interest in punishing the wrongdoers and deterring future

Continued on next page.

leaks outweighs any burden on news gathering, and no privilege covers the communication between source and reporter. The news value associated with leaking Plame's employment is limited to its impact on the credibility of her husband, and continued public debate about President Bush's speech. The damage to the covert intelligence-gathering functions is comparatively great, and the slight news value does not justify privileging the leaker's identity.

▶ *ANALYSIS*

The First, Second, Third, Fourth, Fifth, Ninth, Tenth, Eleventh, and D.C. Circuits have all held that a qualified reporters' privilege exists. Thirty-one states have "shield" laws protecting journalists' anonymous sources. As to Miller (P), her coverage of the Bush administration's conclusions about Iraq's alleged weapons of mass destruction has been proven false, and the *New York Times* publicly apologized for her reporting. She retired from the *Times* on November 9, 2005.

■═■

Quicknotes

GRAND JURY A group summoned to investigate, inform, and accuse persons of crimes when sufficient evidence exists to do so.

SUBPOENA A command issued by court to compel a witness to appear at trial.

■═■

Morales v. Portuondo

Convicted murderer (D) v. Prosecutor (P)

154 F. Supp. 2d 706 (S.D.N.Y. 2001).

NATURE OF CASE: Application for writ of habeas corpus.

FACT SUMMARY: At defendant's post-trial hearing to set aside his conviction, he sought to introduce four witnesses who would testify to statements made by a person who actually committed the murder for which defendant was convicted. The motion was denied on the grounds that the statements were inadmissible hearsay, a new trial motion was refused, and defendant sought a writ of habeas corpus.

RULE OF LAW
A defendant may introduce hearsay statements made under indicia of reliability that would not otherwise be admissible if the exclusion of these statements would amount to a denial of the defendant's right to "a trial in accord with traditional and fundamental standards of due process."

FACTS: Morales (D) and Montalvo were convicted for the murder of Jose Antonio Rivera. After their sentencing, Jesus Fornes approached Father Joseph Towle, Montalvo's mother, Morales's (D) attorney, and a Legal Aid attorney with the confession that he was the murderer and not the two convicted. Morales (D) filed a motion to set aside the verdict, but upon the Legal Aid attorney's advice, Fornes invoked the Fifth Amendment and refused to testify. The Legal Aid attorney and Father Towle could not testify because of privilege. Montalvo's mother and Morales's (D) attorney testified to Fornes's statements, but the court denied the motion and refused to order a new trial. Years later, Fornes was killed in an unrelated accident, and Father Towle executed an affidavit attesting to Fornes's statements to him. Morales (D) filed a writ of habeas corpus, seeking the admission of Fornes's statements on the grounds that their exclusion was a denial of his due process rights.

ISSUE: May a defendant introduce hearsay statements made under indicia of reliability that would not otherwise be admissible if the exclusion of these statements would amount to a denial of the defendant's right to "a trial in accord with traditional and fundamental standards of due process"?

HOLDING AND DECISION: (Chin, J.) Yes. A defendant may introduce hearsay statements made under indicia of reliability that would not otherwise be admissible if the exclusion of these statements would amount to a denial of the defendant's right to "a trial in accord with traditional and fundamental standards of due process." The

statements do not qualify for an exception to the hearsay rule, but they are "vital" to Morales's (D) defense and have sufficient indicia of reliability. Fornes's "confession" to four different individuals alone indicates trustworthiness, but the statements were also made in circumstances under which Fornes had no motive to lie. As far as privilege, Fornes had every assurance that his statements to Father Towle and the Legal Aid attorney would be kept confidential. Fornes's statements to Father Towle are perhaps covered by the priest-penitent privilege. Father Towle, however, has determined that the statements were made in an informal confession, thus he is able to testify to them. Had the statements been a formal confession, even Fornes's death would not allow Father Towle to reveal them. Similarly, the statements to the Legal Aid attorney are covered by the attorney-client privilege. Death does not dissolve that privilege; however, exclusion of the statements would render Morales's (D) trial fundamentally unfair. Admissibility of such statements in that circumstance is secured in the U.S. Supreme Court case of *Chambers v. Mississippi*, 410 U.S. 284 (1973). Morales's (D) trial was fundamentally unfair due to the exclusion of Fornes's statements and his writ of habeas corpus petition is granted.

ANALYSIS

Certain statements are protected by privilege forever, even after the privilege holder's death. This can create a no-win situation as in the *Morales* case where his innocence could be demonstrated if only the privilege could be dissolved. The U.S. Supreme Court addressed those circumstances in the *Chambers* case which allows otherwise inadmissible hearsay evidence to be admitted to protect the fundamental fairness of the judicial process. It is possible, however, that had Fornes's privilege claims been stronger (e.g., a formal confession to Father Towle), an innocent man could still be in prison.

Quicknotes

HEARSAY EXCEPTION Out-of-court statement made by a person other than the witness testifying at trial that is offered in order to prove the truth of the matter asserted, and is admissible at trial notwithstanding the fact that it is hearsay.

PRIVILEGED COMMUNICATION A statement made by an individual, which is protected from disclosure at trial as a result of its being communicated to a person with

Continued on next page.

whom the declarant shares a relationship that is protected by law.

WRIT OF HABEAS CORPUS A proceeding in which a defendant brings a writ to compel a judicial determination of whether he is lawfully being held in custody.

CHAPTER 12

Lawyer-Client Privilege and Privilege Against Self-Incrimination

Quick Reference Rules of Law

People v. Gionis

State (P) v. Ex-husband (D)

Cal. Sup. Ct., 892 P.2d 1199, 9 Cal. 4th 1196 (1995).

NATURE OF CASE: Appeal from reversal of conviction.

FACT SUMMARY: Defendant's friend, an attorney, testified for the prosecution at defendant's trial for conspiracy to commit assault on his ex-wife. The testimony concerned statements defendant made to the friend concerning the ex-wife and a threatened assault. Defendant's conviction was reversed on appeal on the grounds that the statements should have been protected by the attorney-client privilege, and the state appealed.

🏛 RULE OF LAW
Attorney-client privilege does not protect statements made to an attorney, even if the statements concern legal matters, if advice is not sought from the attorney in his professional capacity or if the attorney has already refused representation.

FACTS: Thomas Gionis (D), a physician, and John Lueck, an attorney, were friends and had a business arrangement. Gionis's (D) wife served him with divorce papers and Gionis (D) became upset and asked Lueck to come to his home. Lueck was very clear in refusing to represent Gionis (D) in his dissolution proceedings, but went over to offer support to his friend. Gionis (D) made statements concerning his ability to "really take care of [his wife]" in a way that no one would suspect him. Gionis (D) and Lueck discussed some aspects of his dissolution case, including the benefit of a change of venue, but Lueck repeatedly informed Gionis (D) that he needed to seek representation. At a later day, Gionis (D) showed up at Lueck's office and requested that Lueck make a court appearance for him because his attorney was out-of-town. Lueck reluctantly did so but did not again represent Gionis (D). Months later, Gionis's (D) ex-wife and boyfriend were viciously assaulted. Gionis (D) was indicted for conspiracy to commit assault and the State (P) argued that he orchestrated the entire assault. At trial, Lueck testified to the statements Gionis (D) made that day. Gionis (D) was convicted, but the appellate court overturned his conviction on the grounds that Lueck's testimony was inadmissible due to attorney-client privilege. The State (P) appealed.

ISSUE: Does attorney-client privilege protect statements made to an attorney if advice is not sought from the attorney in his professional capacity or if the attorney has already refused representation?

HOLDING AND DECISION: (Baxter, J.) No. Attorney-client privilege does not protect statements made to an attorney, even if the statements concern legal matters, if advice is not sought from the attorney in his professional capacity or if the attorney has already refused representation. Lueck was explicitly clear in his refusal to represent Gionis (D) prior to going to his home and hearing the statements. The mere fact that some of the conversation between the two men touched on legal issues does not create an attorney-client privilege. Additionally, Lueck's sole instance of representing Gionis (D) was an emergency basis and did not create an ongoing attorney-client relationship. Gionis (D) was speaking to a friend when he made his statements to Lueck and they are therefore not covered by attorney-client privilege. Reversed.

CONCURRENCE AND DISSENT: (Kennard, J.) Although the conversation at issue was not a circumstance in which Gionis (D) was seeking legal advice from Lueck in his professional capacity, privilege may have nevertheless attached. Once Lueck offered Gionis (D) his professional advice that Gionis (D) should seek a change of venue, Gionis (D) was acting in his professional capacity and the attorney-client privilege attached. The privilege did not attach to Gionis's (D) statements of his ability to "take care of" his wife because they were declarative statements not intended to elicit advice. The privilege attached to the change of venue portion of the conversation was harmless, however, because it was irrelevant to the charge of conspiracy to commit assault.

DISSENT: (Mosk, J.) This was not a case of one friend calling on another for support and advice. The two men had a professional relationship. Lueck testified that Gionis (D) had often provided him professional favors and Lueck therefore did not feel imposed upon in answering Gionis's (D) legal questions. Nothing indicated that Gionis (D) did not intend for their conversation to be confidential. The Concurrence and Dissent also misses the mark in separating the friendship from the professional relationship during their conversation. Attorneys often hear personal information from their clients that does not pertain to the legal issues at hand. That does not make those portions of the conversation non-privileged. Requiring the privileged conversation to pertain only to legal issues would not promote the rationale behind the privilege.

▶ ANALYSIS

Attorneys are often asked legal questions by people at parties, by friends, and by family members. Attorneys often answer those questions without hesitation and with

Continued on next page.

neither party intending the establishment of an attorney-client relationship. Perhaps the defining factor should be whether the client intends for the conversation to be confidential and conveys that to the attorney at the time of the conversation. Allowing the privilege to attach to any conversation addressing legal issues, however, will severely curtail the conversations attorneys can have in everyday situations.

■≡■

Quicknotes

ATTORNEY-CLIENT PRIVILEGE A doctrine precluding the admission into evidence of confidential communications between an attorney and his client made in the course of obtaining professional assistance.

ATTORNEY-CLIENT RELATIONSHIP The confidential relationship established when a lawyer enters into employment with a client.

VENUE The specific geographic location over which a court has jurisdiction to hear a suit.

■≡■

Williams v. District of Columbia

Whistleblower (P) v. Government (D)

806 F. Supp. 2d 44 (D.D.C. 2011).

NATURE OF CASE: Motion to exclude the inadvertent disclosure of privileged evidence.

FACT SUMMARY: In the course of Williams's (P) lawsuit against her former employer, the District of Columbia (the "District") (D), the District (D) inadvertently produced a purportedly privileged communication which it later sought to exclude from trial.

🏛 RULE OF LAW
Privileged information that has been inadvertently disclosed can be excluded if reasonable steps were taken to both protect the information from inadvertent disclosure and then to rectify the mistake once discovered.

FACTS: Christina Conyers Williams (P) brought suit against her former employer, the District of Columbia (the "District") (D) for retaliation based on testimony she provided before the District of Columbia Council. Pursuant to discovery, the District (D) inadvertently produced a purportedly privileged communication from the District's (D) general counsel. Months later, the District realized its disclosure and sent a letter to Williams (P) directing her to return the document, referencing Fed. R. Civ. P. 26(b)(5)(B). Williams (P) never responded to the notice, and the District (D) did not seek relief during the ensuing two years and eight months of pre-trial litigation. When the parties eventually exchanged proposed evidence lists, the District (D) filed a motion to exclude the inadvertent disclosure.

ISSUE: Can privileged information that has been inadvertently disclosed be excluded if reasonable steps were taken to both protect the information from inadvertent disclosure and then to rectify the mistake once discovered.

HOLDING AND DECISION: (Kollar-Kotelly, J.) Yes. Privileged information that has been inadvertently disclosed can be excluded if reasonable steps were taken to both protect the information from inadvertent disclosure and then to rectify the mistake once discovered. It used to be the case that virtually any disclosure of a communication protected by the attorney-client privilege, even if inadvertent, worked as a waiver of the privilege. However, Congress partially abrogated this relatively strict approach to waiver by enacting Rule 502(b) of the Federal Rules of Evidence which provides that an inadvertent "disclosure [of a communication or information covered by the attorney-client privilege or work product protection] does not operate as a waiver ... if: (1) the disclosure is inadvertent; (2) the holder of the privilege or protection took reasonable steps to prevent disclosure; and (3) the

holder promptly took reasonable steps to rectify the error. . . ." The party claiming that its disclosure was inadvertent bears the burden of proving that each of the three elements of the Rule has been met.

Notwithstanding the easing of the waiver doctrine brought about the enactment of Rule 502(b), the Rule does not remove the parties' responsibility to take reasonable precautions against the disclosure of privileged documents. First, and most importantly, the District (D) has utterly failed to explain its methodology for review and production of discovery. Second, the District (D) has failed to provide a concrete sense of the total number of documents that it reviewed and produced. Third, the District (D) offers no clear picture of the demands placed upon it by virtue of Williams's (P) document requests and the timetable of production. In the final analysis, the District's (D) showing is so cursory and incomplete that there simply is no foundation to evaluate the reasonableness of the precautions taken to guard against inadvertent disclosure.

Even where the holder of the privilege can show that it took reasonable precautions to guard against disclosure, the holder bears the further burden of showing that it promptly took reasonable steps to rectify the error once discovered. In this case, when Williams (P) did not promptly return the communication or otherwise respond to the District's (D) letter, the District (D) was on notice that further action was required. Here, the District (D) took no further action, electing instead to wait years while a privileged communication remained in the hands of a third party to the communication. This sort of indifference is fundamentally at odds with the principle that the attorney-client privilege must be jealously guarded by the holder of the privilege lest it be waived. The District's (D) motion to exclude is denied.

▶ ANALYSIS

What this case shows is that despite the relaxation of the strict rule waiving attorney-client privilege based on inadvertent disclosure, a party can still fail to persuade a court to exclude the material when it does not have procedures in place to prevent disclosure, and then does relatively little to seek its return. Minimal reasonable steps in a timely fashion may have prevented the denial of the District's (D) motion to exclude.

■═■

Continued on next page.

Quicknotes

PRIVILEGED COMMUNICATION A statement made by an individual, which is protected from disclosure at trial as a result of its being communicated to a person with whom the declarant shares a relationship that is protected by law.

■━■

Swidler & Berlin v. United States

Deceased client's attorney (D) v. Federal government (P)

524 U.S. 399 (1998).

NATURE OF CASE: Appeal of refusal to quash grand jury subpoenas obtained by the Office of Independent Counsel during a federal investigation.

FACT SUMMARY: James Hamilton (D), an attorney, sought to quash grand jury subpoenas containing attorney-client materials on the grounds of attorney-client privilege.

🏛 RULE OF LAW
The attorney-client privilege survives the client's death.

FACTS: During investigations of alleged White House travel irregularities, Deputy White House Counsel Vincent Foster met with petitioner Hamilton (D), his attorney, to seek legal representation. Hamilton (D) took handwritten notes at their meeting. Foster committed suicide a few days later. Subsequently, a federal grand jury issued subpoenas for the handwritten notes as part of an investigation into whether crimes were committed during the prior investigations into the travel irregularities. Hamilton (D) moved to quash, arguing the notes were protected by the attorney-client privilege. The federal district court agreed and denied enforcement of the subpoenas. The court of appeals reversed, and Hamilton (D) appealed.

ISSUE: Does the attorney-client privilege survive the client's death?

HOLDING AND DECISION: (Rehnquist, C.J.) Yes. Here, the testamentary disclosure of communications as an exception to or implied waiver of the attorney-client privilege did not preclude the posthumous application of the attorney-client privilege to a grand jury subpoena of the attorney's notes about a conversation which the attorney had with the client shortly before the client's death. The rationale for this testamentary exception is that it furthers the client's intent. The attorney-client privilege must survive the client's death, given that knowledge that communications will remain confidential even after death encourages a client to communicate fully and frankly with counsel. While fear of disclosure, and consequent withholding of information from counsel, may be reduced if disclosure is limited to posthumous disclosure in the criminal context, it is unreasonable to assume that it vanishes altogether. Posthumous application of the attorney-client privilege is supported by the client's concerns about reputation, civil liability, or possible harm to friends or family. Posthumous disclosure of communications may be as feared as disclosure of those communications during a client's lifetime. Furthermore, the attorney-client privilege

is broader than the Fifth Amendment's protection against self-incrimination. Reversed.

DISSENT: (O'Connor, J.) Where the exoneration of an innocent criminal defendant or a compelling law enforcement interest is at stake, the harm of precluding critical evidence that is unavailable by any other means outweighs the potential disincentive to forthright communication. The cost of silence warrants a narrow exception to the rule that the attorney-client privilege survives the death of the client. Moreover, the doctrine should not apply where the material concerns a client who is no longer a potential party to adversarial litigation.

▶ ANALYSIS

The Supreme Court noted that limiting the posthumous exception to the attorney-client privilege to criminal cases or to information of substantial importance to any particular criminal case is not justified. Hence such an exception would not be created. The attorney-client privilege applies no differently in criminal and civil cases, and the client may not know at the time of disclosure whether the information would be relevant to a civil or a criminal matter.

■■■

Quicknotes

ATTORNEY-CLIENT PRIVILEGE A doctrine precluding the admission into evidence of confidential communications between an attorney and his client made in the course of obtaining professional assistance.

FED. R. EVID. 501 Provides that privilege principles shall be based on common law.

FIFTH AMENDMENT Provides that no person shall be compelled to serve as a witness against himself, or be subject to trial for the same offense twice, or be deprived of life, liberty, or property without due process of law.

GRAND JURY A group summoned to investigate, inform, and accuse persons of crimes when sufficient evidence exists to do so.

SUBPOENA A command issued by court to compel a witness to appear at trial.

■■■

United States v. Zolin

Federal government (P) v. Religious organization (D)

491 U.S. 554 (1989).

NATURE OF CASE: Appeal from decision in a tax return investigation action.

FACT SUMMARY: The Internal Revenue Service (P) contended the crime-fraud exception to the attorney-client privilege should allow it to investigate documentary material relating to Church of Scientology (D) activities, but the trial court refused to inspect the allegedly privileged material absent independent evidence of crime or fraud.

> 🏛 **RULE OF LAW**
> A court may conduct an in camera review to determine whether privileged attorney-client communications fall within the crime-fraud exception.

FACTS: The Internal Revenue Service (IRS) (P) sought to investigate the tax returns of L. Ron Hubbard, founder of the Church of Scientology ("the Church") (D). In the course of investigation, the IRS (P) sought access to documents that had been filed under seal in state court in connection with a suit by the Church (D) against one of its former members. The Church (D) objected to production of the documentary material on the grounds of the attorney-client privilege. The IRS (P) argued that the material fell within the crime-fraud exception to the privilege and urged the district court to listen to the tapes in making its privilege determination. Both the district court and the Ninth Circuit refused to apply the crime-fraud exception, finding no independent evidence to support it. The IRS (P) appealed, arguing that the crime-fraud exception did not have to be established by independent evidence (i.e., without reference to the content of the contested communications themselves) and that the applicability of the exception could be resolved by an in camera inspection of the allegedly privileged material.

ISSUE: May a court conduct an in camera review to determine whether privileged attorney-client communications fall within the crime-fraud exception?

HOLDING AND DECISION: (Blackmun, J.) Yes. A court may conduct an in camera review to determine whether privileged attorney-client communications fall within the crime-fraud exception. No express provision of the Federal Rule of Evidence bars the use of an in camera review of allegedly privileged communications to determine whether those communications fall within the crime-fraud exception. Although the Church (D) argued that Fed. R. Evid. 104(a) might be read with Rule 1101(c) to establish that, in a summons-enforcement proceeding, attorney-client communications cannot be considered by the district court in making its crime-fraud ruling, there is no basis for holding the documentary matter in this case must be deemed privileged under Rule 104(a) while the question of crime or fraud remains open. Furthermore, disclosure of allegedly privileged materials to the district court for purposes of determining the merits of a claim of privilege does not have the legal effect of terminating the privilege. The question of the propriety of the review then becomes whether the policies underlying the privilege and its exceptions are better fostered by permitting such review or prohibiting it. The costs of imposing an absolute bar to consideration of communications in camera for the purpose of establishing the crime-fraud exception are too high. The standard that strikes the correct balance is that, before engaging in camera review to determine the applicability of the crime-fraud exception, the judge should require a showing of a factual basis adequate to support a good-faith belief by a reasonable person that in camera review of materials may reveal evidence to establish the claim the crime-fraud exception applies. Moreover, the party opposing the privilege, here the IRS (P), may use any unprivileged evidence in support of its request for an in camera review, even if the evidence (here, transcripts of the tapes) is not independent of the contested communication. Judgment of court of appeals vacated and case remanded.

▶ ANALYSIS

As pointed out by Justice Blackmun in the *Zolin* case, the Supreme Court does not interpret Rule 104(a) in the same manner as it is interpreted under California law (Cal. Evid. Code Ann., 915(a)). Under the Federal Rules of Evidence, Rule 104(a) provides that preliminary questions concerning the qualifications of a person to be a witness, the existence of a privilege, or the admissibility of evidence shall be determined by the court. In making its determination, it is not bound by the Rules of Evidence, except those with respect to privileges. However, Rule 104(a) does not, by its terms, exclude from consideration all materials as of which a claim of privilege has been made. The comparable California Evidence Rule, § 915(a), on the other hand, provides that a presiding officer may not require disclosure of any information "claimed to be privileged" under this division in order to rule on the claim of privilege. The Court in *Zolin* refused to read Rule 104(a) as if its text were identical to the California rule, thereby allowing a more flexible interpretation that lets the district court consider "non-independent" evidence in determining whether in camera review may take place.

■=■

Continued on next page.

Quicknotes

ATTORNEY-CLIENT PRIVILEGE A doctrine precluding the admission into evidence of confidential communications between an attorney and his client made in the course of obtaining professional assistance.

FED. R. EVID. 104 Permits a court to consider all non-privileged matters, whether independently admissible or not, when determining preliminary issues of admissibility.

FED. R. EVID. 501 Provides that privilege principles shall be based on common law.

FED. R. EVID. 1101 Outlines the applicability of the Federal Rules of Evidence to a variety of legal proceedings.

■■■

In re Grand Jury Investigation [Rowland]

Federal government (P) v. State government (D)

399 F.3d 527 (2d Cir. 2005).

NATURE OF CASE: Appeal of order compelling testimony of former chief legal counsel to the Governor of Connecticut.

FACT SUMMARY: In the course of investigating possible criminal violations by Connecticut public officials and employees, a federal grand jury subpoenaed Anne C. George, former chief legal counsel to the Governor. The Governor's office invoked the attorney-client privilege. The district court entered an order compelling George's testimony, finding that the governmental attorney-client privilege was tempered by the government lawyer's duty to the public.

🏛 RULE OF LAW
The governmental attorney-client privilege may be invoked to preclude testimony by a government attorney in the context of a criminal investigation against public officials.

FACTS: In the course of investigating possible criminal violations by Connecticut public officials and employees, a federal grand jury subpoenaed Anne C. George, former chief legal counsel to the Governor. Governor Rowland (D) was under investigation for receiving gifts from private individuals and entities in return for public favors. The Governor's office invoked the attorney-client privilege, and George refused to answer certain questions during the grand jury investigation. The district court entered an order compelling George's testimony, finding that the governmental attorney-client privilege was tempered by the government lawyer's duty to the public.

ISSUE: May the governmental attorney-client privilege be invoked to preclude testimony by a government attorney in the context of a criminal investigation against public officials?

HOLDING AND DECISION: (Walker, C.J.) Yes. The governmental attorney-client privilege may be invoked to preclude testimony by a government attorney in the context of a criminal investigation against public officials. The existence of the governmental attorney-client privilege is not challenged, but only its application in the context of a criminal investigation against public officials. There is also substantial authority for the view that the attorney-client privilege in the context of a criminal investigation of public officials serves the same purpose and with the same force as that in the private context. Though the public attorney owes a duty to the public, as well as to the office of the Governor, the duty to the public is not best served by forcing the attorney to testify against those in office, but in

allowing for the free communication between the attorney and elected officials, so that they get the best legal advice in the course of representing the public. It is crucial that government officials be encouraged to seek and receive fully informed legal advice. Since the attorney-client privilege applies to the communications at issue in this case, it must be enforced. Reversed.

▶ ANALYSIS

Remember that while the attorney-client privilege may apply with equal force to the governmental lawyer-client relationship, the governmental lawyer-client relationship is different from the private lawyer-client relationship. In the governmental context, the lawyer's "client" is the office or agency, not the person who holds the office, and the ability to waive the privilege stays with the office. Thus, an outgoing governor may not assert or waive the privilege she held while in office, and the privilege that applied when she was in office may be waived or asserted by her successor.

■■■

Quicknotes

ATTORNEY-CLIENT PRIVILEGE A doctrine precluding the admission into evidence of confidential communications between an attorney and his client made in the course of obtaining professional assistance.

ATTORNEY-CLIENT RELATIONSHIP The confidential relationship established when a lawyer enters into employment with a client.

■■■

United States v. Hubbell

Federal government (P) v. Subpoena recipient (D)

530 U.S. 27 (2000).

NATURE OF CASE: Appeal from dismissal of indictment.

FACT SUMMARY: Prosecutors served defendant with a subpoena duces tecum, with which defendant complied only after receiving use immunity. Defendant was later indicted for tax-related violations, based in large part on information derived from the subpoenaed documents. Defendant argued the indictment should be dismissed based on Fifth Amendment privilege and a grant of use immunity.

🏛 RULE OF LAW
Document assembly and production has a testimonial aspect protected under a grant of immunity and Fifth Amendment protection against self-incrimination.

FACTS: In a largely unrelated matter to the case at hand, Webster Hubbell (D) was served with a subpoena duces tecum. The scope of the subpoena was quite broad and sought the assembly and production of thousands of pages. Hubbell (D) invoked his Fifth Amendment rights against self-incrimination before the grand jury. Prosecutors granted Hubbell (D) use immunity and defendant produced over 13,000 documents. As a result of reviewing the documents, prosecutors sought and received an indictment against Hubbell (D) for tax-related violations. Hubbell (D) contended he was protected from prosecution by his grant of immunity, but the district court disagreed. Hubbell (D) appealed and the court of appeals dismissed the indictment, requiring prosecutors to demonstrate independent knowledge of the evidence against Hubbell (D) that did not directly or indirectly derive from the document production. The United States Supreme Court granted certiorari.

ISSUE: Does document assembly and production have a testimonial aspect protected under a grant of immunity and Fifth Amendment protection against self-incrimination?

HOLDING AND DECISION: (Stevens, J.) Yes. Document assembly and production has a testimonial aspect protected under a grant of immunity and Fifth Amendment protection against self-incrimination. The act of compiling and producing documents in response to a subpoena has testimonial aspects separate from the contents of the documents. The Fifth Amendment protects against compelled, self-incriminating testimony. The Government (P) resolved the issue by offering Hubbell (D) use immunity. Prosecutors argued that they would not men-

tion or introduce the produced documents at trial, thus they claim not to have violated Hubbell's (D) "use" immunity. The Government (P), however, has already enjoyed derivative use of the documents because the production itself was the first link in the chain of evidence. Hubbell's (D) act involved his thought and effort in locating, assembling, and producing all of the documents sought in the very broad subpoena. The Government (P) has made no showing of independent knowledge of the existence of the incriminating documents or of their contents. The Government (P) compelled production of incriminating documents and cannot benefit from it in contravention of Hubbell's (D) invocation of Fifth Amendment protections and grant of use immunity. Affirmed.

CONCURRENCE: (Thomas, J.) The Self-Incrimination Clause may have originally been intended to protect against the compelled production of all incriminating evidence rather than just testimony.

▶ ANALYSIS

Justice Marshall's separate opinion in *Fisher v. United States*, 425 U.S. 391 (1976), predicted the testimonial aspect of document production as it relates to private documents independently unknown to exist. The admission of a document's existence can certainly be testimonial and should fall under Fifth Amendment protections.

■=■

Quicknotes

CERTIORARI A discretionary writ issued by a superior court to an inferior court in order to review the lower court's decisions; the Supreme Court's writ ordering such review.

FIFTH AMENDMENT Provides that no person shall be compelled to serve as a witness against himself, or be subject to trial for the same offense twice, or be deprived of life, liberty, or property without due process of law.

IMMUNITY FROM PROSECUTION Statutory protection from prosecution afforded to a witness in exchange for his testimony.

SUBPOENA DUCES TECUM A court mandate compelling the production of documents under a witness's control.

■=■

CHAPTER 13

Familial Privileges

Quick Reference Rules of Law

Tilton v. Beecher

[Parties not identified.]

N.Y. Ct. App., 2 Abbott's Repts. at 49, 87 (1875).

NATURE OF CASE: [Nature of case not stated in casebook excerpt.]

FACT SUMMARY: One spouse was called to testify against the other at trial and the attorneys debated the issue.

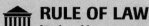
RULE OF LAW
[Rule of law not stated in casebook excerpt.]

FACTS: One spouse was called to testify against the other at trial.

ISSUE: Is there a privilege for spousal communications?

HOLDING AND DECISION: [Judge not stated in casebook excerpt.] Mr. Evarts argued for the plaintiff that the law should not compel one spouse to testify against the other because of the sanctity of the marital relationship. Mr. Beach argued for the defendant that the wife should be able to testify because the marital relationship has already been disrupted by women joining the workforce and becoming independent beings in every other facet of life. [Decision not stated in casebook excerpt.]

▶ ANALYSIS

The old-fashioned and faintly condescending language of this older case aside, the defendant's attorney has a point. Women had recently been "ushered" into leading independent lives through legislative acts, had recently joined the workforce in a noticeable fashion, and were no longer as tied to their domestic duties. Perhaps the defense attorney is arguing that women were no longer under the rule of their husbands, so they should be able to testify if they desired. The spousal privilege, however, is intended to work both ways and is held by the spouse who made the communications. The sanctity of the marital relationship should protect the conversation shared within it.

■▬■

Quicknotes

PRIVILEGED COMMUNICATION A statement made by an individual, which is protected from disclosure at trial as a result of its being communicated to a person with whom the declarant shares a relationship that is protected by law.

■▬■

Trammel v. United States

Convicted drug trafficker (D) v. Federal government (P)

445 U.S. 40 (1980).

NATURE OF CASE: Appeal from convictions for conspiracy to import and importing heroin.

FACT SUMMARY: Trammel's (D) wife agreed to testify against her husband in return for lenient treatment for herself, but Trammel (D) argued he had the right to prevent her from testifying against him.

🏛 **RULE OF LAW**
A criminal defendant cannot prevent his spouse from voluntarily giving testimony against him because the privilege against adverse spousal testimony belongs to the testifying spouse.

FACTS: In return for lenient treatment for herself, Mrs. Trammel, an unindicted coconspirator, agreed to testify against her husband at his trial for conspiracy to import and importing heroin. The district court ruled she could testify to any act she observed during the marriage and to any communication made in the presence of a third person but not as to confidential communications between herself and her husband because they fell within the privilege attaching to confidential marital communications. On appeal, Trammel (D) contended that he was entitled to invoke the privilege against adverse spousal testimony so as to exclude the voluntary testimony of his wife. The court of appeals rejected this contention and affirmed the convictions.

ISSUE: Can a criminal defendant invoke the privilege against adverse spousal testimony so as to prevent his spouse from voluntarily offering adverse testimony against him?

HOLDING AND DECISION: (Burger, C.J.) No. Inasmuch as the privilege against adverse spousal testimony belongs solely to the testifying spouse, a criminal defendant cannot invoke the privilege to prevent his spouse from offering adverse testimony against him. The *Hawkins* case, [*Hawkins v. United States*, 358 U.S. 74 (1958)], left the federal privilege for adverse spousal testimony where it found it at the time, thus continuing a rule which barred the testimony of one spouse against the other unless both consented. However, since that 1958 decision, support for that conception of the privilege has eroded further and the trend in state law is toward divesting the accused of the privilege to bar adverse spousal testimony. The ancient foundations for so sweeping a privilege involved a conception of the wife as her husband's chattel to do with as he wished, and they have long since disappeared. Nor is the desire to protect the marriage a valid justification for affording an accused such a privilege. If his spouse desires to testify against him, simply preventing her from doing so is not likely to save the marriage. Affirmed.

▶ **ANALYSIS**

The Model Code of Evidence and the Uniform Rules of Evidence completely abolished the notion of privilege against adverse spousal testimony and limited themselves to recognizing a privilege covering confidential marital communications. Several state legislatures have followed suit.

Quicknotes

FED. R. EVID. 501 Provides that privilege principles shall be based on common law.

SPOUSAL PRIVILEGE A common-law doctrine precluding spouses from commencing actions against one another for their torts.

United States v. Rakes

Federal government (P) v. Husband (D)

136 F.3d 1 (1st Cir. 1998).

NATURE OF CASE: Appeal from grant of motion to suppress evidence.

FACT SUMMARY: Defendant and his wife were victims of extortion and had several discussions concerning the alleged threats. The prosecution sought the admission of these marital communications, but defendant claimed protection of privilege for confidential marital communications.

🏛 RULE OF LAW
Confidential marital communications are not forfeited or waived absent wrongful complicity merely because the communications involve criminal matters.

FACTS: Stephen Rakes (D) and Julie Rakes, husband and wife, owned a South Boston business which drew the interest of James "Whitey" Bulger. The Government (P) believed that Bulger threatened the Rakeses and forced them to transfer their business interests to an associate of his for a fraction of the business's worth. Before a federal grand jury, Stephen Rakes (D) denied the threats and the extortion, so the Government (P) indicted him for perjury and obstruction of justice. The Government (P) sought to introduce several communications between Stephen Rakes (D) and Julie Rakes concerning the alleged threats and extortion. Stephen Rakes (D) moved to suppress on grounds of privilege for confidential marital communications. The district court suppressed all but one statement because it involved a communication to a third party. The Government (P) appealed, claiming privilege was waived or forfeited because Stephen Rakes (D) was discussing criminal matters as a participant in the extortion.

ISSUE: Are confidential marital communications forfeited or waived absent wrongful complicity merely because the communications involve criminal matters?

HOLDING AND DECISION: (Boudin, J.) No. Confidential marital communications are not forfeited or waived absent wrongful complicity merely because the communications involve criminal matters. Stephen Rakes (D) and Julie Rakes were not "participants" in the extortion, but victims of it. Their discussions concerning the criminal matter never rose to the level of wrongful complicity. Had one or both spouses committed a crime, the crime-fraud exception could perhaps permit the admission of their communications into evidence. Privilege is not otherwise lost when innocent parties share communications that play a role in a crime. Stephen Rakes's (D) communication to a third party also does not waive the

privilege. Stephen Rakes (D) was not sharing information about the communication between him and his wife. He was sharing a story to avoid debt collection. Here, marital privilege for confidential communication was neither forfeited nor waived. Affirmed.

▶ ANALYSIS

The court in *Rakes* was not impressed with the Government's (P) argument that marital communications between innocent victims about criminal matters forfeit privilege. Open communication is important in families and the courts do not want to chill communication between spouses. The privilege even survives divorce, although the communication must have taken place during the marriage.

■=■

Quicknotes

CONFIDENTIAL MARITAL COMMUNICATIONS A communication made between a husband and wife which is privileged at the election of the spouse-witness.

EXTORTION The unlawful taking of property of another by threats of force.

OBSTRUCTION OF JUSTICE The interference with the administration of justice (usually through court process) in any manner.

PERJURY The making of false statements under oath.

SPOUSAL PRIVILEGE A common-law doctrine precluding spouses from commencing actions against one another for their torts.

■=■

In re Grand Jury Proceedings

Government (P) v. Parents (D)

103 F. 3d 1140 (3d Cir.), *cert. denied*, 520 U.S. 1253 (1997).

NATURE OF CASE: Three consolidated appeals for criminal convictions.

FACT SUMMARY: Three cases concerning a parent-child privilege were consolidated on appeal, one from the U.S. Virgin Islands and two from Delaware. In the Virgin Island case, a father was subpoenaed to testify adversely to his son. In the Delaware cases, a daughter was subpoenaed to testify against her father.

RULE OF LAW
Federal law does not recognize a parent-child privilege.

FACTS: Three appeals concerning a parent-child privilege were consolidated into one hearing. One appeal originated in the Virgin Islands, and the other two originated in Delaware. In the Virgin Islands' case, the father of the target of a grand jury investigation was subpoenaed as a witness, and moved to quash the subpoena by asserting privilege under Fed. R. Evid. 501. The father argued that he had a close, loving relationship with his son and, should he be forced to testify, he would not be able to talk with his son without the son's attorney present for the entire investigation. The father's motion to quash was denied because the Third Circuit had not addressed the issue of whether the federal court recognized a parent-child privilege, and all other circuits had refused to recognize the privilege. In the Delaware cases, a daughter was subpoenaed to testify to the grand jury regarding charges against her father for the interstate kidnapping of a woman. She refused to testify and was found in contempt of court. The contempt order was stayed pending appeal.

ISSUE: Does federal law recognize a parent-child privilege?

HOLDING AND DECISION: (Garth, J.) No. Federal law does not recognize a parent-child privilege. A privilege should be recognized only where such a privilege would be indispensable to the survival of the relationship that society deems should be fostered. It is not clear whether children would be more likely to discuss private matters with their parents if the privilege was recognized, or whether a child would know of the privilege's existence, unlike a lawyer or other professional, or whether, even knowing of the privilege, the child would enter into the decision to confide in the parent. Also, a father having knowledge of a child's illegal behavior should be free to take whatever action the parent deems appropriate in the interest of the child. In short, recognition of the privilege will not change the inherent child-parent relationship, but would greatly impair the truth-seeking function of the judiciary. Such a function is recognized in only four states. Congress has not granted authority for the federal courts to create such a privilege, but is free to create one through legislation if it deems it necessary.

CONCURRENCE AND DISSENT: (Mansmann, J.) Fed. R. Evid. 501 already grants congressional authority to recognize a parent-child privilege, since such privilege does exist in the common law of four states. A limited privilege should be recognized in cases of compelled testimony where both child and parent seek the protection of the privilege. The limited nature should remain to encourage a case-by-case evaluation.

ANALYSIS

Even though Rule 501 allows adoption of all common-law privileges, privileges are generally disfavored. As a result, Rule 501 is not interpreted expansively to create a parent-child privilege, even though four states' common laws have already done so. The majority read Rule 501 to grant this power only to common-law privileges that exist in all states, or at least in the majority of states.

Quicknotes

FED. R. EVID. 501 Provides that privilege principles shall be based on common law.

PRIVILEGED COMMUNICATION A statement made by an individual, which is protected from disclosure at trial as a result of its being communicated to a person with whom the declarant shares a relationship that is protected by law.

SUBPOENA A command issued by court to compel a witness to appear at trial.

Glossary

Common Latin Words and Phrases Encountered in the Law

A FORTIORI: Because one fact exists or has been proven, therefore a second fact that is related to the first fact must also exist.

A PRIORI: From the cause to the effect. A term of logic used to denote that when one generally accepted truth is shown to be a cause, another particular effect must necessarily follow.

AB INITIO: From the beginning; a condition which has existed throughout, as in a marriage which was void ab initio.

ACTUS REUS: The wrongful act; in criminal law, such action sufficient to trigger criminal liability.

AD VALOREM: According to value; an ad valorem tax is imposed upon an item located within the taxing jurisdiction calculated by the value of such item.

AMICUS CURIAE: Friend of the court. Its most common usage takes the form of an amicus curiae brief, filed by a person who is not a party to an action but is nonetheless allowed to offer an argument supporting his legal interests.

ARGUENDO: In arguing. A statement, possibly hypothetical, made for the purpose of argument, is one made arguendo.

BILL QUIA TIMET: A bill to quiet title (establish ownership) to real property.

BONA FIDE: True, honest, or genuine. May refer to a person's legal position based on good faith or lacking notice of fraud (such as a bona fide purchaser for value) or to the authenticity of a particular document (such as a bona fide last will and testament).

CAUSA MORTIS: With approaching death in mind. A gift causa mortis is a gift given by a party who feels certain that death is imminent.

CAVEAT EMPTOR: Let the buyer beware. This maxim is reflected in the rule of law that a buyer purchases at his own risk because it is his responsibility to examine, judge, test, and otherwise inspect what he is buying.

CERTIORARI: A writ of review. Petitions for review of a case by the United States Supreme Court are most often done by means of a writ of certiorari.

CONTRA: On the other hand. Opposite. Contrary to.

CORAM NOBIS: Before us; writs of error directed to the court that originally rendered the judgment.

CORAM VOBIS: Before you; writs of error directed by an appellate court to a lower court to correct a factual error.

CORPUS DELICTI: The body of the crime; the requisite elements of a crime amounting to objective proof that a crime has been committed.

CUM TESTAMENTO ANNEXO, ADMINISTRATOR (ADMINISTRATOR C.T.A.): With will annexed; an administrator c.t.a. settles an estate pursuant to a will in which he is not appointed.

DE BONIS NON, ADMINISTRATOR (ADMINISTRATOR D.B.N.): Of goods not administered; an administrator d.b.n. settles a partially settled estate.

DE FACTO: In fact; in reality; actually. Existing in fact but not officially approved or engendered.

DE JURE: By right; lawful. Describes a condition that is legitimate "as a matter of law," in contrast to the term "de facto," which connotes something existing in fact but not legally sanctioned or authorized. For example, de facto segregation refers to segregation brought about by housing patterns, etc., whereas de jure segregation refers to segregation created by law.

DE MINIMIS: Of minimal importance; insignificant; a trifle; not worth bothering about.

DE NOVO: Anew; a second time; afresh. A trial de novo is a new trial held at the appellate level as if the case originated there and the trial at a lower level had not taken place.

DICTA: Generally used as an abbreviated form of obiter dicta, a term describing those portions of a judicial opinion incidental or not necessary to resolution of the specific question before the court. Such nonessential statements and remarks are not considered to be binding precedent.

DUCES TECUM: Refers to a particular type of writ or subpoena requesting a party or organization to produce certain documents in their possession.

EN BANC: Full bench. Where a court sits with all justices present rather than the usual quorum.

EX PARTE: For one side or one party only. An ex parte proceeding is one undertaken for the benefit of only one party, without notice to, or an appearance by, an adverse party.

EX POST FACTO: After the fact. An ex post facto law is a law that retroactively changes the consequences of a prior act.

EX REL.: Abbreviated form of the term "ex relatione," meaning upon relation or information. When the state brings an action in which it has no interest against an individual at the instigation of one who has a private interest in the matter.

FORUM NON CONVENIENS: Inconvenient forum. Although a court may have jurisdiction over the case, the action should be tried in a more conveniently located court, one to which parties and witnesses may more easily travel, for example.

GUARDIAN AD LITEM: A guardian of an infant as to litigation, appointed to represent the infant and pursue his/her rights.

HABEAS CORPUS: You have the body. The modern writ of habeas corpus is a writ directing that a person (body) being detained (such as a prisoner) be brought before the court so that the legality of his detention can be judicially ascertained.

IN CAMERA: In private, in chambers. When a hearing is held before a judge in his chambers or when all spectators are excluded from the courtroom.

IN FORMA PAUPERIS: In the manner of a pauper. A party who proceeds in forma pauperis because of his poverty is one who is allowed to bring suit without liability for costs.

INFRA: Below, under. A word referring the reader to a later part of a book. (The opposite of supra.)

IN LOCO PARENTIS: In the place of a parent.

IN PARI DELICTO: Equally wrong; a court of equity will not grant requested relief to an applicant who is in pari delicto, or as much at fault in the transactions giving rise to the controversy as is the opponent of the applicant.

IN PARI MATERIA: On like subject matter or upon the same matter. Statutes relating to the same person or things are said to be in pari materia. It is a general rule of statutory construction that such statutes should be construed together, i.e., looked at as if they together constituted one law.

IN PERSONAM: Against the person. Jurisdiction over the person of an individual.

IN RE: In the matter of. Used to designate a proceeding involving an estate or other property.

IN REM: A term that signifies an action against the res, or thing. An action in rem is basically one that is taken directly against property, as distinguished from an action in personam, i.e., against the person.

INTER ALIA: Among other things. Used to show that the whole of a statement, pleading, list, statute, etc., has not been set forth in its entirety.

INTER PARTES: Between the parties. May refer to contracts, conveyances or other transactions having legal significance.

INTER VIVOS: Between the living. An inter vivos gift is a gift made by a living grantor, as distinguished from bequests contained in a will, which pass upon the death of the testator.

IPSO FACTO: By the mere fact itself.

JUS: Law or the entire body of law.

LEX LOCI: The law of the place; the notion that the rights of parties to a legal proceeding are governed by the law of the place where those rights arose.

MALUM IN SE: Evil or wrong in and of itself; inherently wrong. This term describes an act that is wrong by its very nature, as opposed to one which would not be wrong but for the fact that there is a specific legal prohibition against it (malum prohibitum).

MALUM PROHIBITUM: Wrong because prohibited, but not inherently evil. Used to describe something that is wrong because it is expressly forbidden by law but that is not in and of itself evil, e.g., speeding.

MANDAMUS: We command. A writ directing an official to take a certain action.

MENS REA: A guilty mind; a criminal intent. A term used to signify the mental state that accompanies a crime or other prohibited act. Some crimes require only a general mens rea (general intent to do the prohibited act), but others, like assault with intent to murder, require the existence of a specific mens rea.

MODUS OPERANDI: Method of operating; generally refers to the manner or style of a criminal in committing crimes, admissible in appropriate cases as evidence of the identity of a defendant.

NEXUS: A connection to.

NISI PRIUS: A court of first impression. A nisi prius court is one where issues of fact are tried before a judge or jury.

N.O.V. (NON OBSTANTE VEREDICTO): Notwithstanding the verdict. A judgment n.o.v. is a judgment given in favor of one party despite the fact that a verdict was returned in favor of the other party, the justification being that the verdict either had no reasonable support in fact or was contrary to law.

NUNC PRO TUNC: Now for then. This phrase refers to actions that may be taken and will then have full retroactive effect.

PENDENTE LITE: Pending the suit; pending litigation under way.

PER CAPITA: By head; beneficiaries of an estate, if they take in equal shares, take per capita.

PER CURIAM: By the court; signifies an opinion ostensibly written "by the whole court" and with no identified author.

PER SE: By itself, in itself; inherently.

PER STIRPES: By representation. Used primarily in the law of wills to describe the method of distribution where a person, generally because of death, is unable to take that which is left to him by the will of another, and therefore his heirs divide such property between them rather than take under the will individually.

PRIMA FACIE: On its face, at first sight. A prima facie case is one that is sufficient on its face, meaning that the evidence supporting it is adequate to establish the case until contradicted or overcome by other evidence.

PRO TANTO: For so much; as far as it goes. Often used in eminent domain cases when a property owner receives partial payment for his land without prejudice to his right to bring suit for the full amount he claims his land to be worth.

QUANTUM MERUIT: As much as he deserves. Refers to recovery based on the doctrine of unjust enrichment in those cases in which a party has rendered valuable services or furnished materials that were accepted and enjoyed by another under circumstances that would reasonably notify the recipient that the rendering party expected to be paid. In essence, the law implies a contract to pay the reasonable value of the services or materials furnished.

QUASI: Almost like; as if; nearly. This term is essentially used to signify that one subject or thing is almost analogous to another but that material differences between them do exist. For example, a quasi-criminal proceeding is one that is not strictly criminal but shares enough of the same characteristics to require some of the same safeguards (e.g., procedural due process must be followed in a parole hearing).

QUID PRO QUO: Something for something. In contract law, the consideration, something of value, passed between the parties to render the contract binding.

RES GESTAE: Things done; in evidence law, this principle justifies the admission of a statement that would otherwise be hearsay when it is made so closely to the event in question as to be said to be a part of it, or with such spontaneity as not to have the possibility of falsehood.

RES IPSA LOQUITUR: The thing speaks for itself. This doctrine gives rise to a rebuttable presumption of negligence when the instrumentality causing the injury was within the exclusive control of the defendant, and the injury was one that does not normally occur unless a person has been negligent.

RES JUDICATA: A matter adjudged. Doctrine which provides that once a court of competent jurisdiction has rendered a final judgment or decree on the merits, that judgment or decree is conclusive upon the parties to the case and prevents them from engaging in any other litigation on the points and issues determined therein.

RESPONDEAT SUPERIOR: Let the master reply. This doctrine holds the master liable for the wrongful acts of his servant (or the principal for his agent) in those cases in which the servant (or agent) was acting within the scope of his authority at the time of the injury.

STARE DECISIS: To stand by or adhere to that which has been decided. The common law doctrine of stare decisis attempts to give security and certainty to the law by following the policy that once a principle of law as applicable to a certain set of facts has been set forth in a decision, it forms a precedent which will subsequently be followed, even though a different decision might be made were it the first time the question had arisen. Of course, stare decisis is not an inviolable principle and is departed from in instances where there is good cause (e.g., considerations of public policy led the Supreme Court to disregard prior decisions sanctioning segregation).

SUPRA: Above. A word referring a reader to an earlier part of a book.

ULTRA VIRES: Beyond the power. This phrase is most commonly used to refer to actions taken by a corporation that are beyond the power or legal authority of the corporation.

Addendum of French Derivatives

IN PAIS: Not pursuant to legal proceedings.

CHATTEL: Tangible personal property.

CY PRES: Doctrine permitting courts to apply trust funds to purposes not expressed in the trust but necessary to carry out the settlor's intent.

PER AUTRE VIE: For another's life; during another's life. In property law, an estate may be granted that will terminate upon the death of someone other than the grantee.

PROFIT A PRENDRE: A license to remove minerals or other produce from land.

VOIR DIRE: Process of questioning jurors as to their predispositions about the case or parties to a proceeding in order to identify those jurors displaying bias or prejudice.

Casenote® Legal Briefs